To Dave about Alaska

Gary Gunkel

11-17-2012

COURAGE AND CONVICTION

COURAGE AND CONVICTION

An Alaska State Trooper's Journey Through a
Life of Principled Law Enforcement

L. Gary Gunkel

authorHOUSE®

AuthorHouse™
1663 Liberty Drive
Bloomington, IN 47403
www.authorhouse.com
Phone: 1-800-839-8640

Some of the names have been changed to protect the innocent and others, because I have no way to find them.

First published by AuthorHouse   01/25/2012

ISBN: 978-1-4685-4569-2 (sc)
ISBN: 978-1-4685-4568-5 (hc)
ISBN: 978-1-4685-4567-8 (ebk)

Library of Congress Control Number: 2012901103

Printed in the United States of America

Any people depicted in stock imagery provided by Thinkstock are models, and such images are being used for illustrative purposes only.
Certain stock imagery © Thinkstock.

This book is printed on acid-free paper.

Because of the dynamic nature of the Internet, any web addresses or links contained in this book may have changed since publication and may no longer be valid. The views expressed in this work are solely those of the author and do not necessarily reflect the views of the publisher, and the publisher hereby disclaims any responsibility for them.

Thank you

Beth and Mark Carrick, Mark and Luke Gunkel, Gregg Gunkel, Thank you for all of their help and guidance and editing in getting this book finished.

Pat and Phil Edwards Thank you for all your help and encouragement.

Jim Crawford Thank you for gathering up all the loose ends and putting them all together to make a presentable finished product. Without your experience and expertise and editing I would have been lost.

I want to thank the Lewiston Morning Tribune for letting me use their articles from the past to get the proper time range of my book and the happenings of those events.

Last and most important my wife and best friend Ann. Over the four years it took me to get this book together, Ann kept it going just by doing the small things that competed for my time. With our business there never was time to accomplish everything. It was very tempting to just throw it all aside and un-clutter my life. Ann never hesitated in furnishing the necessary love and affection to keep our family front and center and in so doing keeping this book on track. Many is the time Ann would drop everything and come to read through the section I was working in to make sure it was flowing properly. To help on the difficult areas and even now to smooth the process. My daughter Karen Anghel and all of my grand children have contributed greatly inspiring me to complete this project.

PROLOGUE

The following is a Father's Day tribute written by my daughter, Beth Carrick for her church's newspaper in June 1988.

A Firm Foundation Transforms a Teen's Life

My dad's mother was a person of small stature and big ideals. From her petite frame came more love of life, love of people, kindness and bigheartedness than one would have thought possible. The love of Christ shined through her and this was evident to everyone who knew her.

She loved her children, and was their biggest enthusiast. My father, now 6'4" was not always so tall and in his younger years had the unfortunate experience of being chased home by the neighborhood bully on a regular basis. After weeks of trying to find a peaceful solution to this problem, my grandmother decided to intervene. One afternoon hearing the usual commotion outside, she threw open the window, leaned out and yelled with all her might: "Hit him, Gary, hit him." Dad says he did and that was the end of that problem. Father's Day isn't usually the time one remembers grandmothers. For me, however, it is this kind of old fashioned heroic support of one's children that comes to mind when I think of my father and Fathers Day.

The heritage my grandmother instilled in my father has carried over a generation and I have benefitted from it. The Bible says if we profess our faith, the Lord will defend us before God our Father. Here on earth I know I will always have a defense in my dad.

My father is an eternal optimist with incredible zest for life that is coupled with an adventuresome spirit. These qualities have led our family up the West Coast and around Alaska. Through it all I have been exposed to some great experiences. Dad has pushed himself to excel in his various careers and interests. These include dog sled racing, photography, bush piloting, commercial fishing and law enforcement.

Dad has always trusted in God for leadership and direction, and has continuously given God credit for his successes. This living by faith has been a constant proclamation of God's faithfulness. I was raised in a Christian home, but of all the "teaching" I've been exposed to, nothing speaks as much to me as these undeviating actions of trusting God.

As I look back, the most important thing my dad did for me must have been extremely hard. He allowed my brother, sister and me freedom to fail or succeed and encouraged our own opinions. With dad's strong personality this was a true act of self denial. The chain of command in our house started with God, but was followed very closely by my father. It would have been much easier for him to dictate our lives—but instead, our opinions were accepted (though sometimes reluctantly) and our independence encouraged.

Near the end of my senior year of high school I was having an identity crisis. Facing the process of growing up, yearning to be independent and at the same time uncertain about leaving the security of home. These fears were still with me the day my dad and I had the opportunity to go on a cattle drive. We rose to the cold dark of a 3:00 morning, loaded our horses and drove to the neighbor's winter pastures in the foothills of the Blue Mountains. As we arrived, a glorious sunrise gave the surrounding hills a glow that took our breaths away.

We met up with other men who assigned dad and I the task of herding the cattle down a small canyon. As we approached the first cows, we were unsure of our ability to make these big-eyed creatures move anywhere, to say nothing of in a specific direction. Our first tentative yells sounded pretty silly, but before long we were racing all over, yelling and whooping at the top of our lungs. Emerging from the canyon, we faced a hill that seemed to go straight up. Pulling our horses by the reins and slapping the cattle preceding us, we made it up that mountain. I was startled when seemingly in the middle of nowhere we came upon a beautiful corral nestled in a stand of pine trees.

Exhausted, dirty and sore I sat on the fence with the hot afternoon sun beating down on me. I watched intrigued, while the men roped the calves and treated them for pink eye. There was my dad, handsome and tall in his brown cowboy hat, wrestling 200 pound calves. As I watched, I felt peace about my future. God had given me a great father and a great foundation. I thank God for his continuing love, for my grandmother, my father, and my heritage.

Present

A moment, so peaceful, gives time for a person to reflect on where he's been, who he is, and what might lie ahead. Today was filled with those moments. It was April 27th, 2008 and I was working in our booth at the Asotin County fairgrounds. Our early morning espresso sales had been brisk, but now had slowed down. Ann, my wife, had gone home to pick up more supplies and I was at the booth by myself. Last night, Saturday, the animals had been auctioned off. The only people around this morning were the kids that had early morning barn duty and a few supervisors. The rest of the Sunday crowd was just starting to stir and come out of their campers.

Asotin County has the first fair of the year in the state of Washington, and always over the last weekend of April. This works out quite well for our family business, as it is the first major event of the year for what I call our "monkey business." These latter years of our lives, we are slowing down, but still have one drive-thru espresso location, a coffee roasting business and a food processing plant. We produce assorted baked goods, a full line of chocolates and fudges, and of course, lots of coffee, which we sell through our Internet website.

It was around 8:30 a.m. and I was thinking that we would be loading up our coffee booth later in the afternoon after another successful fair. The warmth of the April morning sunshine felt good. While I stood there soaking it up, Sergeant Eric Spaulding of the Asotin County Sheriff's Office walked by and stopped to visit. Eric started telling me that he and several other law enforcement officers had been talking about the Asotin County fairs of the early 1980's. "That was just before you were elected county Sheriff, Gary." Eric said there had been a couple officers present that had worked those old fairs. They told about the fights going on everywhere and the big street dance down by the county courthouse and the Snake Pit, a bar set up during the fairs across from the courthouse offices in the evening that did a big business selling beer to anyone, regardless of age, that could walk or crawl to the door. The Snake Pit was the big drawing card in town and had established a rowdy reputation in those days. There were lots of drunks, women, men, and even kids present, with many disturbances. At one legendary riot the Asotin County Sheriff called for assistance from Clarkston Police Department, Lewiston Police Department and the Washington State Patrol. The drunken crowd damaged several patrol vehicles as well as a lot of private property. The county fair brought a repeat of this occurrence three out of the four years before I became sheriff of Asotin County.

Asotin County is located in a valley where the Clearwater River joins the Snake River, with Clarkston, Washington on one side of the confluence, and Lewiston, Idaho on the other. Living throughout the valley and within 15 miles of the county is a resident population of over 60,000.

Asotin County, including the 7,000 population of Clarkston and six miles away the 2,000 population in the town of Asotin, was wide open for the consumption and sale of all drugs including alcohol, marijuana, cocaine and heroin. The methamphetamine market was just getting started. The Lewiston, Idaho police had teamed up with the Idaho State Drug Agents and worked drug enforcement on their side of the river with many arrests. The biggest problem the Idaho law enforcement officials were having was that all of the drug dealers started coming across the river into Washington to do their business as there was safe harbor from drug enforcement in Asotin County.

The readily available alcohol and drugs flooded the Asotin County fair with a drunk and disorderly crowd. This easy access coupled with the frequent "keggers" held by the youth brought with it lots of fights, drunk driving accidents and open drug use. Dealing with this activity was a huge challenge to local law enforcement.

The parks built by the Army Corps of Engineers were another law enforcement problem. During the heat of summer the youth would carry in coolers of beer, and as the afternoon got hotter and hotter the beer would flow more freely. According to people living above the parks along the river, there was open nudity and even flagrant sex taking place amongst the hundreds of intoxicated young people present. Complaints went unanswered as some residents reported that deputies said they were afraid to try to enforce the law down there.

I was not aware of all these problems when I first started to run for sheriff, but now I am getting way ahead of myself.

About that time a customer walked up and Eric carried on his patrol, but he had broken open the floodgates of my memory . . .

pg. 90

pg. 100

pg. 5

pg. 79

pg. 141

pg. 198

pg. 197

pg. 126

pg. 124

pg. 231

pg. 276

Chapter 1

My mother and father were concerned that I would never grow up. I was not a bad kid but I was always doing something different. I fully embraced life, enjoying every single moment of it. I still do.

After high school and a stint in the service, I had put together a dog team of Irish Setters, which had earned the reputation as the fastest dog sled team in the lower 48 states . . . most of the time. To help support my passion of dog sled racing, I did construction work, and worked for the forest service running a crew of fire fighters in the summer, while living in the most incredible area of the United States . . . the Sierra Nevada Mountains of California. Beginning in September, I spent the biggest part of my time in the outdoors, hunting, training sled dogs and getting ready for the winter racing season. Both Ann and I raced teams of our Irish Setter sled dogs all over the western US. From our home near Lake Tahoe, we raced in California, Nevada, Oregon, Colorado, Utah and Arizona. Most sled dog races were tied in with winter carnivals and our team of Irish Setters was always a crowd favorite, likely due to their uniqueness. While at first being regarded the "underdogs" (no pun intended), we quickly overcame the myth and usually beat the traditional teams made up of huskies.

Ann was a registered nurse, making a living for our family in the winter, while I would supplement our income with prize money won at dog races. She also helped with the training. In order to have the greatest chance of winning, I would take our best dogs for my team. Ann would make a team out of the remaining dogs and enter whatever class (three dog, five dog, or women's class) we thought would win us the most money. While I basked in the glory of winning, Ann would take her team of dogs and also do very well, often winning her division.

In December of 1964, at the age of 26, I had an incredible experience that would shape my life forever. This "defining moment" opened my eyes to a whole new world of possibilities, giving me a completely different view on what I could accomplish, allowed me an avenue to develop a unique background of skills and prepared me to take on enormous tasks and prevail at great odds.

On a Sunday morning I answered the door to find the local pastor asking if I did any rescue work with my dog team. When I asked what the problem was he said that on the previous morning, four young people, late teens and early 20's, had driven up the Mount Rose highway to look at the snow had not returned, and their folks were very worried about them.

Saturday had been a very nice day until early afternoon, when a blizzard had blown in with high winds and near zero temperatures in the mountains. The missing people had apparently driven up the highway in the morning and when the blizzard hit they were unable to get off the mountain.

I had been preparing to train with our sled dog team of Irish Setters for the upcoming race season but was behind in my progress because of a lack of snow. The group of young people were dressed in casual clothing, regular low top shoes and no heavy coats. I told the pastor that I would be glad to see if I could find them. I loaded my seven best dogs into the kennel on my two-wheel drive pickup and tied the sled down on top. The elevation at the north end of Lake Tahoe where the Mount Rose highway starts up is about 6,200' elevation, and as it leaves the Tahoe basin it rises to over 8,900' at the mountain pass leading to the Reno, Nevada area. I had very good traction in my pickup with the heavy dog box in the back, but the two feet of fresh snow that had fallen at the lower elevation along with the heavy winds blowing up the mountain caused near-zero visibility and snow drifts higher up the mountain. I stopped and pointed my pickup back toward the bottom, and started getting the dogs out of their kennel and hooked up.

The ride up the mountain was becoming a difficult endeavor. The wind was quickly forming drifts that the dogs had to fight through, and my apprehension increased as the drifts became deeper and more frequent. Pushing on towards the big meadow below the summit, the dogs continued to meet the challenge. Just before reaching the meadow the road went around a corner with a cut beside the road causing a huge drift that I later measured at 22' high, where the day before the road had been completely bare of snow.

I met a cross-country skier that had tried to find the lost group near the big drift and stopped to talk to him. The visibility went from about 30 yards to zero with every gust of wind. The skier had made it to the old sheepherder cabin just 50 yards off to the north side of the road, and seeing no sign of the lost group he had decided to go back. At that point, he was exhausted and only interested in getting down off the mountain, and I did not blame him. In this weather any mistake could cost a man his life. The skier and I were not far from the sheepherder's cabin yet there was no sign of the ski tracks he had just made in the snow. As he headed back down the mountain he sank into the snow almost to his knees, but his trail was wiped out instantly with the wind. By now there were only a couple of hours of daylight remaining so I decided to only go the mile or so to the summit. If those missing young people were up there I feared they would not make it through another night. My dogs were still going strong, but the uphill climb was starting to take its toll on them. The wind was blowing at our backs as the dogs bucked the drifts and increased in intensity as we climbed to the upper mountain meadows. I was getting in over my head and I knew it.

When I was a little boy I professed to be a Christian, but had very few times asked Christ to take over for me and show me the way. I have always been very self-reliant. Now I was scared! So it was no trouble for me to turn to Christ and ask Him to lead me to those people. I passed where I knew the sheepherder's cabin was located. The conditions now were such that I could not even see the cabin. The team and I pushed on up the mountain and in another three quarters of a mile I came upon the car, nearly covered with snow. Judging by the black around the exhaust, the car had been running, but now had stopped. The windows were iced over and it was impossible to see inside.

My heart fell all the way down to my feet, and I was having a difficult time breathing. I just knew they would be dead. I went over and opened the door, and was greeted by four very cold and frightened, but alive people. They said that the car was all but out of gas and they were scared, and did not know what to do.

I knew we did not have much time, so I let my instincts take over. I got the strongest looking guy of the four and put my snowshoes on him. I told him to head down the mountain to the sheepherder's cabin, then sent him on his way. I put the girl and other two guys on the dog sled. We went about 50' but the narrow racing sled runners cut through the soft snow down to the gravel. There was no way my dogs could pull that load under those circumstances. The guy wearing my snowshoes had disappeared into the storm and appeared to be doing well when last I saw him. There was no other alternative, so I unloaded the sled and told the three to follow my trail and make their way on down the road watching for the snow poles that marked the roadway. They started the difficult journey down on foot, the two boys helping the girl navigate the growing drifts. Telling them to keep moving and not stop and that I would be right back, I set out in search of the guy that had left earlier on my snowshoes. The wind was erasing his tracks as fast as he was making them. When I passed the location of the sheepherder's cabin, the blowing snow completely wiped out any view of it. I could not even see Duff, my lead sled dog who was just a few yards in front of me. This was a full-blown blizzard and the wind was cutting deep. I was in trouble again, and the weight of responsibility I felt was enormous. I had these people I was supposed to be rescuing scattered all over the mountain in a raging blizzard! I thought, *OH LORD, help me get this together!!!* I was dead serious about asking for help.

About that time Duff came upon the guy on my snowshoes. We found him about a half-mile beyond the cabin. He was in desperate condition. I quickly removed his snowshoes, wrapped him in a tarp and put him on the sled. Donning the snowshoes, I ran back towards the cabin. Just as I made it to the cabin I spotted the others. The two boys were now dragging the girl between them, as she was unable to move under her own power. I ran to meet them and picked her up. The run back to the cabin carrying her through waist deep snow was the longest hundred yards of my life. The blizzard, physical exhaustion, and snowshoes made it almost impossible. When we reached the cabin I immediately started a fire in an old wood stove. After making sure the three were all right I gave them the task of breaking apart a wooden table to keep the fire burning.

Feeling my own strength starting to fade, I ran back the half mile to the guy on the dog sled and got him back into the snowshoes. After rubbing his legs and arms I got him moving towards the cabin by breaking a trail in snow that was now above my waist. When the cabin came into view my heart sank. The entire cabin was engulfed in smoke and appeared to be on fire. When we opened the door I was relieved to find that it wasn't on fire, but they had not closed the lid on the wood stove. After closing up the stove, the fire began to draw properly and the cabin quickly cleared of smoke. Turning my attention to the kids, I could see no frost bite on any of them. The cabin was very small at about nine feet by eight feet, with a small table and a bunk. At this size it heated up very fast. I told them to keep the fire going that I was going to get help and a ride home.

Dog sled racing

After snowshoeing back to the dog sled I found the dogs buried in the snow. It seemed like forever getting them lined out, but I still could not get them moving. Duff would try but Spook would not get up so I finally I had to unsnap Spook from the gang line. By this time the cold was beginning to take its toll on me, and my fingers would not work very well. It seemed as if it took about 10 minutes to get him unsnapped. Now, without Spook and by taking all the weight off the sled, the dogs started moving. It was a difficult decision to leave Spook behind. He was a faithful friend, but I had to get help for those kids. I was completely exhausted and about to run out of gas myself. I had been pushing hard non-stop for nine hours without a break or any food. Now the wind was right in our face and it was getting dark. For the last hour and a half I had been running on nothing but adrenalin. The exertion was now catching up with me and I had built up quite a sweat fighting through the deep snow. The icy wind was now cutting through my clothes and freezing all the way to my skin. After a half mile I was able to step on the sled runner occasionally, and finally we were moving steadily again. We pushed on for another mile through the blizzard when I faintly heard something behind us. I turned to see Spook catching up with us, boy was I glad to see him!

About half way down the mountain I met the big rotary plow that was used to keep the pass open. After telling the operator so he could radio where they could pick up the lost kids, we moved on down the mountain. At the lower elevation the wind was hardly blowing. Exhaustion had all but completely set in and the dogs and I were really glad to see the pickup. Although I was not aware of it at the time, I was experiencing hypothermia. One thing I was painfully aware of was that my feet were frozen and I was really cold. It usually takes about fifteen minutes to get my gear and the dogs loaded but this time it took forty minutes. My fingers were cold and very stiff and due to my hypothermic confusion nothing seemed to work right. When I got to my parents house, my wife, Ann who is a registered nurse, and my mother took care of me and I was able to finally unwind. It took hours for me to warm up. I literally steamed as the fireplace began melting and drying me.

I received a thank you phone call that the young people were safe, followed up with a very nice card. The kids gave me full credit for saving their lives. They told me that they were nearing the point of freezing to death, as their vehicle was out of gas. They had nothing to eat since breakfast the day before, and were losing hope of being saved. They recounted the whole experience to me. *"Then all of a sudden you opened the door of our car and took over, and we knew our problems were over! You said you would get us to a cabin and get a fire going, then go get help for us"*.

It is still amazing to me how when I relied on Christ, He took over and gave me the uncommon strength needed to accomplish the task. By allowing Him to be my guide, we got everybody rounded up and into that cabin. The location of the sheepherder's cabin and the fact that the old wood stove was still there was a miracle in itself.

Learning this lesson early in life was an incredible gift. *I FOUND THAT I COULD DO ANYTHING THROUGH CHRIST.* For me the main thing was to get myself out of the way and let Christ work through me. Sometimes, as I later discovered, that was a bit more difficult than it sounds.

Chapter 2

For the past couple of years, I had been working for the US Forest Service as a fire boss. Running an eight-man fire crew out of Truckee, California. I had turned in an application to go to smoke jumper's school the next summer, and just after the first of the year I was notified that I had been accepted. Ann and I had also been thinking about going to Alaska. Now we were faced with some major decisions. Should I stay in the Sierra Nevada's and go to the prestigious smoke jumper's school to become a career Forest Service employee . . . or should we go to Alaska? Well, after a few days of indecision, Ann and I started planning for a move to Alaska.

When our family first got to Alaska in the mid 1960's, I found a job as a night janitor at a large hotel. The job brought in some money, but did not cover all of our living expenses. The best thing the job did was provide days free to look for another job. I did not go to work until 3 p.m. and got off work at 11 p.m., so I could get a good night's sleep and be off early the following day, job-hunting.

My law enforcement career started by chance in Anchorage, Alaska. I had gone into the fire department to apply for a job. The man at the desk said that I was too late as they had just gone through the testing/hiring process, and now had a list. It would be another two years before they would be taking applications again. He did say that I was, however, just in time to apply for a job as a police officer if I was interested. They would be taking applications for another week before the testing began. The prospect of becoming a police officer brought a burning excitement down deep in my chest. I walked out of the fire department and had to take a deep breath, wondering, *what is wrong with me?* The only time I could remember this type of excitement was when I was a little kid looking forward to Christmas, or the wonderful excitement I felt when I'd met this beautiful young woman named Ann, who had agreed to marry me years earlier. So with anticipation I went into the police department. I was not nervous, but I was excited as I took the application and listened to the man that advised me to get it filled out and return it as soon as possible.

The next day I turned in my application, and a few days later I received a call for an interview. After two more interviews, a written test, and a polygraph test, I received notice to report to the Anchorage Police Academy where I would begin training in two weeks. The excitement had started to calm down, but I knew that I was where I was supposed to be.

During graduation ceremonies at the police academy, we were standing in line as they presented each of us with our badges. Officer Strong, standing right in front of me, received the last of the old numbers, badge #1. I received the first of the new badges, badge #69. I thought at the time that it would have been great having badge #1, but little did I know the significance of that badge and its developing history in the Anchorage Police Department.

We then took an oath that as police officers we would protect the public by enforcing the City of Anchorage ordinances, regulations and State of Alaska statutes to the best of our ability. To me this was a very serious oath, and I felt a shiver run up my back and my body stood a little taller. I was assigned to work with Officer Cranton, a lead officer to finish my training. My very first day was one I will never forget.

Monday found us on the day shift and everything started out quietly. Then we were dispatched to a three story apartment where a young woman had returned home from working the midnight shift and was not able to get into her apartment. She stated that her husband should be home, that he had called her that night, but that he wasn't answering the phone that morning and she could not get him to come to the door. She seemed quite concerned about her husband, so we went to the manager for the keys. We were finally able to get the manager to come to the door, but he had no way to get through the dead bolt inside. After forcing entry into the apartment, we found the husband lying on the bed, dressed in nothing but his wife's underclothes and a clear plastic bag over his head secured with a rubber band around his neck. *No wonder she was concerned*, I thought to myself. He was, of course, dead.

On a dresser at the foot of the bed was a box about six inches square with several small light bulbs of various colors alternating on and off with no obvious pattern. There was a small aluminum pie plate with part of a tube of glue in it on his night table. It appeared that he had been sniffing glue. Officer Cranton studied the box of lights for a few moments and finally he said; "Those lights don't do anything for me."

We found four pages of well used hand-written notes lying on the dresser next to the light box with directions on how to achieve sexual gratification by cutting off your oxygen. The idea was to stop just before you went unconscious. *He obviously waited too long*, I thought again.

One of my last training segments had outlined this very thing, and at the time I remember thinking that I would likely never see anything like that. Boy was I wrong, and I *sure* didn't think it would be on my first call. Still, I was not too far off as this would be the only call of this nature I responded to during my entire law enforcement career.

Our training included spending two weeks at the city prison farm, where the inmates cut their own firewood, raised their own vegetables and potatoes, and cleared more ground for the farm operation. I also spent two weeks working in the city jail system processing and handling prisoners.

At the academy we received very intensive training on how to put a case together. In the 1960's Alaska did not have an abundance of attorneys. The courts were set up for police officers to file their own complaints, prepare affidavits for search warrants, and complete most of their own legal work in misdemeanor cases. Years later, while fighting in the courts with judges and prosecutors who undermined cases and some who actually disobeyed the law, I knew exactly what to do. The legal background I learned in the early days was invaluable.

After a couple of months my lead training officer signed off and I was on my own. This was the first time I ever looked forward to going to work. We would check our assigned area and go out on patrol. If there were any calls or problems in our patrol area the dispatcher would contact us by radio. A normal shift of patrol officers consisted of seven different patrol areas, two traffic officers, a sergeant and a shift commander. We would report for duty thirty minutes before shift started to get briefed on what was going on. It was also not unusual to have one to three auxiliary officers report in to ride along with the regular officers.

One of our captains told us stories of how they had to do it in the old days. The police department was located near 4th and C Street, which was in the middle of all the bars and the "red light" district of Anchorage. There was a very tall pole that indeed had a red light on top of it. If the dispatcher received a call they turned on the red light and it was the responsibility of the officer on the street to contact the dispatcher to find what the call was about. That was back in the early 30's. Things had not changed that much; we were still in the center of the red light district, but now we had radios for communication.

What I found most interesting about patrol was you never knew what you might get dispatched to. It might be an armed robbery or a domestic disturbance. I loved going out on patrol because anything could happen and it usually did. I did not like to see the end of my shift coming, or for that matter the end of my workweek. Every call could be a new problem. One of my favorite assignments was foot patrol. Fourth and C Street was the hub of the area, with eight square blocks of bars, hotels, tattoo parlors, dance clubs, eating places, strip joints and hock shops. The personnel from Elmendorf Air Force base and the Army at Fort Richardson patronized this area. Saturday night after payday was a wild time in Anchorage.

I was 6'4", weighed 240 and was able to take care of myself, so I drew a lot of foot patrol. One Saturday after the servicemen's payday in our pre-shift briefing our patrol supervisor, Commander Prater, asked, "Who's on foot patrol tonight?" Our sergeant answered, "Gunkel!" Commander Prater got a smile on his face, then continued with what was an annual speech.

"Gentlemen, as you know, it is time for the potato harvest on the city prison farm. You know that it gets very uncomfortable for the street people in the cold of winter. Their answer to the cold is to commit some type of crime so they can spend four to six months in jail where they have a warm place to sleep and lots of potatoes and moose meat to eat all winter." The city farm kept a crew on call 24/7 to pick up all moose road kills for meat processing and freezing for the inmates at the city farm.

"I have just been notified that the harvest starts next week and they are short of workers on the farm. I do not want any bad arrests, but if you come across any good arrests do not pass them up." Commander Prater concluded his comments and the briefing was over. It was 3:05 p.m. and I headed out for the swing patrol on foot.

I walked down C Street to the alley between 5th and 4th Streets and turned west. A few doors down the alley I saw a group of men involved in a dice game. There were eight of them, and gambling was against the law. They did not see me coming up behind a box holding several garbage cans. I watched them for a few minutes, then got on the portable radio and called Commander Prater to come down and transport eight prisoners. When he pulled into the alley the eight gamblers bolted in the confusion. I cut off their escape route and Prater just opened his back door and a few of them climbed right in. I gathered up the money and dice, and when the second patrol vehicle arrived we loaded up the rest of the gamblers. It took four hours to process and book the prisoners. As soon as I completed all my reports I returned to my patrol assignment.

Another officer, Robert Texas and I had a friendly competition going on at that time. That month he was working traffic duty in an area that was mostly residential on the outskirts of town, with a couple of small shopping centers. I was working the red light district where there was excellent potential for arrests. The competition was to see if I could make more arrests than he could issue traffic tickets. We were running pretty close and it was getting near the end of the month when I made the eight arrests for gambling. That put me in the lead and I barely edged him out.

Early the following month I was working the Spenard area of town and was dispatched on a call. A woman had called in stating that a man in the house was holding her against her will. The call was not in the district I was working but right next to it in Robert Texas' area. He was on another call, so I responded. The house was set back about 60' from the road and it was about an hour before dark. The lawn ran all the way to the small 30' x 40' house. The door was located in the middle and there was no cover. I went to the door and knocked but did not get an answer. The third time I knocked, a man opened a small, four inch square panel located in the top half of the door. He asked what I wanted and I identified myself as a police officer and said that I needed to talk to the woman that had called the police. He said there was no woman inside, so I asked if a woman had left the house recently and he said no. I then asked if he would mind if I looked around in his house. As he opened the door I could see he was holding a semi-automatic handgun in his right hand, pointed at the ground. The gun was in a full cocked position and his finger was on the trigger.

My first thought was to get close enough to grab him, but I quickly ruled that out. I was at least two to three strides away from him with no place to seek cover, so all he had to do was point and shoot. My next thought was to get my weapon unsnapped so I could shoot first if he made any aggressive move at me. Again I asked if the woman who had called police inside? He looked at me in a puzzled manner and I thought, *maybe I can talk my way out of this.* He had not started to raise his weapon yet so this seemed like the best course of action. Once more I asked about the woman and that time the question set him off. "I wish people would just leave me alone!," he growled, and his gun hand started to move. I reached for my weapon just as another police car pulled up. My concentration was focused on the man with the gun, when I heard Robert Texas' friendly voice boom out "Hi John, how are you doing?"

Robert had sized up the situation and instantly started out across the open lawn while talking in a friendly manner. The man, surprised by the greeting from Robert, responded, "Oh, hi," and his aggressive manner melted. Robert continued in a calm conversational voice, "John, why don't you give the officer your weapon." John's demeanor completely changed, and as he handed me his weapon butt first, he said, "Be careful, it's loaded." Thanks to the fast thinking of Robert Texas, I had just escaped a very dangerous situation. He had truly saved the day.

Most officers who approached the scene as Robert did would have grabbed their shotgun and stayed behind the protection of their patrol vehicle. In this situation, that would have been very dangerous. The woman that called in the incident had run next door where she was waiting for the police to arrive. Robert took a real chance, but his familiarity with the man and his instinctive actions paid off big time for everyone present.

The rest of the story did not end so well. About eight years later, Robert Texas was patrolling on the night shift. While walking down an alley he noticed a broken window and stopped to investigate. As he peered inside he caught a face full of buckshot fired at point blank range, killing him instantly. Sometimes things do not work out as we would like them to. I owe Robert Texas a huge debt, maybe even my life. *Lord thank you for the times he and I shared, and for watching over and guiding me. Please continue to take care of Robert's family.*

Chapter 3

I had been working as a police officer for just over a year in the City of Anchorage, and there had been a rash of armed robberies. At that time I was working my six months as one of the two traffic units in the city. If there was a traffic accident, I would be the first officer called. If there were no accidents I would patrol the area with the greatest potential for traffic problems. My unit was always equipped with radar (radar was fairly new at the time), which I used for monitoring traffic speeds. As always I attended the daily pre-shift briefing to stay up on any potential problems. There was not much going on other than the occasional traffic stop.

It was a beautiful spring morning on a day shift. I went to the east end of town, working my radar on the morning commuters. All was well. Then I set up just outside the entrance to some new housing tracts on the road called Fireweed Lane. There were no homes where I was set up with my radar. The area was just being developed, so I had picked a short stretch of quiet road with a wide spot that gave me room to park on the edge. With this location, my radar could read about a half mile back. I had only been there five minutes when my rear view showed a vehicle headed my way. A quick glance at the radar meter showed the vehicle to be approaching at 48 miles per hour. That was 13 miles per hour over the posted speed limit. I had just calibrated my radar unit that morning so I knew it was reading accurately.

I turned on the red lights as the vehicle approached, and as he went by I pulled onto the road behind him, turning on the siren. His speed did not change so I jammed the gas pedal to the floor and quickly caught up with him. As I was reaching for the radio mike to report that I was in a vehicle pursuit, he started to slow down. I came up behind him and radioed the license number, vehicle description and stop location to my dispatcher. As I got out of my vehicle it was difficult to ignore the beautiful spring day, but my attention became riveted on the driver. Approaching on the driver's side, I stopped by his back door. Looking over his shoulder I could not see both his hands. He had to twist around at the waist to see me. I asked for his registration and drivers license, staying behind him. He started fumbling around saying it was his wife's car, then reached across to the glove box looking for the papers. As both of his hands appeared, I moved up to the car just behind his front door. He still had to twist around to see me. Finally he looked behind the visor and found the registration. After looking closely at the registration he handed it to me. Again, I asked for his driver's license. The young man, around 20-years-old, reached into his back pocket, then said he had left his wallet at home. When I asked his name he gave me the name on the registration. I took the registration and returned to my patrol vehicle while keeping an eye on him.

I called the dispatcher and asked her to run the name on the registration. I was looking for his driving record and current driver's license, but since I had no date of birth on this guy I did not expect much. When the search came up blank, I requested that she check the phone book for a phone number using the address and name on the registration. When the dispatcher dialed the number she got no answer. Still in my patrol car, I filled out a ticket for speeding and not carrying a valid operator's license. I completed the ticket entering the name and address that was on the registration. The dispatcher tried dialing the number one more time, with no answer. So I returned to the driver and, after receiving his signature promising to appear, I sent him on his way. Little did I know that this man was up to no good.

Three days later I learned the whole story because this young man was in the headlines of every news agency in Alaska. He had been arrested just after robbing a liquor store. Three days before the robbery he had stolen a car to use in the robbery. When questioned, he said that right after he had stolen the car he had been stopped for speeding (that was where I entered the picture). The person interviewing the suspect asked what happened, and the suspect stated that the policeman had caught him with radar. He said, "I was going to kill him, because I had just stolen the car, but I never got the chance. I had my 44 magnum loaded and cocked under the driver's seat. I just couldn't get a good shot at him."

The robber had gone to the liquor store across from Merrill Field, the small plane airport, just after shift change in the afternoon. A half mile east of the liquor store there was a dirt road that entered the brush and small trees, and continued to a dead end overlooking Ship Creek. The road was only a couple of hundred yards long. The officer patrolling that area had just gotten a cup of coffee and parked there to drink it. Just as he turned his patrol car around at the end of the drive, the liquor store was robbed. The call went out, dispatching him to the liquor store robbery along with the description of the getaway vehicle. Before the dispatcher had completed her report, the officer interrupted her radio transmission and shouted over the radio, "I almost hit him!" Responding to the call the officer had sped out the dead end road. The robber had turned in the road where they met head-on, nearly causing an accident. Quickly, other officers surrounded the wooded area and a police dog was brought in. The handler, with three others started tracking, and a short time later the dog found the robber and pounced on him, and prevented his attempt to shoot at the officers. He never got off a shot.

Just a routine traffic stop! Just a routine traffic stop? Yes, just a routine traffic stop.

Thank you Lord!

We thought the successful arrest of this robber might reduce the number of armed robberies from small beer outlet stores, liquor stores, and convenience stores but it didn't seem to have any effect at all. The detectives started working stakeouts where an off-duty police officer would go into a place they expected to be hit and wait for a robbery. They thought the Brown Jug liquor store in the Government Hill area near Elmendorf Air Force Base was due to be hit anytime. One of the detectives attended our pre-shift briefing and reviewed some of the tactics they intended to use on the stakeouts. One proposal that concerned me the greatest was that they would carry a shotgun, but without a round in the chamber. They felt that when the bad guys showed up, the sound of racking the round into the chamber would serve to demoralize them when confronted and they would give up.

If I was to face an armed robber my weapon was going to be loaded, including one in the chamber! There was no way I was going to give the bad guys a head start on me!

That night I was assigned the patrol in the Government Hill area, and later I was to stake out the liquor store until it closed. I called Ann about three hours into my shift to let her know I would be a little late getting home that evening and told her about the stakeout.

Ben Strong, another one of our officers, had come in for the pre-shift briefing even though he was off duty. The evening was pretty slow, with little going on. About half way through my shift I was told that Ben had volunteered to do the inside stakeout at the liquor store and had gone ahead to the store a bit earlier.

Ben and I had gone through the academy together, and then ended up on the same shift. We got to know each other pretty well. Ben was quiet and laid back. He was also an excellent police officer. There were three different liquor stores, in my area. Because it was a slow night, I had patrolled each store several times. Eleven p.m., the end of my shift, was fast approaching so I made one last tour of the liquor stores. The last store I checked was the Brown Jug, the one Ben was staked out in, and all was well. I finished my patrol and returned to headquarters. There were no reports left to do so I went off duty about 10 minutes after 11:00 and drove home.

I was listening to the radio on the way home, and as I entered my driveway the announcer broke into the middle of a song and said, "We interrupt this program to report there has been a gunfight at the Brown Jug liquor store in the Government Hill district of Anchorage, and a police officer has been shot to death!"

I turned around in the driveway without stopping. The thought hit me like a ton of bricks. *I was supposed to be in that liquor store, not Ben!* It was a half-hour drive back to the station and I kept going over my actions that evening. *Was there anything I could have done differently?* There was one police car in the station parking lot and it started to leave as I drove up. Every vehicle was out with three to five officers in each one. Every police officer in the department had come in to help in any way they could. Two detectives were interviewing a suspect, and another one was waiting for them. Finally one of the detectives said to the suspect, "Ok Dewey, I saw you limping when you came in, drop your pants and show us where Ben shot you during the holdup." He immediately stood up and dropped his trousers and pointed to what appeared to be a gunshot wound in his upper leg. They finished the interrogation and went after a warrant for Dewey's brother.

What apparently happened was that the two suspects entered the Brown Jug, announcing to the young female clerk that it was a holdup. They then placed the clerk in the restroom, telling her not to come out for thirty minutes. Ben, in the back of the cooler, waited until the clerk was out of the way before attempting an arrest. He stepped out with his riot gun loaded with buckshot. One of the suspects fired a shot at him hitting him in the upper chest with a 30-caliber semiautomatic, causing Ben to drop the riot gun. Ben then pulled his 45-auto and emptied the clip shooting at both the robbers as they ran from the store. Ben then went over to the counter and dialed the police department number, and when the dispatcher came on the line, Ben told the dispatcher "Holdup at the Brown Jug liquor store in Government Hill." The dispatcher then heard him hit the floor as he fell dead.

Ben Strong, wearing badge #1, was the first police officer killed in the line of duty in the Anchorage police department. This was a very sobering experience for everyone in the department, the entire law enforcement community, and especially in the Gunkel house. As I received the news about the shooting over the radio, Ann was watching it on TV. In my haste to return to the station, I had not stopped to tell my Ann that I was ok. I had, however, told her earlier in the evening that I was going on stakeout duty in that very liquor store. Now Ann, hearing news of the shooting on TV, thought she had been widowed. When I returned home later she was very happy to learn that I was alive. After she explained precisely how she felt going through this experience it crushed me to realize what I had put her through. We had two beautiful daughters with another baby on the way, and I was humbled by Ann's concern.

Still, the job was incredible; I knew I had found my profession. Law enforcement was remodeling my life and giving me greater responsibility. I not only had to answer to my God, but also to those that depended on me.

Chapter 4

Anchorage, Alaska Police Department 101 was my law enforcement learning ground. My mom and dad had taught me to respect those that are older than me, and all women. When I was in high school In Richmond, California I found there were exceptions to most every rule. Richmond High School was located in the California Bay Area and was the largest three-year high school in the United States. The classes were quite large and the high school was spread out. The population was 60 % black and 40% white. If there were prejudices I was not aware of them.

When I entered high school I remember mom and dad's instructions. They gave me the do's and don'ts regarding the opposite sex. Richmond High was the most painful training ground of all, as I remember. I messed up and it was in front of tons of people and escape was painfully slow.

Jim Elsberry, a good friend in high school, and I had a long way to go across the high school campus to our mid-afternoon class. I had been late several times and now the teacher had little patience with me. It was now a sentence of thirty minutes after school for every offense. The first part of the journey was down a long hallway packed with kids. Jim was too polite and always got behind in this hallway. This day, the teacher of the class we had just gotten out of held us a couple of minutes, so the hall was really crowded. I told Jim to keep up with me and we would make it. I turned around to head out, then reached behind me and grabbed Jim's T-shirt so he would not fall behind. Just then I heard a loud voice shouting behind me, "BOY, WHAT YOU DOING?" I turned around and what I saw set the hair on the back of my neck and head straight up. Instead of Jim's shirt, I had grabbed this big black girl's left breast. I froze for just a second and took it all in. This poor girl's eyes were as big as saucers and her mouth was wide open. I have always been a man of quick action, so I immediately turned her loose and proceeded to vacate that area. The place exploded in an uproar of laughter, and as I took one last look back, some of the boys that witnessed this mistake of identity were rolling on the floor out of control and hysterical. No one in the school's history, before or since, ever made it down that hallway as fast as I did that day.

The next lesson I encountered that involved a woman also took place at Richmond High. In one of my classes this young black girl around my age of 17, started coming by my desk and hitting me in the shoulder. I did nothing to provoke her behavior and did nothing in return, but every day she would repeat it. Her swing improved by the day and was getting harder and harder. Believe me, this was no love tap. At first I thought the teacher did not see what was happening, but then I caught her looking away just after I had been hit. I did not know this girl, and could not remember ever seeing her before. This girl had very broad shoulders and swung her punches just like a boy. I was getting very embarrassed because no action was being taken to stop her. The young woman was acting completely like a bully. I was concerned about hitting a girl, but at the same time I was also becoming afraid of her.

After a month had gone by with her punching me every day, I finally decided I would have to do something about it. Just as I expected, at the next class she came in and swung hard hitting my shoulder. I instantly stood up from my desk and hit her shoulder a little harder than she hit me, which surprised her. I kept my hands up in case she became aggressive, but that stopped her. She later told me to come out to the Big R in front of the school and she would be there with her boyfriend right after school. I went out to the Big R after we got out and was relieved to find that they did not show up.

That teacher knew that I was going to have to take action, not her or the school. When I finally did what needed to be done, the problem went away and I learned another lesson: Give girls and women all the respect they will allow, and then do what needs to be done. As Christ illustrated with the woman at the well, he knew what and who she was, but gave her all the human respect she would allow him to give. She responded in a positive way.

It was a Sunday morning and all was quiet on foot patrol in downtown Anchorage. I went several blocks to the area where the big hotels were, then received a call that there were two women fighting in a bar located at 5th and C Street. I started that way and got there 10 minutes later. As I entered the bar, I noticed the bartender was watching two women that were kind of struggling with each other. There was no one else in the bar and I went over to separate them. At this, both women became agitated at me and they both jumped on me hitting, scratching and trying to bite me.

I only had one set of handcuffs, so I grabbed the more aggressive of the two. She had long hair so I pushed her to the floor and quickly stepped on her hair, pinning her head to the floor with my left foot. Then without moving my foot I was able to spin the other woman around and get the cuffs on her hands behind her back. The bartender still refused to help, so I radioed for a prisoner transport with one hand while controlling the handcuffed woman with the other hand, and kept the other woman pinned to the floor with my foot on her hair.

The bartender said that he had no idea what they were fighting about. It did appear their biggest problem was they had too much to drink. I waited until my prisoner transport arrived to let the woman off the floor. It was a good thing because as I let her up she began fighting again. She immediately found herself in handcuffs too.

The women working the streets were definitely of a different sort. This was new to me. I remember in the academy the instructor stated that after working with these women for a while the first thing that will go through your mind when you see a woman is, "I wonder what her price is." I had not yet reached that state of mind, but my education was definitely growing.

Chapter 5

Our family had been in Alaska for a year and a half and had increased by one. Mark arrived on the scene to join his two older sisters, Karen and Beth. I was very pleased with life, and Ann was a very busy mom.

My parents could take it no longer. With a brand new grandson in Alaska, and not having seen the rest of our family for that year and a half, they were on their way to see us. They called the day before they were to arrive and said that they would be in about noon the next day.

That was perfect. I was working the day shift that month, and as usual I was doing foot patrol. As most of the street people did not get up and around until 2:00 or so in the afternoon, I told Ann to bring my parents downtown to see me when they got in. I would be in the area of 4th Avenue and C Street.

Ann arrived with mom and dad about 11:30 a.m. and I got in the car with them. We had visited only a few minutes when I received a call of a fight in progress in the bar right across the street from where we were parked. I told them not to go anywhere and went across the street and into the bar.

The bartender saw me come in and came over to tell me they had gone into the bar next door and pointed to a door connecting the two without going out onto the street. As I entered the next bar, the bartender was pointing to the problem. Two men were pushing each other and it appeared they were ready to start exchanging blows. I went over and attempted to cool them down. The biggest one threw a punch at my face, hitting me on the shoulder as I ducked. I grabbed him and shoved him towards the exit and started herding the other one along. Both of them turned to fight me just inside the door. I pushed both them through the door and the other one hit me on the arm as I followed them out onto the sidewalk. I grabbed one and put him up against the wall, then did the same with the other. I had a handful of each guy's collar, and they settled down as I instructed. I called for a prisoner transport, and waved to Ann, mom and dad as we went off to book the bad guys.

The arrests certainly were not planned, but I am sure that being able to see me doing my job with no problems helped put my parents at ease about me being able to do police work. This reminded me of one of my earliest memories while living in Richmond. I was in the 4th or 5th grade and a boy in my class was always picking on me. There were several boys that hung out with him, but Jackie was the tough guy. My folks had taught me not to fight, so I did not fight. As Jackie pressured me to fight him I became afraid of him. There were always four to six guys with him, and they all wanted me to fight Jackie. These boys had gotten in trouble at school so they would always wait until after school and try to catch me on the way home.

One day my dad was home early and saw these boys chasing me to the house. Then they stood outside chanting, "Gary is a chicken, Gary is a chicken," over and over. Dad wanted to know what was going on, and when I told him, he wanted to know if I had done anything to any of them. I told him no, and when he asked how long this had been going on, I told him they had been at this since we had moved there. My father then told me I had to stand up for myself. "You apparently have done all you can do to avoid fighting, so now you have to fight that Jackie kid, and if you don't I will give you a strapping! You have to take a stand, Gary." By this time, Jackie and his buddies had already left.

The very next day I tried a new route home, but these guys were on to me. I came from a different direction, with them all behind Jackie. This time there were more of them, maybe 10 or more. My mom came to the door as I hit the bottom step. Seeing the look on her face stopped me in my tracks. The gang circled around Jackie and me. I was scared. His friends started rooting for him, saying, "Get him

Jackie! Hit him in the face! Come on Jackie, you can do it! You got the chicken cornered now! All he has is his mother! Mama's little boy, mama's little boy! You can whip him Jackie!"

I looked up at my mom and she came down a couple of steps. She did not look afraid at all. She said, "Gary, just double up your fist and hit him in the face!" For my mother to say something like that was highly unusual. I would do anything for her . . . and suddenly I was not afraid any more. I had tried everything to avoid fighting and these boys would not leave me alone. My mom had tears in her eyes, and recognized the problem. Now I could see she was agreeing with dad 100% even though she had never spoken against his instruction for me to fight.

I turned around and waded into Jackie, hitting him two or three times, and it was all over. Jackie's friends were stunned at first, now mom started shouting, "Gary is the winner! Gary is the winner!" Then they all chimed in, "Gary is the winner! Gary is the winner!" Jackie even chimed in with them. We stood around for a few minutes and there was nothing but friendly talk. The other boys then started wandering off. At school, Jackie and I became great friends. I had learned another lesson in life; stand up for what is right.

When dad came home from work that night, he and mom made me out to be a hero. Looking back, I can see life's lessons that I have learned just by living them. These lessons have shaped my ability to handle real life problems in law enforcement and life as we live it. Only consider force when all else fails. Always look for guidance from Christ. As it was, mom allowed Christ to work through her in the guidance of her young son. She guided her son in the way he should go . . . Now he will not depart from it.

Chapter 6

It was late summer. Mom and dad had left Alaska and gone back to their home at Lake Tahoe. Their visit had brought out more of my past and I could not put it out of my mind.

A year before I had graduated from Tahoe Truckee High School in Truckee, California, I had joined the United States Marine Corps Reserve. I went to the Naval Reserve unit in Reno, and there I was taken over to the Marine training area on the same base. This is when I learned that the Marine Corps was the foot soldier for the Navy.

Still in my senior year I was really enjoying school. I was happy go lucky and well liked by all my teachers. To my parent's dismay, getting good grades was not my highest priority. My science teacher, Mr. Dewhurst even made a special deal with me to get extra credit and allow me to get a passing grade in his class. But taking my Marine exam proved to blow my cover with him.

The Marine entrance exam was conducted at the Naval Reserve in Reno, Nevada. The exam was long and took several hours to complete. It was a general aptitude test that you couldn't really cram for so I just dove in. The next day at home they called me and asked if I could report back to their offices. When my father and I returned the next day, there was some sort of training program going on with Navy personnel. As we sat and waited I noticed a steady stream of people coming into the room. Some nodded, acknowledging me and others just looked at me. Finally an officer came in to talk to us.

The officer introduced himself as the Faculty Commander and said "Congratulations, Gary, you have just passed your entrance exam with the highest grade ever recorded here." In complete disbelief, my father said, "Are you sure?" The officer assured him that I had passed the test much higher than anyone else. Then the officer asked me, "Are you sure you want to join the Marines and not the Navy?"

I was feeling pretty good about myself when I went to school on Monday. My science teacher was waiting for me. "Gary, I am on to you now!" After asking him what he meant by that, he stated that he was an officer in the Naval Reserve. At the weekend meeting he'd just attended they told him about this really smart kid from Tahoe Truckee High School who had aced the Marine exam . . . "And when I found out it was you, I was amazed! You have just been goofing off here!" Whoops! Not only had he found out, but also he told all the rest of my teachers. It was a good thing I only had half of a year to go at that time.

.

My parents were very proud that I was able to graduate, but wished that I had tried to get better grades in school. When they took me to the airport to leave for San Diego and active duty in the Marines, my mom had those tears in her eyes again. Soon my world changed. The fine people at the Marine Corps boot camp were not impressed with my intelligence. Or if they were they did a great job of hiding it.

After boot camp we were moved to Camp Pendleton in the rugged coastal mountains of Southern California. There I went through basic infantry training, then on to advanced infantry training.

The reserve unit I joined in Reno was only an hour or so from our home at Lake Tahoe. While in this infantry unit I spent the next seven and a half years polishing my boots, learning how to dress like a Marine, act like a Marine and walk like a Marine. We got lots of practice on the shooting range, where I qualified Expert with the M1 rifle, and the Army .45-caliber pistol. We also learned skills in hand-to-hand combat, how to shoot all the weapons at our disposal and ongoing in-house training through the reserve unit in Nevada as well as other Marine training facilities.

The Marine Corps is where I learned real discipline, and how to accept responsibility for my actions. Christ knew I needed the type of discipline that the Marine Corps administered. They were very good at making me think before talking. Semper Fi!

Chapter 7

I became interested in the Anchorage auxiliary police officers that came in and worked with us for no pay. They would show up for our pre-shift briefing and we had the opportunity to visit with them. These officers had attended a training course, including firearms safety. They were also required to qualify in order to carry a firearm. They were trained in backing up the regular officers and most were good at what they did. These guys came from all walks of life. The auxiliary officers liked the excitement and teamwork just like the regular officers. The only difference was our level of experience and the fact that we got paid.

Real police work is not like what you see on TV shows. On TV, every program will have one or two cases that are really significant or serious. The typical police officer may only be involved in a few of these cases throughout his entire law enforcement career.

One Saturday evening in late summer several auxiliary officers showed up to ride on patrol. One auxiliary officer decided he wanted to walk foot patrol with me. I was delighted to have the company. That Saturday was a military payday, and there were lots of young guys in and out of the bars and cafés down town. It was a warm and beautiful evening.

My partner, Roger and I had just come out of the alley between 6th and 7th Streets, and turned north. We both saw a young man across the street heading the same direction we were walking. He was wearing a pistol in a holster on his belt. He was about 50 yards ahead of us as he walked into a small café. There was no law against carrying a weapon out in the open, but carrying a concealed weapon was prohibited. Nevertheless, it was very unusual to have someone openly carrying a weapon in the city.

We crossed the street and headed for the same café he had disappeared into. I told Roger to stay near the door in case this guy headed that direction after we got inside. As we went through the door we spotted the man with the gun standing at the rear counter talking to the cook through the opening above the counter. He was facing away from us and I wasn't sure if he had seen us or not. I kept walking and had to go around a row of tables while Roger waited by the door.

The place was packed with every chair occupied. Everyone in the room saw us come in and they were watching the man with the gun. The cafe immediately became quiet as I observed the man unsnap his holster and grab his weapon. As he began to pull his gun, I moved in behind him, drawing my own weapon.

The only sounds in that busy café were the sliding of chairs and people diving for cover. As the man's weapon started to clear the holster, he reversed direction and jammed it back into his holster. It was then that he noticed the eerie silence around him. Not a soul was talking. He turned around and his face went white as he found himself looking down the barrel of my revolver. Taking full advantage of his shocked surprise, I quickly covered the space between us and in one movement snatched the gun right out of his holster. Taking him firmly by the arm, I escorted him to the door with my knees shaking and my mouth as dry as the desert sands. Roger had stood his ground and we had come out on top. As with any dicey situation, when the action is over you closely evaluate your actions. It was very sobering to realize just how near we had come to an up-close-and-personal shoot-out. While Roger still looked stunned, I was deep in thought, analyzing my actions. In this business, part of our behavior is to continually learn and improve so we can maximize our survivability and that of others on the streets. Roger still looked stunned as I uttered a short prayer under my breath: *Lord, thank you for watching over me and delivering all of us in that café safely from near disaster.* We completed a check on the suspect and ran the numbers on his weapon. There appeared to be no problem, just a case of poor judgment.

We started back down the alley we had just walked out of, this time heading east. After walking a couple of blocks we went past the Alley Cat Bar and noticed a couple of men having what appeared to be a heated argument several yards down an alley across 4th Avenue. Roger was a couple of strides behind me as we headed towards the two men. Only one of the men saw us as we walked up; the other had his back to us. I had barely gotten out the words, "OK, what's going on here?" as we approached and I was still speaking as I started past the man with his back to me. Just then I saw him reaching for a gun from a shoulder holster, his actions indicating his intent to shoot the other man. There was no time for further talk, nor time to even attempt to draw my own weapon. I could only go with my instincts.

My only chance was to get control of his weapon, so I lunged at him from more than a stride away. With my eyes fixed on the gun, I grabbed gun, his hand and everything else I could get a hold of. Grasping firmly, I jerked straight up and the man found himself off balance and on his tiptoes. I then twisted him violently, using a hip throw and causing him to hit the alley surface hard on his back and right shoulder. As he fell, this maneuver jarred the gun loose. I now had both hands on his wrist and gun hand and my knee in his ribs. Roger came forward to help me handcuff the suspect after I secured his weapon.

We got the suspect to his feet and I called for the prisoner transport. I noticed that Roger's face was a chalky white. After getting the prisoner booked for attempted murder Roger's color was beginning to improve. He told me that he just remembered that his wife had wanted to do something with him that night so he had to leave early. I sincerely thanked him for the assistance.

I saw Roger on several more occasions, but he never volunteered to walk with me again. I am convinced that Christ had a whole league of guardian angels watching over me. Roger had experienced two very serious incidents during that evening foot patrol. He did very well, and did not back down. He was there for me to the conclusion of each incident. I really did appreciate his dedication to the job, and the backup support he provided.

While this type of work is incredible and will bring out the best in most men, I have also found it can bring out the worst in some.

There were lots of prostitutes operating in and around Anchorage when I was there working as a police officer. There were a lot of pimps, each with several prostitutes working for them in specific areas, and they did quite well. When one of pimps would get ambitious and a try to move his operation into another's area, things would sometimes get serious and a fight would break out. Other times, the fights would be between the pimps and their own prostitutes when the girls were caught freelancing.

Early one afternoon while on vehicle patrol in a section of town known for its abundance of prostitutes, I heard one of our units get dispatched to a shooting. Shortly after the officer arrived, the dispatcher gave a description of the suspect vehicle that had fled the scene. The vehicle was a new white Cadillac with a black man driving, and a black woman passenger. Soon after, I met a vehicle that matched the description of the suspect vehicle. It was going the opposite direction so I turned on my lights and siren and made a U-turn. I pulled up behind the Cadillac, which was doing about 45 miles per hour in a 30-mile zone. We made two turns in the next six blocks and now I was able to determine that the vehicle was headed to the hospital. When they arrived at the hospital the driver quickly hurried around to open the door for the woman passenger. She got out of the Cadillac holding a pillow to her stomach. She took a step then stopped, bending forward clutching the pillow to her stomach, saying "Ohhhhhhhh, Ohhhh, I've been shot." Then she would take another couple steps, then bend over clutching the pillow to her stomach, again moaning, "Ohhhhhhhh, Ohhhhhhhh, I've been shot." I asked her where she had been shot and she straightened up and pointed to her head. There was a bullet hole in her forehead. She responded, "It went in here and out here." pointing to the back of her head. Then she took another few steps and bent over clutching the pillow to her stomach. "Ohhhhhhhhhh Ohhhhhhhh, I've been shot."

There was no doubt that she was emotionally upset. She knew that she should be dead, especially with the entrance hole in her forehead and the exit hole in the rear of her head, but there she was walking around. We got her into the emergency room where a doctor was on the scene immediately. While he was checking the victim I was with the suspect. When I asked where the weapon was that shot her he said it was in his car. So we went out to his vehicle where he pointed to the weapon laying on the seat. It was a .38 Special with a 2 ½ inch barrel. About that time the detectives arrived. We went inside and found that the bullet had penetrated the skin, and had circled her head just under the skin and had exited at the rear of her head, without penetrating the bone. Apparently this woman had gone into another pimp's area and he got upset and shot her. Then her pimp had taken the gun away from the shooter and brought her to the hospital.

More of the "Red Light" surfaced around the large hotels. I was involved in one particular incident at the Anchorage Westward Hotel. The evening had a bit of snappy weather. The temperature was in the mid-20s with a wind of about 15 miles per hour, just cold enough that a light jacket felt good. I was in a patrol vehicle working the down town area. The call came in a little after midnight. There was a woman with a knife in the lobby of the Anchorage Westward Hotel and she was threatening anyone that came close to her. I entered the hotel and the desk clerk pointed to the back portion of the lobby. There was a young woman approximately 25 years old. As I started back I could see a man and a woman apparently employees of the hotel, attempting to engage the suspect in conversation. As I got closer I could see the young woman had a pocketknife with a blade four inches long in her right hand. The hotel employees were attempting to get her to leave the hotel, but she was having nothing to do with them. I asked her if I could give her a ride anywhere. And she ignored me. Apparently she had talked with a man who had asked her to come up to his room. And the hotel staff would not let anyone not registered go upstairs. This woman was apparently high on something as she was very spacey and could not carry on a conversation. I got too close to her and she brandished the knife at me. The male hotel employee circled around behind her and came up to help disarm her.

He reached around her and pinned both her arms to her sides as I moved in trying to get hold of her right hand with the knife. She immediately bent her wrist and cut the employees arm, causing him to let go of her. She then moved towards me with a strong round house swing coming from below her waist with the knife towards my stomach. I reversed direction with my hips, sucking in my gut and barley avoided the knife. I still do not know how she missed me as she followed through getting close to me, so all I had to do was reach out and grab the knife hand as it reached the top of her swing, spin her to the floor and disarm her. Checking the weapon later we found it to be very sharp with a sweeping curved cutting edge. It was a serious weapon. And the prosecutor filed serious charges against her. Assault with a deadly weapon. *Lord thank you once again for being there and watching over me.*

They made me out to be super-cop, but I know how close I came to getting cut wide open. I had completely underestimated that woman and the speed and power of her attempt to get that knife into me. *Lord I thank you from the bottom of my heart, for delivering me home to my wife and family safe and sound that night.*

The court case was pretty interesting. The defense attorney portrayed me as a big bully pushing around this poor defenseless little woman. He asked if I was in uniform and when I said I was, he asked if I had on my gun belt and weapon. I said that I did. He asked how tall I was and I answered 6'4" and I weigh 230 pounds. He responded by asking what were you thinking when you stood in front of this little woman? I said I was thinking I wish she would let me get her a ride home. I told him, one of the hotel employees came up behind her and as I started forward, she started a vicious lunge at me with what now looked like a machete headed right for my stomach. I backed up and sucked in my stomach, and somehow avoided getting sliced open. Her lunge carried her up to my shoulder and I was able to get hold of her hand and knife and disarm her. I did not have time to get scared before, but I made up for it afterward. We won the case and she was off to prison.

The first two years of law enforcement in Anchorage were a real education for me on how to and how not to do things on the street. I truly loved the job and the excitement that came from helping people. I would occasionally think back on what really brought me to Alaska but the fullness that I embraced this profession with did not leave much time for other things. I loved the outdoors, fishing, hunting and all the many outdoor sports, but it was easy to get caught up in the battle against the criminal element.

Ann and I had been raised in the big city atmosphere, but then mom and dad had moved to Lake Tahoe high in the Sierras, and Ann's parents had moved out of the city into what was then the small city of Martinez, California. We decided that is how we wanted to raise our kids, in rural, small town USA.

Right after we moved to Anchorage we did take a trip down the Kenai Peninsula to the Ninilchik River as a family outing. We rented a small cabin and spent two nights. The silver salmon were running and I was able to catch several silvers running around six to eight lbs. each, and several trout. Mark, our son had not arrived yet, but our daughters Karen and Beth really enjoyed being able to reel in the fish. Ann was just glad for a family break even though the finances were pretty tight, as Alaska is an expensive place to live.

One of the ways we were able to cut corners was in our babysitting. I was in a rotation working one month day shift, then the next month working swing shift, then rotating on to the graveyard shift. Ann would set her hospital schedule to be one shift ahead of me so we could watch for each other as I was going in to work and she was coming home. I would have the kids with me then switch them on to Ann. This was marriage by shift, and neither one of us liked it, but it got us through some tough times.

While we were going through this time our pastor was preaching about Christ's teaching in the Bible about tithing. Ann and I both felt we should be giving to the local church but there was no way we could do that as we were both working hard and long and it was taking every cent we had, and still the month was too long for the money. Finely, after praying about it we decided that we were going to do it anyway. The Bible says to give 10% of our income, so we did exactly that. We cannot tell you how it happened but for the first time since we had moved to Alaska we had money left over at the end of the month. We double checked our bills and found them to all be about the same, and still there was money left over. We had trouble with whether we should be tithing the before taxes amount or the after taxes amount. That first month was the after taxes amount, but a little later we decided to give 10% of the before taxes amount. Now it was even easier to get through the month. Again we did not get an increase in wages, or a reduction in the bills that came in. It was just easier and we had more to spend. I would challenge anyone to accept Christ's teaching in the Bible about tithing to Him, and apply it to themselves. The results were incredible. We did nothing different during that first month, other than give the money to the church before we paid any bills, or bought anything else

Our fishing trip also alerted us that there were other possibilities. There are law enforcement needs and nursing needs in the small towns also. Alaska did not have a county form of government; instead they utilized a borough form. And in the 1960's there were no police entities in the boroughs. There were only a dozen or so towns that had police departments, and the State Troopers were the police for most of the state. At that time there were only 129 State Troopers covering the whole state. After talking with a few State Troopers I found that on a busy day when I was working in Anchorage as a city traffic control officer I would do more accident investigations in one day than most State Troopers did in a year. Another consideration was the rate of pay. If I was getting State Trooper pay, and we did not have to pay a babysitter and gasoline for another vehicle going round trip to Anchorage every day, Ann would not have to work. Now that was a goal worth working towards.

California was where we lived before Alaska, and we were trying to compare the Alaska State Troopers with the California Highway Patrol. That was like trying to compare oranges with apples, as they were completely different agencies. The California Highway patrol was mostly highway patrol and related work on the highway corridors, with a few exceptions. I got to thinking more and more about the Alaska State Troopers, and the opportunity of possibly getting a bush post, where I could really see some wild and remote areas. And where we could find the rural atmosphere that was so prevalent in the shaping of this country. The name "The Last Frontier" really had some truth in it.

Chapter 8

I finally I went by and spent an hour or so getting information about the State Troopers. This really did intrigue me and at the end of the interview the officer I talked with said the magic words I'd heard before: "You have come by at just the right time, we are just now getting ready for the new generation of Alaska State Troopers. We have made a deal with Sheldon Jackson College in Sitka and this will be our first academy there. The training will last three months, and cadets will be living on campus and receiving the training right there in Sitka. The applications will close in just a few days, so hurry and get your application in." That is exactly what I'd been told me at the Anchorage PD when I had inquired there two years before.

That evening I hurried home with my application and Ann and I had another big powwow over the pros and cons of this career change. As usual the subject came up, I wonder what Christ would have us do. We prayed about it and we both felt there were doors open for us to proceed on with the plans. Ann has always seemed to know ahead of time when there is a change in direction coming for our family and she got to work at home, and I got the application process started. I filed the application, took the tests and after a short week and a half I got a letter of acceptance and was told to report in two weeks to the Alaska State Troopers Training Academy in Sitka, Alaska.

We got Ann and the kids airplane tickets to California, as they would spend the whole time I was in training with her mother and then my mother letting grandparents spoil their grandkids.

I gave the Anchorage Police Department two weeks' notice that I was leaving. There was a semi-pro baseball field in Anchorage, and an industrial baseball league in town. I was the center fielder for the police department team, and we had two more ball games left in the season. The very next game after I had given notice I was out in center field with a guy on 2nd base and two outs in the 6th inning. It was a very close game and we wanted to win as these guys were in first place.

We were not in the running, somewhere around fourth place, but for the glory we were playing all out. The batter hit a blooper out into shallow center field. There is no way the shortstop could get to that ball so I was giving it all I had. The shortstop was thinking the same way, that there was no way the centerfielder could get to that ball. No one saw the danger of a crash so no warning went out. I could see that I might have a chance in an all out dive for the ball, so I put my glove out and went into a flat dive, The shortstop thought the same thing and running as hard as he could made one last dive while still looking back over his shoulder at the descending baseball.

I remember seeing the ball just clear his glove and felt it hit the pocket of my glove at the same time his face hit me dead center in the chest breaking his glasses and knocking him out. The collision completely deflated my chest, leaving me breathless. I began to think I would never breathe again. The umpire was the first to arrive and he ran around the pile looking for the ball. I was so completely without air I could not say anything or even wiggle my foot. Finally the umpire came over and picked up my hand with the glove on it, and opened my glove. Seeing the baseball buried deep in the pocket he signaled and yelled, "You're out!" It took 15 minutes for us to get off the field. I was not able to do anything with my arms and the little air I took in was extremely painful. At the hospital the doctor said I had suffered an extremely severe bruise to my lungs and sternum and said I should do nothing strenuous for the next month and a half.

I explained to the doctor about the State Trooper academy and he said you could do only what your body will allow you to do. The doctor gave me a letter and a week and a half later I kissed my wife and family goodbye for three months, and off I went. In Sitka we assembled at the training academy and checked into our rooms. I was in a dorm room with six other guys on the second floor. This class was the first one at the new academy location in Sitka. The next morning they assembled the entire class and welcomed us. They gave us an outline of the classes we would be taking and what was expected. The one thing that really jumped out and grabbed our attention was when they announced, "We expect to lose up to forty percent of those sitting here today." Every class was a must pass with no exception.

I was granted light duty for the first week, and then I participated to the best of my ability as my injuries allowed. It took me about three weeks to be able to keep up with the group, then my speed and stamina came back quickly. I was not one of the leaders, but I consistently came in the top 10 positions.

I found that the classes with the state troopers academy were much more intense and went into more detail than my training with the Anchorage police. For instance, the hand to hand combat had several holds, throws and blows that you could deliver to gain the advantage of a person that was combative. I had been through the Anchorage Police Department, and the United States Marines hand to hand training, and while they also demonstrated throws and holds and ways to gain advantage of your opponent, I found a few bits of information that really enabled me to be successful when the outcome was really serious.

Our instructor told us that we would be taught many holds, throws and blows, but that we should only focus on two or three that worked for us. "Unless you are constantly working out and can become proficient with all the holds you learn, then just stick to the few that you know how to use proficiently. If you have to stop and think of what to do, you have just lost the advantage, and probably the battle."

We spent some 20 hours getting our hand to hand tools sorted out and picking what works best for each of us. For this whole course segment we were paired up. I was the second largest so I got my practice with the biggest guy. He weighed 40 lbs. more than I did and was three inches taller than me . . . and there was no fat on any part of his body.

One of the throws we learned was how to deal with your opponent who came running at you from yards away with the intent of tackling you or knocking you sprawling. We were on the beach and I was supposed to grab George's shirt and fall onto my back pulling him down while placing my foot in his gut and hanging on to his shirt as he went over me well, George got up a head of steam and I missed his shirt when he hit me, so he knocked me another 15 yards down the beach.

I felt I had been rolled over by a steamroller. The instructor said that is exactly the way not to do that move. I fully agreed with him. So we went through it in slow speed, That gave me a chance to feel the right way of getting it done, George walked up and I grabbed his shirt and rolled over backwards placing my foot in his gut, but lost my grip on his shirt about half way through, so as George went over he went sailing like a big bird right on down the beach. The idea of this throw is to hang on and as George lands on his back the momentum brings me up on top with the opportunity of handcuffing him.

George was a good sport, and he kept working with me. It took about 30 minutes and I finally got everything coordinated and made three good throws in a row. I have used this throw or some variation of it a few times since, and every time it has been successful.

The hold I learned that I have used the most can be very dangerous. It's called the sleeper. We received instruction that started in the classroom. It is simple, by cutting off the blood to the brain you pass out in a matter of seconds. If the blood is cut off completely for more than about a minute the person can die. Those of us that wanted to learn this hold received some very intense training. We would practice on each other with at least two observers paying close attention every time the hold was applied. Once learned, this hold is the most effective way to gain control, leaving no after effects of any kind. It is easy to apply. The rules I set for my-self is to never put a person out, just apply until they start feeling warm and fuzzy. It works every time, and gives me a greater margin of safety. The positives about the sleeper are it does not involve choking or using a nightstick, and it does not bruise the suspect or the person applying the hold.

We were also instructed in riot control, how to determine whom the agitator was, and to go after that person. By successfully controlling the leader the riot would melt away. This got a discussion started and as I looked back now at my experience in law enforcement, I found that I had been using the same type of reasoning in taking care of problems as I was dispatched on calls where someone was causing a problem. Remove the problem and everything settles down. This did not necessarily mean to arrest the person; if the problem could be taken care of by getting one person to leave, that was fine also. But if it did require an arrest, and there was resistance, the sleeper hold was quick and easy to settle the unruly one down and transport them off to jail with no fight involved. After the academy, several of these nuggets became instilled in my methods of handling unruly individuals throughout my law enforcement career.

As the three month academy progressed I was gaining knowledge in all areas. I was exceptionally open to new ways to increase positive impact on the community, while at the same time I was learning how to be of greater service to those within the community by reaching out and participating in different community activities such as basketball, baseball and local conservation or sports clubs. This group believed that conservation is not preservation, but that by controlling the harvest in any area depends on the amount of animals existing, and especially the male to female population. The key is getting to know the district and adjusting the harvest throughout the area the same as a good trapper would in his area. He will take only the largest male animals and stay away from the females and younger, smaller animals, only taking what is necessary to maintain an even balance.

Chapter 9

There was just over two weeks to go when I was called in to talk to the Academy Commander. Needless to say I was apprehensive about what to expect since we had lost a large number of cadets to that point. Then I was really flattered when the Commander advised me that myself and one other fellow would be graduated early from the Academy because of manpower needs in the Anchorage area. I did not have to accept this early graduation. I could stay and finish the academy if I wanted. I had been there for almost two and a half months, and that meant two and a half months away from my family especially Ann. It was an easy decision and all I could say was, *Lord, thank you.*

That means I had no other tests to take (I had already passed the toughest ones), but the most important was that in two days I was going to see Ann, and we could celebrate together this change of direction in 'our' profession. Ann would not have to work anymore. She could be a stay at home mom and get involved in any community or church activities she felt led to do.

I met Ann at the airport, and she informed me that our kids stayed with my mom and dad to continue the program to further spoil them. My mom was really disappointed as the two weeks of planned events with our children and the chance to visit with Ann were cut short because of my getting out of the academy early. It was fun being free and by ourselves for a few days, but we both looked forward to our kids arriving back home with us again. We did not have any idea how short the time was that we would have before we were getting ready for our next major move. It was just shortly before my class was scheduled to graduate.

I was now an Alaska State Trooper, and on my first duty assignment in Anchorage. I was aware of the very good reputation the State Troopers enjoyed, but did not know how they had acquired that status. The large class I was in had raised the total number of State Troopers to 126 Commissioned Officers. If you take Texas, the second biggest state, you can drop it into Alaska three different times and still have room left over. That gives you a little idea of the huge size of this extremely rich place. Only first class cities were eligible to have their own police departments, which include only a dozen or so cities in the whole state. The State Troopers were the only police protection everywhere else.

Several of those early State Troopers were outstanding heroes in saving lives early in the Valdez earthquake. People in the Valdez area and along the roads up and down the Alaska Peninsula that were damaged, cut off and endangered, several State Troopers drove as far as they could then took to the roads on foot to check on people at different locations who were unable to get out of where they were. The State Troopers earned the respect of the citizens of Alaska by helping them against incredibly long odds.

In another instance the mayor of Cordova, in desperation called the governor pleading for the governor to send a detachment of State Troopers to his town as people on one side of town had risen up against those from the other side of town and at anytime they expected one side or the other to open fire. There were no roads in or out of town, so the only way to get there was by airplane. The governor responded that he would send the State Troopers. The mayor was the first one to get out to the airport when the flight came in. He saw one State Trooper get off the airplane, and hurried up to him and asked where are the rest of the troopers? The State Trooper looked around and asked, there is only one town isn't there? And the mayor nodded, yes. So the State Trooper responded it will only take one trooper then. Within a couple of days the problems had all been resolved, and the State Trooper was able to leave.

In our training I found out that the State Troopers have the responsibility of serving civil papers for the court system. This, for the most part, was a drag, having to serve paperwork, but we received lots of detailed instruction on civil service. If we got careless we could assume the liability in someone's case. That was an unpleasant thought.

Generally, that is one of the chores that the day shift draws. I was in a new subdivision south of Anchorage, looking for an address that was very elusive to find. It was 10:00 a.m. and I had given up. The only way I was going to find the address to serve this paper was to find someone in the area and ask directions. It seemed that the house numbers were going backwards with a few left out. There was no accurate address sequence. That is probably why this civil paper had not been served yet. I was making one more swing through the area, and then I saw someone out in her yard. A woman was lying down near the sidewalk that went by her house. The only problem was she was wearing a bikini bottom and nothing else.

I made another swing through the neighborhood, but still did not find anyone else I could talk to, so I went by the bikini bottom again and she was still there. I stopped the patrol vehicle and got out. I walked over to where she was lying on her stomach. She raised her head and looked at me, and I looked straight into her eyes and never looked away from her eyes. I asked directions and she told me where that address was. I was very polite as I repeated the instructions she had given me. When she nodded that I had it right I thanked her, still being very careful to only look her directly in the eyes. Then I left.

I went on to serve my paper and as I was leaving the neighborhood I noticed that the woman I first talked to was no longer in her front yard. I found that by not looking at what the woman was displaying, she knew exactly where my eyes had looked and more importantly where they had not looked, and by not prolonging the stay, just taking care of the business at hand, I did get the civil paper served.

There were also a few arrest warrants that had not been served, but for those there was lots of detailed information. One warrant in particular was a young lady with a failure to appear warrant issued by the court. Fancy Nancy was a topless waitress and nude dancer at one of the nightspots outside the Anchorage city limits.

When a State Trooper would attempt to locate the young woman during working hours, she was never there. The State Trooper would try and check ID's on the dancers and girls waiting tables but when they are only wearing a G string or bikini bottom there is no place to carry an ID. The girls would have to go to their dressing rooms, where other girls were at various stages of dress to retrieve their ID's and somehow they were never able to catch up with that particular elusive young woman

It was a situation where a group of young women were able to make you feel very uneasy to say the least. I decided this could be approached in a different way. I went out to the club in the early afternoon, when there were only two vehicles in the parking area. There was one topless woman behind the bar talking to a male customer. I stopped at the far end of the bar and the man left the building when he saw my uniform.

The woman bartender came down and stopped in front of me and asked if she could help me. Looking her in the eyes I explained the problem of the warrant issued by the court and asked if I could get the home address of the young woman. I was told they could not give out anyone's home address. After we talked for a few minutes, eye to eye, she reached down and pulled the tank top from around her waist up covering her breasts. She then told me to come to the bar and ask to see Fancy Nancy the next evening when she would be there working.

The next night when I went to the place the temperature was 15 degrees outside. And like the last time I was in full uniform. I contacted the bartender and he said she would be right there. When she walked up it was obvious that they had not told her I was coming to meet with her, as she was wearing nothing but a G-string. *Lord what am I doing here?* I informed the young woman she was under arrest for failure to appear. I am sure the instructor at the State

Trooper academy would agree that this one time I did not have to do a search. I could see everything so there would be no need . . .

Now the tricky part, Fancy Nancy asked if she could get her long coat as it was cold outside. I said yes, but I would have to search it first. So off we went into the dressing room where she gave me her long coat and does a slow 360 degree turn around in front of me, showing that she is not armed. I felt my face turn a bright red and quickly cleared the coat for her to put on, then we headed out to the patrol vehicle. It must take them an awfully long time to put on all that make-up!

I cuffed her with her hands in front (I did not want a surprise opening of the front of her coat as I had already seen more of her than I wanted). I immediately called the dispatcher that I had a female prisoner that was wearing nothing but a G-string and an overcoat. I gave my location and reported in every two minutes all the way to jail. At the jail I took the prisoner in to the booking area and both lady dispatchers had to come and see this prisoner. There were several men in the area, but it was the women that were the most curious.

After work that evening I went home and took Ann in my arms and just held her tight. *Lord, thank you for our two little girls and little boy. Show Ann and I how we are to raise them to follow you.*

Chapter 10

It was now the fall of 1968 and Ann and I were in Anchorage for a few weeks helping out with the short staffing in the Anchorage detachment while I was apparently being evaluated. I was asked if I would like to take over a one man post in Glennallen, Alaska. The town is located 200 miles south of Anchorage, an interior highway post with a population of approximately 800. I told them that I was very interested, so they sent me out to look at Glennallen and the area. I spent the day with the State Trooper that had been there for two years.

We toured the local holding cell, trooper office, met the State Fish and Game officer and the head of the state road department and went to the mission hospital and medical offices. They only had one doctor and several nurses who were grossly overworked. The doctor and nurses did an enormous amount of quality work with very little support or supplies. We also went to the local Bureau of Lands, Alaska's equivalent of the US Forest Service.

The State Troopers residence is located at the local airport in Gulkana, maintained by the federal government. Also living there is the crew running the flight service station. Jack Wilson had a hanger located on the airport where he did work on his airplanes, and other private aircraft in the area. The office also maintained by Jack was his headquarters for his air taxi service. Jack Wilson at the time I was there held the record for landing and then taking off at the highest altitude in the world. Jack was also a widely known bush pilot that flew all over Alaska and was an exceptional glacier pilot.

At that time in 1968, the geographical area covered by the one Glennallen trooper was about 80 miles to the northwest of Glennallen, south about half way to and then going south all the way to Valdez on the coast in an arm of Prince William Sound. The district following the route the Alaska oil pipeline was going to take on its route from the North Slope to a port in Valdez. To the north, the Glennallen district ended at the Paxson junction, turned north at the junction and went about thirty miles further north along the Caribou highway.

Going southeast down the Copper River runs an old road that was built originally as a railroad bed from Kennecott Copper mine. This old railroad crossed a bridge over the Copper River to town, and went all the way down to where the fresh water met saltwater at the ocean. There is no area that you can access in a vehicle.

The highway continued southeast out of Glennallen towards Tok, where it turned south to the Nabesna Community and extended back towards the beautiful Wrangle Mountains.

Draw a line in the state of Washington right down the center of the Cascade Mountain Range from the north border with Canada to the south border with Oregon and the area that is east of the cascades is roughly the size of the Glennallen one trooper district I would be covering. There were over 600 miles of Highway and the towns of Valdez, Glennallen, Nabesna and several smaller settlements. There were also three Indian villages and several hunting camps with countless bush airstrips scattered through out the area.

This was all good hunting country with lots of moose, caribou, Dahl sheep, mountain goat, black bear, grizzly and small game, including timber wolf, wolverine, lynx, beaver, land otter, and others.

Then there was the fishing, some of the best in the world. King salmon, grayling, red salmon (sockeye), silver salmon (coho), rainbow trout and Dolly Varden trout. This is what I came to Alaska to experience. But somehow I got side tracked with life and trying to make a living.

There were some negatives to being the State Trooper I was to replace as he stated that he did not remember how long it was since he had a day off. His average workday was eleven to twelve hours a day, and all he was doing was answering calls.

Glennallen is the first place I saw hamburger for sale at over $5.00 per pound, and remember, that is back in the 1960's! The other groceries were about twice as much as they were in Anchorage and they were not cheap in Anchorage either.

When I got home, Ann was already packing. This certainly was a direct answer to our prayers. My hunting would now be a necessary enjoyment, as we would need the meat hunting could produce.

Chapter 11

Ann and I had met in the First Baptist church in Richmond, California. We had an on-again off-again romance in high school that was interrupted with my folks moving to Lake Tahoe.

Mom was really impressed by Ann, who she had gotten to know quite well from our earlier time together. My sister Patty and mom got together after I got back from my six months active duty in the US Marine Corps and pushed and persuaded me to call Ann who was in her final year of nurse's training in the county hospital in Oakland, California. I made a trip to the Bay Area to take a friend of my folks home from Cedar Glenn Lodge at Lake Tahoe. I was spending the night at my aunt's house, only a couple of miles from the hospital where Ann was in training.

Actually, I was very open to dating Ann as I had always liked her, but so did several other guys. I had not talked to her for a year or so, and I was a little timid about calling, but I called and said I was in town for just the evening and asked if we could get together. Ann said she had a date in a couple of hours, but come on over. I did and despite those circumstances we had a good time. I was very interested in Ann and she appeared similarly interested in me. But this romance was not like dating the girl next door. I lived over two hundred miles away from her. I asked Ann for a date for the following Saturday. I picked her up at the hospital and we went to the Contra Costa County Fair. We spent several hours there through the afternoon and into the evening. We were mostly walking and talking and getting re-acquainted. We were on the midway when one of the vendors called to me "Bring your pretty little wife over here and win her a prize" That caught me by surprise but I did go over and try, but missed the milk bottles with the baseballs.

I have to say that having a beautiful girl like Ann as my wife sounded pretty good. The following Friday evening, I again picked Ann up at the hospital shortly after she got off work. We went out and had a quick meal and left for Lake Tahoe. Ann had been able to get the whole weekend off so we were able to get out of town. Mom, dad and the whole family and crew for the motel were waiting for us to arrive. We got there late and stayed up talking for a couple of hours. Saturday morning we played tourist with some time on the beach, a little water skiing and some boat riding. Then back to Cedar Glenn Lodge for some R & R around the pool. My folks had been in the motel business quite some time and a lot of our guests were really old friends. This romance between Gary and Ann was a very popular subject around Cedar Glenn Lodge, so when the lovely Ann arrived on the scene she was the center of attention. Ann was kept busy with our crew from the motel, but especially mom and dad's friends and guests from the motel.

I had planned a hike in the mountains. I wanted to be alone with Ann, and only Ann. It was about 4:00 p.m. and the summer evenings did not get dark until about 9:00. There is a road that leaves Lake Tahoe right as you enter Kings Beach referred to as the Truckee shortcut. The road goes right by the golf course and heads up the mountain going over a little pass and works its way down and out of the hills to a large flat with scattered pine trees and meadows on its way to the town of Truckee.

About two miles before getting out of the trees and reaching the Truckee flats there is a draw the goes off to the right, and that is where I took her. We got out of my pickup truck and started up the left side of the draw working up along the draw, climbing the ridge. About a mile from the road the trees thin out and we could look back down the draw and see that the bottom opened up into a very pretty grassy meadow. A small grove of Aspen trees were scattered along the far edge of the meadow. A small spring entered the top of the meadow and worked down towards the grove of Aspen trees. While we were still on the ridge, the shadows were growing longer. Just at that time from across the canyon came the call of a lone coyote with its voice echoing back and forth across and down the canyon.

Ann moved closer to me and I took her hand and put my arm around her pulling her close. I had found this special place several years earlier and wanted to share it with her as I was really taken by its beauty. I wanted to show her more so we started off the ridge and worked down into the draw towards the spring where it entered the meadow. We stepped over the spring, and walked across the meadow. We were both overcome with the beauty of the area. Going down to the aspen trees I took her hand and we entered the edge of the trees and there overlooking the meadow and spring was an aspen tree with carving on the bark. I pointed to the tree and Ann went over and saw the carving that said "Gary Loves Ann." It was obvious that the carving was several years old, as there was a date that took the age back to our high school days. This impressed both of us. I knew that this young woman was the one Christ had selected for me, way back then. All these things did not just happen accidentally. I showed Ann that my feelings dated farther back than both of us realized. Ann melted into my arms and we just held each other close. WOW!

We shared a fruit and nut candy bar sitting on the ground and leaning back against the tree watching the water going down to the meadow. Then I showed Ann how to drink from a small stream, one of the sweetest springs I ever drank from. We got back to the road just before dark and went back to Cedar Glenn. I took Ann back to Oakland and her school at the hospital the next day, and as I drove back to the lake all I could think about was her.

I had to see her again so I went down again the following Friday night and stayed with my aunt and uncle in Oakland and picked Ann up Saturday morning. We drove over to Santa Cruz on the coast and spent the day on the beach, doing lots of talking about the future, and discussing our plans. After taking her home that evening I decided to stay the next day. So I picked her up early, but it took me until afternoon to get the courage to ask her to marry me. I was blown away when she said, "Gladly!"

I returned home with the main task of getting Ann a set of rings. As soon as possible I returned back to the Bay Area to ask her mom and stepdad for her hand in marriage, and give Ann the rings.

Chapter 12

I lived at Lake Tahoe with mom and dad, younger brother Gregg and the motel crew that consisted of three other girls in the same age group as us kids. Mom took in a similar crew every summer to help clean the motel. They were all like family and I did get a lot of ribbing from my sisters and the all girl crew. Our dinner table was big and round. My sister, Patty worked at the bank, and asked, "When are you going to get Ann a ring?" Actually I had already bought her a ring, but did not plan to tell them until I had given the ring to Ann. I was not about to give those girls more to tease me about. So I said I am not going to buy a ring. It was obvious that I am a lousy liar, and they were all over me.

I had been saving my money to buy a rifle that I really wanted. And they all knew about it. Patty asked, "Did you buy the rifle?" and I replied no. Then Patty said, "I saw a big check come through on your bank account from Rogers Jewelers." And I wanted to crawl under the table. I usually did a little better than hold my own against all these gals but they really piled on this time.

Finally, I did admit that I had bought Ann a ring and they all broke out cheering. I was red as a beet and was really flustered. They would not let me eat another bite of dinner, they wanted to see the ring, I looked at mom and she was on their side. I was proud of the rings I had bought for Ann, they were really good looking and larger than most I had seen. The engagement ring had one large diamond with two smaller diamonds, one on each side. And the wedding band had four small diamonds. This young woman really had my attention. I went up to my bedroom and got the rings and took them down to the table and they were all waiting for me. I took the rings to my mother and gave them to her. She opened the box and I saw the tears come to her eyes. She obviously approved, and passed the rings on to the others. I was pleased with the response from everyone there. I just hoped Ann would feel the same.

I went down again on the next weekend and was really pleased by Ann's response to the rings. Later that night we were at Ann's home. Her mom Georgia and stepfather Johnny were watching television in the living room. We sat down for a short time and I finally got up the nerve, and went over and turned off the TV. I said I have a question I needed to ask. Johnny said what is it? So I said "I am asking for Ann's hand in marriage. But I want you to know we are planning on moving to Alaska." Johnny said, "Is that all?" And her mother said "No," not objecting to us getting married but to us moving to Alaska. Then Johnny said, "Now turn the TV back on!" Johnny, Georgia and Ann all three laughed at the expression on my face.

We were married four months later on my birthday in December. Ann was apologetic about picking my birthday for our wedding but I was all for it. I have never received a birthday gift that meant so much to me.

Now several years later all these things were coming together. It is very interesting how God will answer our prayers, and prepare us to be able to fulfill what he has in mind for us. I continue to thank God for bringing us together, again and then again. I am so appreciative for my mom's work to point me in the proper direction when choosing the right young lady to live with and work together in raising a family up under the shelter of God's umbrella, and for keeping us together, with exceptionally good health.

Chapter 13

Shortly after the State Trooper academy and my short tour in Anchorage, we moved to Glennallen in early summer of 1968, and settled in for our first trooper post. There was never a lack of work to do. I worked in a couple of fishing days catching a nice mess of grayling, which are similar to trout. We heard that the salmon were running in the Copper River and were told that the only way to catch them was to use a dip net. The Copper River is very muddy as is true of most glacier-fed rivers. Nearly all of the smaller rivers that originate at the Wrangle Mountains originate from glacial water and feed into the Copper River. As it works its way around to Nabesna, the Gulkana River enters the Copper River about five miles north of Gulkana Airport. The Gulkana River is one of the smaller rivers and has clear water. This country has a little of everything.

Going by Gulkana air field a few days after we moved there I saw a small cub-like aircraft that was newly painted, with a for sale sign on it. I went in to Jack Wilson's flight service and asked about the airplane, and found it was a tandem Taylorcraft with a 65 horsepower engine. Jack said the airplane was in good shape and would be an excellent first airplane to learn to fly in. The airplane was rated a three place aircraft, with the pilot in front and a slightly wider seat in the back rated for two.

I'd been thinking about learning to fly and this was exactly what I was looking for, an aircraft, that was inexpensive and a good airplane to learn in. The type of flying I wanted to do dictated a "tail dragger" aircraft. I was interested in getting into those hard to get to areas for the hunting and fishing. Ann and I also wanted to explore Alaska's rich history with all of its areas to still discover, and rediscover. This airplane does not have an electrical system. To start the airplane, you have to prop it. That means you physically pull the prop through, one pop at a time until the engine starts, and then you get in the airplane and drive. That also means there is no radio in the airplane, so unless you buy a portable hand held radio there is no communication. And very little heat is available. When the weather gets really cold, 20 degrees or colder, you do not feel any heat. You just leave the defrost vent pulled so as to keep the front windshield defroster open with heat from the motor. When it gets down to 10 degrees give or take a little, there is no defrost action. This is one of the inconveniences of an airplane with no electric system, but the price was right, $2,600. Lack of an electrical system does not make the airplane unsafe, just inconvenient, and there are always ways to work around the different inconveniences.

There are hundreds of miles of beaches that can be searched and explored in Alaska, and just thinking of the new areas accessible through flying got me excited. But first I had to learn how to fly. Mike Stone, Jacks number one pilot also held a certificate as a flight instructor. I bought all the books needed to learn about flying, navigating, and rules of what to do and what not to do. And then with Ann sharing my enthusiasm, we bought the airplane and I started doing the paperwork and taking flying lessons.

On one of those early flights, I took off with Mike in the rear seat. It was a nice afternoon and the temperature around 30 degrees. We flew by some low clouds but as I started to turn to the left the stick would not move. So I told Mike that the stick was stuck and he said, "I have it." I then took my hands and feet off of the controls and Mike took over. After a few minutes or so Mike said, "You are right, it seems to be jammed." Then he asked in a friendly voice, "Are you ready to meet your maker?" I responded, "I am ready when He is ready for me. How about you?"

I knew Mike had only been married a couple of months, and he responded, "I would really like to kiss my wife a few more times." I laughed and said, "Now that you mention it, so would I." "Ok." he said, "You take over and I'll tell you what to do. This will be a good experience for you."

There was no wind so using the foot pedals on the rudder I skidded around and headed back to the airport. We lined up a long way off and I used the foot pedals to keep the right and left in line and backed off on the throttle to lose altitude, then added throttle when we needed to gain altitude. We had a little bump as we touched down at the airport. *Wow that was easy!* I was feeling my confidence building.

After getting safely on the ground we went looking for the problem, and found it right away. The fabric on the back of the wing where the ailerons were attached was not glued completely to the wing and it was touching the aileron. There was condensation in that little cloud we had flown by which caused the cloth to freeze to the aileron, not allowing the stick to move. We had neither one of us put much pressure on the stick, and that's all we had needed to do that time. You might guess that my pre-flight on the airplane really improved after that experience. Fixing the problem was easy.

In a very short time I had soloed and was able to progress each time I found time to fly. I followed the list of requirements I needed to accomplish and within a few months I had my license. The type of flying I wanted to do could be a little hard on me and my airplane so I asked Mike if I could hire him to make a bush pilot out of me, or enough of one that I would not get into trouble.

Mike said I have always wanted to trap and I hear you are a good trapper. You get skies on your airplane and I will show you what I know about bush flying, while you show me what you know about trapping. The next year I received an incredible education in flying, or probably even more importantly, in flying safely.

Shortly after getting an airplane we got the chance to rent a 160-acre homestead with a home and space to build an airfield runway just behind the house. We were 10 miles north of Glennallen, and life felt well.

Life as a State Trooper on a highway post was very busy. Once every two weeks I would drive to the small town of Valdez on the coast. This was before the oil pipeline was built, and the pipeline was only a rumor at that time. I would drive down and serve any legal papers that needed serving, check in with the city mayor, the Chief of Police and his one man police department. Then I would take care of any problems that happened outside the city limits.

The two main sources of income in the area at this time were commercial fishing and the state mental hospital. This trip the hospital had requested that I transfer a mental patient from the Valdez hospital to Anchorage. This is accomplished by picking up the patient and driving back to Glennallen, then on to the post in Palmer. One of the State Troopers out of Palmer would come to meet me and then take the patient on to Anchorage.

This time was a little different. After we were approximately 40 miles out of Valdez, my mental patient told me he had played a trick on the hospital orderly. When he had come around with the pills they always gave to patients who were moving from one hospital to another, he had not taken it. That pill was to have calmed down the patient so the person transporting would have no problems. He reached into his shirt pocket and showed me the pill. I chose not to turn around and drive back to the state hospital again, so I just kept going.

About 10 minutes later he looked out his passenger door window and said did you see that? And I responded no, what did you see? He said that guy on a motorcycle was trying to pass us on the right side? I said I had not seen that. According to him every couple of miles that guy would try to pass us again on the right. He had a vivid imagination, and it kept the trip lively. I did not have any problems with him nor did the other trooper.

A few weeks later I received a call from the mayor of Valdez that his Chief of Police had left town in a hurry the day before. The story he heard was that his Chief of Police had been in the bar down by the city dock and there had been some altercation between him and some others. The result was that someone had taken the policeman's pistol and thrown it in the bay, then had thrown his badge into the bay, and then had threatened to throw him into the bay if he did not get out of town. He apparently believed them as he left town and did not contact anyone in the area.

I went right down to Valdez but no one had seen anything or heard anything. I did have a report that the Valdez Chief of Police had made it into Fairbanks and did not have a pistol or a badge with him.

One of my first adventures with the airplane was discovering that the Gulkana River had a run of king or Chinook salmon in it. I was flying down the Copper River and as I came by the junction where the Gulkana River joined the Copper River I saw the clear water of the Gulkana pouring into the muddy Copper. I circled a short distance up the Gulkana then flew the bottom several holes down to the Copper River. I saw several nice kings lying in those holes. Whoopee!!

Then I flew along the Copper River looking for a place to land and there was nothing. I went back and looked at the salmon again and boy were they beautiful. Then back to the Copper River again there was only one place that I might make a landing, so I flew in for a closer look. There were some awfully big rocks scattered along this gravel bar, but it was the only possible place to land. Back to see the fish again . . . well maybe, then I flew back to the potential landing spot. Those fish would sure be good eating. It was now obvious that this was the only place in the area that would provide a safe landing. So I set up to bring it in slow and easy, nose up, throttle back, and stall it in, just right, short roll and WE MADE IT!

It was about a half of a mile back to the Gulkana River and I caught one nice 24 lb. king. I flew home feeling pretty proud of myself. Then two days later I went down and tried it again. Again I was able to land safely and catch a nice fish. Getting lined up for another take off on that sand bar I started to roll the plane forward and after increasing my ground speed I pulled back on the stick, the main landing gear came off the ground but because I held the stick back the tail remained down just off the ground, and there was a loud BANG as the tail wheel struck a big rock very hard. The airplane stayed in the air with no apparent problems. After gaining altitude I opened the door far enough to see there was no tail wheel . . . oops!

Instead of flying to my landing strip at home I flew into Gulkana as there was staff working the flight service station, and I wanted help available in case I should need it. I lined up with the airport and flew down the runway at 50' off the pavement. Not landing, and staying in the pattern and going around again, and did not land this time again staying in the pattern. I saw one of the crew come out and give me the green light to land acknowledging I had a problem. As I went by the cross taxiway to Jack Wilson's hanger I saw Jack and another person getting into a pickup starting down to the runway.

I stayed in the pattern again, only this time I landed. And there was no problem. The tail wheel had been attached to the leaf spring at the rear of the tail and the spring came down and trailed along behind. I got out thinking Mike was right, keep your head and with this airplane you can walk away from about anything. This plane will not quit flying until around 31 miles per hour, so it can be slowed down very slow, removing lots of the potential for damage. With the tail wheel leaf spring dragging along the runway it was like throwing out an anchor. By giving the plane a little throttle I was able to lift the tail and by pushing the stick forward so the tail was off the ground, I could move around at ease.

In a short time we were back in business with a new tail wheel and tail spring. I also learned a valuable lesson, if you cannot get a clear place to land, DO NOT LAND! Those salmon I caught were very good eating, but they were very expensive.

Alaska State Trooper Gary Gunkel

Chapter 14

I received a call from the State Trooper stationed in Tok, saying the border patrol had reason to believe that a bad man from Canada had crossed the border into Alaska. He had departed Tok an hour ago en route to the Anchorage area. The suspect was believed to be a terrorist in Canada, and there was a warrant for his arrest for murder. I attempted to reach Terry, the Fish and Game protection officer in our area, but he was out of the area. I left Glennallen looking for a dark green four door sedan unknown make, with Canadian license plates. A Caucasian was said to be driving the vehicle with three passengers. The information stated that he might be dropping off the passengers.

As I was driving north towards Tok, about an hour and fifteen minutes out of Glennallen, I met a dark green sedan being driven by a single Caucasian male. Once I was out of sight I turned around and began pursuit. I was on the radio trying to make contact with anyone. After three attempts I gave up. The suspect was driving the speed limit as I came up behind him, and turned on the red lights. Once he stopped, I got out of the patrol vehicle with my riot gun, jacked a shell into the chamber, and approached the vehicle with the barrel pointed straight up in the air and the butt of the shotgun in the crook of my arm. I was behind him about half way between his rear fender and the driver's seat before I could see both of his hands. I went ahead and approached slowly asking for his operator's license. He got his wallet out but dropped it three times before he found his operator's license. His back seat was filled with luggage and personal items. It was obvious he was moving. And there was no place for three passengers. I asked his destination and he stated that he was a teacher and was on his way to Glennallen where he was going to teach this year. I thanked him and wished him well and made my way back to my patrol vehicle where I removed the double 00 buck shot cartridge from the chamber of my shotgun and turned around making my way back towards Tok Junction again.

I did as before checking every side road and business that was open all the way to Tok Junction. But never did make contact with that bad guy.

It was times like that I really felt all alone. But I was determined to take every precaution I could to remain safe while at the same time doing my job to the best of my ability. I was determined to not become another statistic.

I had good friends that were teachers in Glennallen and Larry told me I should have heard the story that new teacher told of the State Trooper who stopped him on the highway coming into Glennallen. He said that the State Trooper was very polite, but handled that sawed off shotgun like he knew how to use it. There was a social event that we were invited to about a month later. The new teacher was there, and we all had a good laugh over it.

Glennallen, the Wrangle mountains and surrounding country was a hunter and fisherman's paradise. There were lots of Dall sheep, mountain goat, moose, caribou, grizzly, brown and black bear throughout the range. There was also a treasure of small animals. This is where I learned how to fly in the mountains. My little 65-horsepower Taylorcraft airplane performed great at lower altitudes, but the higher elevations were a challenge.

I took a week and a half vacation and a good friend, Allen, Ann, the kids and I went hunting in the McCarthy area and surrounding mountains. We established a base camp and went sheep and goat hunting using the airplane to get into base camp and then doing lots of walking. We were able to get a couple of nice Dall sheep rams, and I missed a nice mountain goat. Allen only had three days, but we were able to get his ram on the second day. I got a nice ram from the same herd that Allen took his sheep.

After taking Allen back out to his pickup on the main road system, the kids, Ann and I landed at the town strip at McCarthy. McCarthy has its own road system, and while there used to be a considerable number of people scattered through the area, there were far fewer now. In fact, people were few and far in between in that area of Alaska. After they shut down the copper mines and the gold diggings died out, McCarthy became isolated. Several of the smaller bridges between the Copper River and McCarthy washed out, which caused problems crossing the Copper River so people had pretty well left.

I was able to introduce Ann to Mr. and Mrs. Jackson. They owned a small house in McCarthy and spent the summer there from early spring to late fall. Up until that year they enjoyed the peace and quiet of the backcountry living. The Jackson's were a delight to visit with. They also had an old jeep that they used to travel around the limited road system of the area. There was no electricity in McCarthy except their small generator, which they did not use very often as it was very expensive getting fuel. Every time I came to town I would stop and check on the Jackson's. This year they now have some unwanted neighbors in town that stay up late at night partying. Depending on the day there are from three to eight people in the campsite. The group is from Cordova, and they arrive and depart by air taxi service.

The State of Alaska had a work shop located in the area where they would fly a couple of men in for a week or so when they needed some work done on the area road system. In the old days the transportation in and out was a railroad that ran from Cordova on the coast up the Copper River to the town of McCarthy. The railroad had been owned and operated by the copper mine. When they shut down the copper mine they also shut down the railroad.

We had a nice time doing some exploring, visiting the town of McCarthy and checking the other airstrips around the area. One of these was a gold mine that had a very wide and long airstrip that was sitting on a fairly steep hill. It was important to always take off going downhill and land going uphill.

Ann and I landed at that old gold mine airstrip and hiked the two miles to the gold mine. It was mostly a placer operation that had a bunkhouse, a dining hall that looked like they had just walked out and left the dishes still sitting on the shelves, and the silverware still in the proper containers. There were blankets, sheets and pillows just waiting for the crew to return. The whole place was wired and had indoor and outside lights. All of the electric power for the camp was furnished by a generator, which had been removed. But everything else appeared to be there and ready to go. They had diverted a stream through a short duct way to where a hydroelectric power plant had previously been. The whole camp area was very neat and well kept with toilets, showers with hot water, and completely self-contained. To see all the buildings and supplies still in place was a treat. We were careful to leave everything as we found it.

Sheep camp Beth, Mark, and Karen

We went back a year or so later to find that all the dishes had been broken and the place had been badly vandalized. We felt lucky at having seen that camp as it had been before.

Vacation was over and it was time to get back to work. I had made contact with the Cordova Police Department checking up on the camp with the Cordova people. They were surprised to find they were still in the area, as the leader of the group had a failure to appear warrant,.

I got hold of Jack Wilson at the flying service and arranged for a charter flight into McCarthy. Jack set the flight up for Mike to take me up there in his Cessna 185 the next day leaving at 10:00 a.m.

After landing at the McCarthy airstrip, we walked into town and to the camp site. Everyone was still sleeping. Mike having furnished transportation for them in the past pointed to the leader's tent. The leader, a James Bettencourt, came out of his tent rubbing his eyes. There was a table in the center with a baggie full of marijuana, and another partially full bag right beside it. I identified my-self as an Alaska State Trooper, and his smile turned to a frown. He asked what I was doing here in McCarthy, turning to look at his marijuana. I replied that I was here to arrest him for failure to appear in court, and now it looked like there would be additional charges.

I took him into custody and seized the marijuana. James Bettencourt was not a happy camper, and neither were the other two people there in camp. They told James that they would be leaving in a couple of days, and then made arrangements for transportation out with Mike, who was accompanying me.

Chapter 15

It was mid-morning and I was behind a school bus entering Glennallen. School was out for the summer but there were some fires going on in the area and the Bureau of Land Management had leased some school buses to transport fire crews. There were several big rough looking guys looking out the rear window, and two of them started gesturing at me with their hand and their middle finger extended, in other words giving me the finger. They turned in to the local Land Management headquarters so I followed them in and stopped behind the bus.

They were not getting off so I went over and got on the bus. My intention was to find out if there was anything wrong that I could help them with. I was only able to identify one of the guys that belonged to one of the hands. The minute I stepped on the bus I knew there was a potential problem. This was not your average fire crew. There were lots of comments, so I attempted to separate the one I could identify by asking him to come off the bus. He got up and started off the bus coming from the rear, and every one of the others got up and followed him off.

This problem was escalating rapidly. This group surrounded me and started closing in. I had to take command immediately, or I was in trouble. I took the problem guy by the arm saying you are under arrest. He said what for, and I responded "indecent language in public" as I turned him around. The 23 other gang members were closing the circle around us again. I took my prisoner and started for my patrol vehicle. At the very last second the gang parted and let us through. I stopped at the passenger door and put handcuffs on my prisoner and opened the door helping him into the vehicle. The other guys were getting more upset each minute. I knew I had been successful up to this point by surprise, as they had never had anyone stand up to them before, especially with the odds so much in their favor. As I went around the patrol vehicle my knees were shaking, *and again I said, thank you Lord.*

I later found out that this group was from the motorcycle gang known in Alaska as the Brothers, started by a couple of the Hells Angels out of California. I also found that four of the local guys working in the tool shed had observed what was going on and had knocked the heads off their Pulaski's with the intention of backing me up with what amounted to pick handles for clubs, if the need arrived. I did not know any of these men; they just felt the obligation to backup their State Trooper if he needed it. This projection of attitude is what makes it possible for one man to be effective in enforcing the law against long odds, where there are so few officers.

I took my prisoner to our local holding cell at my office and locked him up. Almost immediately the phone was ringing. The local head of the BLM was on the phone. He stated that he was having problems with the Brothers motorcycle group of fire fighters. When I had left they had erupted in loud cursing and unruly behavior. They stated they would not leave until the trooper brought back their brother. I told him you are the head of the local BLM station and these people were under your supervision. Tell them I said if they did not behave in an orderly fashion you are to order them off the property, and then call me again. If they fail to leave, I will be right over to take any trespassers on the property to jail. The boss called back about 15 minutes later and said they were getting on the bus again, but they were very unhappy. They said they were going back to Anchorage to get reinforcements to come back and bust their friend out of jail. I thanked him for the information and asked if they had done any damage, to the property. He stated he did not think so. I told him to be sure and call again if he had any problems.

I was busy the rest of the day getting all the paperwork done for the arraignment the next morning. I was not sure what would happen when that bunch reached Anchorage, but that was not going to happen for several hours since it was 200 miles out to Anchorage. Later that evening I received a phone call from an Anchorage State Trooper wanting to know what I had done to get the Brothers motorcycle gang all stirred up. I told him not much, that one of them gave me the finger and I just arrested him. He asked if I still had him and I answered yes I did. He was going before the local Justice of the Peace in the morning. Scott told me that the Brothers were organizing a group to come out and bust their friend out of jail. We thought we would come out and reinforce you for this hearing. Do you need any special weapons? I responded my riot gun is adequate. Two men drove out from Anchorage but none of the Brothers showed up.

The Justice of the Peace that was conducting the hearings called the proceedings to order and read the complaint against the prisoner, which stated that he had used obscene language in public by waving his hand with his middle finger extended at a State Trooper. The prisoner stated that he had not said anything. The Justice of the Peace asked the prisoner to show the court his wave at the State Trooper. The prisoner took pleasure in giving me the finger in court. The judge said, "I have traveled all over the world, and that is known universally as—you! I find you guilty." I was relieved, *thank you Lord for protecting me.* That was my first incident with the Brothers motorcycle gang.

My supervisor and next up in chain of command was Corporal McConahay, the commander of the Palmer Post in the Matanuska Valley. Palmer had a police department and a good size population of approximately 5,000 people, 60 miles east of Anchorage. The Palmer Post was very busy with me located in Glennallen as a satellite. There was another area that Palmer was responsible for and that was Talkeetna. For me to get there I had to drive southwest to Palmer approximately 140 miles, then turn North and drive to the end of the highway to the small town of Talkeetna. They were very busy in the Palmer, Wasilla area and surrounding valley so every three weeks or so I would get a call to go to Talkeetna area to answer several complaints. It required one or two nights away from home in order to answer all the complaints in this area. One of the problems that is ongoing was aircraft vandalism. There were several guides and outfitters working out of the small airport there. It was the closest airport to the Mount McKinley National Park and was the origin for mountain climbing expeditions, wildlife sightseeing trips and hunting trips outside the park.

This problem was very serious as the vandalism sometimes might not be discovered until an outfitter had taken off, putting everyone in the aircraft in danger. The only laws in the state that addressed the problem was a misdemeanor vandalism charge that gave out fines up to $999.00 and/or up to one year in jail. The state had recently brought in a new felony vandalism charge, but the law had not been used yet. I was working with the Assistant Attorney General for the area over the telephone. We put together the first case of felony vandalism to an aircraft.

In this particular case the suspect was a good friend with someone in the flying business. The suspect went over to one of his friend's competitors and cut part of the landing gear partially through. This could cause possible damage and or injury to anyone flying in the Piper PA-18 Super Cub airplane on any landing or take off.

I was able to put the case together and get a confession from the suspect. I arrested him and he was sent off to Anchorage for transfer into the Anchorage criminal justice system. That case certainly put a damper on vandalizing aircraft in the Talkeetna area.

Chapter 16

I woke up to another 40 degrees below-zero day. The still and calm, crystal clear days permit you to see the four peaks of the Wrangle Mountains one hundred twenty miles away like they are just across the street. Only in Alaska have I witnessed weather creating such pristine beauty. I had been running my trap line pretty regularly but this weather is extremely hard on equipment. A little before noon I was on my way to the airport, in Gulkana. Starting the vehicles at home, we just plug them into a small pump with an electric heater installed in the water system and the whole water system in each vehicle stays nice and toasty. To check the trap line the project starts at home.

For trapping in 40 degrees below zero I wear insulated underwear both uppers and lower, with a cotton t shirt underneath, In case of sweating the cotton will pick up that moisture. Then I put on a pair of heavy, loose fitting wool trousers, and a heavy wool shirt. Next is a pair of insulated overalls, then a heavy down-filled overcoat with a hood fringed with wolf that pre-heats the air as you breathe through the fringe around the hood of the parka. The hands are very important. I liked a pair of fuzzy monkey-faced gold color gloves fitted loosely underneath a very large pair of moose hide mittens. The back of the hand on each mitten was coyote fur. These mittens are lined with tightly woven wool that came from my Marine Corp winter trousers. The mittens were my outerwear, but the monkey-faced gloves were used when I was doing something that required using my fingers.

Getting out of my pickup the cold snow squeaked and crunched with every step I took. I got out two lengths of stovepipe each with ninety-degree elbows, and a blowtorch. This is my improvised engine heater. I opened the bottom of the engine cover and point the elbow up towards the oil pan at the bottom of the engine and light the blowtorch. As soon as I have the torch burning well I direct the fire into the pipe. The flame is only going about half way down the pipe but lots of heat is being blown right up onto the pan of the engine and is being trapped under the insulated engine cover.

After 20 minutes the whole engine compartment had risen to a balmy 50 degrees and is ready to start. While waiting for the blowtorch to do its job I pre-flight the airplane, then remove the blowtorch and engine cover. Then I get hold of the prop and pulled it through. One pull and the engine roared to life.

Before going to the airplane I went over to the flight service station and filed a flight plan including the time I would be back. After storing my rifle, the engine insulation cover, and a small duffel bag in the airplane, I climbed in and taxied out to the runway. Wow, what a beautiful day. Checking the thermometer on run-up I found the temperature had now dropped to—41! In winter the plane has skis for landing gear. The run up to the end of the airstrip was complete and we started down the runway. There are no brakes when flying with skis. After checking both magnetos I set the selector back on both mags and away we go taking off to the northwest out of Gulkana. I climbed out to 2,000 feet keeping my eye on the thermometer. As my plane climbed altitude the thermometer also rose until the outside temperature was at minus 20 degrees. That is still cold but is what is referred to as an inversion, where a colder air mass is trapped by a warmer layer overhead. There was approximately a foot and a half of snow with some frost that had created a winter wonderland.

I arrived at the lake and checked closely for overflow water on the ice and could see no evidence of any so I decided to land. I had not planned on being out long, but I had made several trapping sets on this end of the lake and a couple on the other end, and at a small lake a few hundred yards away I had also set a snare for a beaver. First I went over and checked the beaver snare. There was a very big beaver in the main house on this lake. I only wanted that big blanket size beaver, so I had set the snare a long distance out from the house. None of the smaller beaver should be venturing that far away from the lodge. It appeared that the set had been disturbed but the ice had frozen back over so it took me about 15 minutes to break it open again. I was rewarded with the biggest beaver in the colony. I carried my prize back to the airplane and then trekked around the lake to where I had made several sets. A large male lynx had made several trips through here but I had not been successful in catching him yet. On my next to last set I found him. I gathered my trophy and then quickly returned to the airplane to leave it, then I headed down to the other end of the lake to see if that wolverine had come back. And again, in my last trap, there he was. Wow! What a day on the trap line. Not many sets but I was rewarded generously.

Now it was time to get back to the airplane and out of there. It had already been longer than I had planned. I loaded up my catch and turned on the ignition and went out and grabbed the prop. On the first pull the engine popped to life, I raced for the throttle, it coughed, sputtered, I'm almost there, baby, hang on . . . then the engine died just as I grabbed the throttle. Uh-oh! My greatest fear was being realized. I had flooded the engine in that impossibly cold weather and there was no way I was going to get it started.

I knew better. I should have left the insulated engine cover in place while I was away from the airplane. I checked the temperature and now it was down to 44 degrees below zero. I had enjoyed a very beautiful late afternoon, but now I had better get ready for a really long cold night. I had some matches in my emergency gear, but I did not have the blowtorch. I located a couple of trees that had died and were lying down. I started breaking off limbs and building a woodpile. By this time I was an hour late returning to Gulkana on my flight plan. Mike knew my flight plan and where this lake was located as he had accompanied me here a couple of times. I knew he had been out of the area on a charter so he might not be back in time to come and check on me. I had taken my sleeping bag out of the airplane along with a few other things that would have come in handy. I thought I might do well and wanted room to get the fur home. Whoops, it was going to be a long night. I went back to my anticipated fire site and was getting ready to start my fire, when I heard an airplane off in the distance. I hurried back to my airplane and to my great relief; here comes Mike in Jack's super cub. What a beautiful sight it was as he made one pass by and set down so gently and taxied up to my airplane. We tried to start my plane again but could not get it started, we loaded up my gear and pelts and he took me back to Gulkana. Man, was I relieved to be going home. I later found that Mike almost stayed in Talkeetna the evening before, which would have caused me considerable problems with a long cold night. I did try the matches the next day and found they must have collected some moisture in the past, because they would not light.

Good Guy Trapper, Nabesna Country

The next morning Mike and I flew back out to my plane with the stovepipe and blowtorch, and we were successful getting the Taylorcraft to start right up. I had made another mistake, but again a greater power than I had taken over and bailed me out. I learned a valuable lesson with that excursion. It never ceased to amaze me how faithfully Christ was watching over me. As others have said, sometimes it appears that there is a whole legion of guardian angels watching over me. My thanks seemed so inadequate for what Christ has done for me.

The next week Terry, the Fish and Game protection officer called to see if I could accompany him on a long snow machine trip into the back country after a bad guy. Among other things, there was also an arrest warrant for car theft for this fellow. He had a base camp seventy miles off the road where he had been trapping through the winter. We were hoping to catch him at his base camp, and not have to search for him out on his trap line.

We left Glennallen at 6:00 a.m. to drive the 95 miles to the end of the Nabesna road. We were about 10 miles from the end of the road when a pack of wolves ran across the road in front of us. The wolf is a shy animal that is very seldom observed in the wild. This was a truly unexpected surprise. In another 15 minutes we were at the departure point. We unloaded both snow machines from the trailer, checked the fuel and added another five gallons on the sled behind Terry's machine. We headed down the trail after our criminal. We were averaging about 15 miles per hour, and the temperature was between 25 and 35 below zero. We pulled into the good guys camp a couple hours later hoping to find him home. After a short stop visit, we were on the trail again searching. We found that our man had not been over this way. We were not seeing much in the way of game, but we were seeing lots of tracks, as the animals were scrambling out ahead of the noisy approach of the snow machines. A few hours later we located the bad guy's camp and placed him under arrest without incident. Terry took him on his snow machine and I followed, as we headed back out. It took another four and a half hours to get out of there. The sun had gone down and by the time we loaded both the snow machines we were running out of daylight. We pulled out as dark closed in. A couple more hours on the road and we were back in Glennallen again. That was 190 miles total in the pickup, and 140 miles on snow machines at sub-zero temperature. A long day indeed, we were both very glad to be home that evening.

In late spring the Gulkana River gets a nice run of king salmon. I found this out by accident. Everyone else in the area had said there was an occasional salmon in the river, but too few to consider a run and as a result only rarely did anyone fish it. Where the Gulkana crosses the highway, there is a native village with a hundred or so people living there, a church, 10 or 12 houses and a small store. I went by the village and crossed the bridge over the Gulkana. There was a small van pulled off the road and a man was working a small gas stove, cooking something in a frying pan. I walked over to visit and found out he was an Anchorage fisherman who had traveled over 200 miles. He had stopped there to try fishing and had been right in the middle of some very good king salmon fishing. He had caught a 48 lb. fish!

It was not very long before I was a regular on the Gulkana River and knee deep in some of the best salmon fishing I have ever experienced. Karen, our oldest daughter, would go fishing with me and be all over the river bank, up and down both sides of the river. Whenever I got a fish on I'd hand the fishing rod to Karen and she would attempt to reel it in. Soon she ran out of gas so I usually helped her land the fish.

On one trip I watched a king rise way out in the river so I cast the lure to that spot. My heart jumped as I saw a big swirl of water as a huge king salmon hit the lure. I quickly set the hook and once again gave the rod to Karen. She locked her knees and braced against the pull of the big fish. I made a fast grab and caught her and the fishing rod just before they hit the water. My little Karen tried, but did not have a chance with a fish that big. I took the fishing rod back and tried to turn the fish. It had reached the rapids and I had to follow it down to the next hole where the water once again slowed down, but the big King was not slowing down. As we were running out of slow water I tried again to turn him and had to dig in my heels. I had been following down the banks of the river as fast as I could, but could not catch up with him and I was running out of line in my reel. So I set the drag a little tighter . . . and pow! He took almost all my line, and another Gulkana monster salmon tale was born . . .

I have caught kings up to 53 pounds in the Gulkana River and none of them felt anywhere as powerful as Karen's monster. Since then, the Gulkana River salmon run has become very well known, and the nice quiet fishing we once had experienced was no more. It has become famous for it's king salmon runs.

Chapter 17

When moose and caribou season opened in late summer and early fall, there was always an increase of traffic in our area. As soon as we received our first snowfall in September the Caribou would start their winter migration. Shortly after, here come the hunters.

Late one Saturday afternoon I was out patrolling and received a call from Ann on our radio that a gunshot victim was en-route to the mission hospital. I went immediately to the hospital to check on the injured victim. He was conscious and alert, but had been shot center in the chest with a .375 H&H magnum rifle. He and his partner had parked near Paxton Lodge and gone in hunting by snow machine. They were about six miles off the highway when they spotted caribou. They stopped the machine and the friend riding behind on the sled fell. Seeing the caribou trying to flee he hurried to get his rifle untangled from the blankets and it accidentally discharged. The bullet struck the victim, George Thompson in the chest. The temperature was around -20 degrees and both hunters were cold. An emergency bandage was applied and the victim was loaded on the sled for the long trip back to the road. At the highway the hunters contacted the Lodge about the accident, and the nearest hospital, which was Glennallen was notified.

Under good conditions it would have taken an hour and a half for the drive to the hospital, but there was a light snow falling so it took almost twice as long. At the hospital the doctor was busy trying to stabilize the wound and running a blood test at the same time. They had already called Elmendorf Air Force Base to arrange an emergency transport. It was going to take a couple of hours to get an aircraft ready to fly in the cold weather, but the rescue was under way.

The mission hospital had only one doctor on staff, and a very limited number of nurses. They did an amazing amount of work for such a small staff. This hospital was staffed, supplied and operated completely through donations. They received living expenses through church donations for their support. It was an incredible experience working with these people. This is the true example of living by faith. The doctor came in and asked if he could talk with me so we went into another room and he asked if I would be able to stay with the patient while waiting for the Elmendorf medical evacuation. I was glad to be of what little help I could.

George was fully conscious and aware of everything that was going on. He asked about his wife, but we had not been able to contact her. We tried to reach her several times. George asked what his chances were in making a recovery. "George, as you know, I am not a doctor, but your doctor is very good at what he does. We do have an air evacuation, coming out of Elmendorf Air Force Base. They should be here in about an hour. This type of a wound is their specialty."

I was feeling the need to talk to George about his relationship with Christ, but felt inadequate in bringing Christ into the conversation. "George do you attend church?" "My wife is Catholic, I have been to her church a few times." I really wanted to bring the question of his salvation up, but for some reason I was a miserable failure.

The phone rang and we were notified that the airplane from Elmendorf Air Force Base had arrived at Gulkana Airport. So we took George over and put him on the military aircraft which took off immediately for the one hour flight back to Elmendorf.

I checked at the hospital the next morning and was told that George Thompson had died before the aircraft had landed. I felt guilt in the fact that I had not given him the opportunity to accept Christ. I had not only let George down, but that I also let down Christ who had given me this opportunity.

Christ talking to Peter (and to me): "Before the cock crows you will deny me." Please Lord, give me the strength to do better the next time.

Chapter 18

It was about a week later that I received a call about a young man, 19 years old and in a wheelchair who was drunk and causing problems in Gulkana Indian village. It was 8:30 at night when I arrived and started looking for the man. The complaints from the villages always came from the tribal Chief. They would not call the State Troopers unless the village was unified and had decided that the culprit needed some time in jail before coming back. In other words, when they had enough, it was time to get him out of there.

I was reluctant to arrest someone in a wheelchair, so when I finally found the man I was thinking I would find a place to let him cool down and sleep off his drunk. But this guy was completely out of control. He decided he had enough of me and wheeled around to run. He was very good in that wheelchair and could get in and out of tight spots quicker that most men on their feet. When he hit an open stretch outside it was amazing how fast he could accelerate and maneuver.

I finally cornered him in one of the residences in the village, but he was outmaneuvering me and was about to get away again, so I leaped across a bed and reached across his chest to stop him. He grabbed my left hand with both of his hands and with tremendous arm and upper body strength crammed my hand into his mouth and bit my fingers. His jaws were like a steel trap. I felt his teeth crunch into my left center finger just above the finger nail, catching part of the fingernail. I could not get my hand out of his mouth. His Jaws were closed like a vise. It was like hitting your finger with a hammer, but instead of just a blow, the teeth kept that continuous and horrible pressure.

Later, in court the judge asked, "Then what did you do?" I answered the judge by saying, "I doubled up my right fist and hit him in the head as hard as I could." When the judge asked again, "What did you do next?" I answered, "I hit him again, two or three more times, until he opened his mouth and released my fingers." Then the defense attorney asked me in cross examination, "You mean that you are telling this court that you struck a young man confined to a wheelchair all his life in the head with your fist?" I answered, "Yes, I did." Then he asked, "Are you sorry for your response?" I answered, "Yes. I am left handed and I have quite a bit more power in my left hand than my right hand, so I was wishing he had my right hand in his mouth instead. Then I could have hit him harder and hopefully caused him to quit biting sooner."

The jury was on my side and we won the court case for assault of a police officer. That finger has been a problem to this day. The right side of my center fingernail of my left hand keeps getting ingrown from the bite injury that happened while arresting that young man in a wheelchair.

I had let my guard down when I found out the cause of the problem was a young man, approximately 19 years old, confined to a wheelchair. I know that none of these villages call unless there is a major disturbance. They will take care of the problem themselves. That is the last time I relax until the problem is taken care of. Every time that fingernail gets ingrown I remember my mistake.

Frost on wings and will not fly!

Chapter 19

It was one of my rare days off, and the morning was beautiful with a fair amount of frost. I had not put on the wing covers the night before as I was not planning on flying the next morning, but I couldn't resist. I tried to sweep the frost off the airplane wings, but very little would move so I rolled the airplane so it would be in the sun. But at 20 degrees the sun was having very little effect on the frost. I got a ladder and a rough towel and tried rubbing the frost on the leading edges of the wings. This seemed to smooth it out quite a bit, so after waiting another hour I decided it was ok to take off.

I got the engine running with no problem. I was on the homestead with the runway in the field behind the house. I had laid out the runway so after getting off the end of it you would fly off a bluff with a few scattered trees along the edge. There was a pile of brush and small scrub trees near the end of the runway, about 75 yards before reaching the bluff. I had burned the pile of brush and small trees, but it needed some more work to remove what was left of the small pile. The runway was 900' long, which was plenty of room for my little Taylorcraft airplane. My driveway crossed the very end of the runway on its way to our house and there is forest across the north end of the field and the trees were 75' to 100' tall. Because of the trees I would take off to the south and land to the north, unless the wind dictated differently.

That morning I taxied down to the north end of the runway, warmed up the engine for a few minutes, then I started my takeoff roll. My ground speed got up to normal takeoff speed of 45 miles per hour, but the airplane would not fly, I should have shut it down immediately, but I was confident it would lift off. As I approached the end of the runway it still would not fly, so I used a trick that Mike had taught me. As I went over the end of the runway where the driveway went across, I had the nose up using the control stick. I pushed the stick forward and then quickly pulled it all the way back and immediately shoved the stick forward again bouncing the airplane into the air, just clearing the brush pile. I was sure it would fly, so after bouncing it into the air I brought the stick back to the takeoff position, but the aircraft just settled back to the ground just beyond the burned brush pile. I did not have room to get it shut down so I shot across the short open ground and over a couple of fallen trees, knocking off the landing gear, crushing the bottom of the fuselage, and bending the prop. The bent prop killed the engine, and I slid to a stop right at the edge of the bluff.

The greatest injury was to my ego. Up until now I had seen what an airplane could do but now I had a valuable lesson in what it could not do. I was feeling pretty good about bouncing the airplane over that brush pile, but the down time and the cost of putting the aircraft back together was a bit of a shock. Lesson learned: NEVER, EVER, try to fly aircraft with any frost on its wings. Use the wing covers, put it in the hanger, or wait for Mother Nature to warm things up.

One of the biggest benefits that I received from this crash was getting the feel of the aircraft when you almost have it flying, but not quite, and what happens when you do not have the lift of that smooth airflow as it goes over those wings at a speed needed to keep the aircraft in the air. I did not realize it at that time, but I was accumulating the do's and don'ts needed to get an airplane in the air and keep it in the air for that extra second or two that could determine whether you would live or die.

Thank you Lord for watching over me once again, and delivering me from my foolishness.

After getting the Taylorcraft flying again, I did a lot of flying up, around and through the Wrangle Mountains. The one major drawback with the Taylorcraft was it would not hold our entire family. In fact, it was underpowered any time there was more than one person in the airplane. There were a lot of strips in the high country that I could not get in and out of because of that, so I began looking for a more powerful, early model 180 Cessna. The first models were very lightweight and had a large engine with a constant speed prop. It was also a very good bush airplane because it had a tail wheel instead of a nose wheel as later models have. The tail wheel puts the balance point back instead of forward.

The Taylorcraft had served me well, and I had learned how to fly it well. I was also hearing rumors that there was a good trooper bush post coming open. A bush post is one that is not on the highway system. So when I got the opportunity to get a good Cessna 180 with fairly low hours on the engine, I jumped at it. I got a ride to Anchorage and was checked out for flying the Cessna 180, made the deal and flew it home. I was amazed at how much room there was inside the aircraft compared with my little Taylorcraft. Now it was time to get acquainted with the larger Cessna, and land it on some of the backcountry airstrips. Wow! This was really a great airplane.

The Taylorcraft did not have flaps, but was still able to slow down and land at 31 to 32 miles per hour land speed. The 180 could slow down and land at just under 40 miles per hour with me and no extra weight in the airplane. Those early Cessna's had manual flaps instead of power flaps, which gave you lots of options. You could grab full flaps with no delay, and then dump your flaps, or any portion of them. Coming in slow, just above stall speed, I would grab a full flap position and as soon as the wheels would touch the ground I would dump to zero flaps instantly. This would allow my airplane to not be lifted off by a sudden wind change or a bump and allowed a quicker transition from flying to taxiing; or just the opposite in taking off. I could start takeoff roll with zero flaps, and when ready, grab full flaps at the same time pulling the nose of the airplane directly into the wind as the plane came off the ground. Then, instantly dump a little or most of the flaps, depending how much head wind and ground speed the plane was carrying. This gives the pilot much more maneuverability on that transition from take-off to flying. This also really helps when taking off and or landing with high crosswinds. When you have a strong cross wind, the airplane starts skipping sideways as soon as the weight on those wheels starts getting light. A sandy beach is even worse. But flaps that are not motor driven are a huge advantage, once you get the feel of them.

Gaining experience in this kind of flying makes a big difference when you can feel how the airplane is handling, and you have the experience to automatically make the adjustments.

Chapter 20

I was answering a burglary complaint at a small grocery store 40 miles southeast of Glennallen. Someone had broken into the store the night before and taken some money from the cash drawer. I could not find any clues and the owner had no idea who had broken into his place of business. I looked around the crime scene and found nothing, then checked with some of his neighbors up and down the road.

No one I talked to had seen anything, but at one house a teenage son was acting odd, kind of shy and not wanting to look at me or talk with me. After checking all the neighbors within five miles I went back to talk to the young man. It really surprised me when he admitted to the break-in and gave me the money he had stolen. The owner of the small grocery was amazed and told everyone what a great detective I was.

A couple of weeks later Corporal McConaughy, my supervisor from Palmer, came to town with a copy of a letter sent in by the grocery store owner to the Commander of the State Troopers along with a copy of the letter sent back to the man from the Commander, saying he was impressed with my work and thanking the grocery store owner for writing.

I found out during Corporal McConaughy's visit that because of the amount of work that went through the Glennallen State Trooper office the previous three years, the last two of which were the work I had done, and the fact that the Alaska Pipeline was going through the Glennallen area on its way to Valdez, they were reassigning me and replacing me with four State Troopers.

Chapter 21

I was offered the opportunity to look at the Naknek post on the Alaska Peninsula. So I drove to Anchorage and then flew commercially to King Salmon, and landed at the airport, which at that time had an Air Force squadron based on one side of the main runway and civilian business structures on the other.

It was even more impressive when they had the hangar doors open on the Air Force side of the runway and you could see the F-111 fighter planes stationed there. They kept the most up to date fighter aircraft they had in those hangers. This was part of the northern line of defense and it was not unusual to see them come and go two at a time. In those fighters it was only a hop, skip and a jump to Russia.

The resident trooper set me up at a room in one of the local canneries, and then showed me around as he explained the post duties. The road system around North Naknek post area consisted of 16 miles of road connecting the coastal village of Naknek with the airport and small town of King Salmon. The State Trooper had living quarters in the old school building in Naknek. They had taken two schoolrooms on the main floor and made them into a three bedroom apartment. Then just across the hall were the State Troopers office, the office and courtroom of the district court, and the Borough offices.

The normal resident population was 600+ people in the town of North Naknek, This soared to over 5,000 for the summer commercial fishing season. There were four bars and one hotel. There were also five canneries, one of which was the Red Salmon cannery that also had a company store called the Red Salmon grocery store. This store had lots of hardware, paints and other supplies located in an adjacent warehouse. The cannery store and the hardware store were also open to the public, as were most of the cannery stores. Due to its location right in the middle of town the Red Salmon stores did considerably more business than the others, so they had a sizable inventory and kept their stores open year round. Just up the street past the Borough/court/Trooper offices was a large bar called Hatfield's, and also a good-sized lumber and hardware store on the outskirts of town.

The Borough offices ran the schools in the area, with a large newly constructed school located in North Naknek. Both North and South Naknek were just up from the mouth of the Naknek River, one on each side of the river.

South Naknek was mostly two canneries and some residential areas. This is one of the few areas where the kids have to catch the school airplane, operated by a local air taxi service to and from school. The Naknek airstrip located right in town with two small plane runways, and three hangers located next to them with gas available. There is also a lake between the airstrips where float planes land.

The winter population is around 1,500 people for North and South Naknek, King Salmon, and surrounding villages, but the area swells to more than 12,000 people during the commercial fishing season in the summer. The town of King Salmon located on the Naknek River at the Civilian, US Air Force Airport, was just beginning to develop a large sport fishing industry with several sport fishing camps located around the area that are serviced and reached mostly by floatplanes. They change to hunting camps in the fall. The population increase is primarily inspired by the opportunity to make big bucks very quickly working in and around the commercial fishing industry. This created the boomtown atmosphere that rules with the laws sometimes getting ignored.

The Alaska Peninsula district starts at Lake Clark and Lake Clark pass on the north end, and goes on down the Alaska Peninsula to Lake Iliamna, then along the Kvichak River coming into Bristol Bay about 10 miles from Naknek. The Naknek district went half way to Dillingham going northwest, southwest down the Alaska Peninsula along Bristol Bay to Egigik, then on to Ugashik and Pilot Point, which is the last community southwest out of Naknek and covered from the Naknek post.

Inland there are several large lakes. Lake Iliamna is a small community with a store and bar, airport with a flight service station, a very short road system and a sports fishing lodge, besides the four different villages around Lake Iliamna itself.

On Lake Clark there is a good size village, and another community that has a commercial hanger that works on small aircraft, a church camp with several residences in the area. Katmai National Monument, and Park, and many commercial fishing and hunting camps are scattered over a vast area. For the most part most of the area is very sparsely inhabited.

I went back home with my head spinning after getting just a quick glimpse of an enormous geographical area with numerous scattered villages, a few towns and one new community at Lake Clark. The law enforcement problems could be very difficult and enough to stagger any imagination, especially on a strike year in the commercial fishing industry.

Chapter 22

As soon as I walked in the door, Ann wanted to know about her new home, the grocery store, the church and the school, which I did my best to describe. And then it was time to pack again. We packed everything but a weeks' clothing for each of us, loaded everything into a truck, said our goodbyes and set off for the Anchorage Airport. With no roads to that part of Alaska, we shipped everything we owned by air to King Salmon.

Our new post meant moving way off the road system to the land of Alaska trophy animals, the best fishing in the world and hundreds of miles of lonely beaches to explore. It was early summer, school was out and a new run of red salmon was just beginning to show up in Bristol Bay, just off of Naknek. They were just getting started processing some of the early salmon catches at the canneries, and the excitement was building.

We flew over in our Cessna 180, leaving Anchorage and flying around the upper end of Cook Inlet, then down to Lake Clark Pass, through to Lake Clark following the North shore line the length of Lake Clark, and along the Nondalton River, which flows from Lake Clark into Lake Iliamna. We then followed the northwest edge of Iliamna to where the Kvichak river exits Lake Iliamna, then headed southeast to Naknek, our new home. We landed in Naknek and met Ed Garver from the Alaska State Road Department. Ed gave us a ride to our apartment and the keys to the State Trooper pickup.

Being on a public highway system with a state highway, even though only a few miles long, means I have to administer driving tests after they have passed their written exams.

The Borough offices did the written tests, so all I had to do was give the driver's test. But that kept me busy every Thursday afternoon. Having worked as a traffic accident investigator in Anchorage made me a very tough guy when it came to passing driver's tests. The very first question I would ask myself is would I want this person driving on a road where my family was driving? If the answer was no, then they had to improve and show me they were safe drivers and knew what they were doing. Sometimes that means coming back several times to retake their driving tests.

I received a call from the South Naknek Bumble Bee Cannery medical clinic that is open only in the summer for the Cannery employees and other people in the area. The doctor in charge, Doctor Johnson is a retired physician from Seattle who is a very dedicated person. He really enjoyed keeping his hand in the profession that he had spent his entire life practicing. The doctor told me of a young girl that was babysitting for a local family in South Naknek while the parents were working at the cannery during the day. She called a friend who helped her bring in the baby boy she was babysitting. The baby had died within an hour and a half of arriving at the clinic, and the doctor did not feel good about the explanation the young girl had given him as to what happened with the baby that caused him to die.

I told him I would be down as soon as I could catch an airplane. It was a beautiful morning so after we landed at the airport, I decided to walk the half mile to the medical clinic. At the clinic I introduced myself to Dr. Johnson and asked what he could tell me about the baby and the cause of death?

The parents had left for work in the morning and everything was fine with the one-year-old baby boy. He was in good spirits when the babysitter came over in the morning. About mid afternoon the doctor received a call from the babysitter saying that the baby was acting like he did not feel well. The doctor said to bring him to the clinic so he could check him out. The baby boy was conscious, but unresponsive and did not know what was happening around him.

Within a half hour the boy was unconscious and fading. He would not respond to anything, and was dead in another hour.

I checked the baby boy over carefully and the only thing I could find was a very light discoloration of the skin on the lower abdomen.

"What did the baby sitter have to say about what happened?"

"She said the baby had fallen off the couch."

"Is that all?" I asked.

"Yes. She did not know of anything else that happened to the baby."

First I went to the parent's home and found both parents very broken up. They were having a very hard time with the fact that their baby boy had been in good spirits and very lively in the morning when they left for work, and before the day was over their son was at the medical clinic and shortly after they arrived, he was dead. Neither of them had been home during the day. They were busy processing a large early run of fish that were coming into the cannery, until someone from the cannery came and told them their boy was in the clinic and they needed to get over there.

My next stop was the baby sitter's house, Jackie Bronson. Jackie was 16 years old, and acted more like a 12 year old. She seemed confused and her mom was just as confused. I explained that I was the State Trooper and understood that Jackie was taking care of the next door neighbor's baby boy and the baby became ill. Jackie agreed that was what happened. I asked what she did next and she said she had gotten a friend to come over to take the baby to the doctor. I asked if anyone else had come over to visit where she was babysitting and she responded no. She told me that she was alone all day. I asked if the baby started feeling bad during the day and Jackie said not until the afternoon. Did the baby hurt himself or did he fall? She told me he fell off the couch. Did he cry? Just a little bit. Did you see him fall? Yes she had seen him fall, but it did not look like he had really hurt himself. The doctor sent someone to get the parents, and said he needed to check the baby over, so she had gone home.

I went back to talk to the doctor and I suggested that we get an autopsy on the baby to attempt to find the cause of death. The doctor had already determined that and fully agreed that was what should be done. I called Anchorage and made the arrangements to get the autopsy underway.

About a week and a half later I received a call from Anchorage telling me that the baby boy had received considerable trauma to the body, the same trauma that would result if the boy had been in a vehicle that ran into a solid rock wall at 45 miles per hour, without wearing a seat belt. The doctor said he would send the written result of the autopsy to my office.

I received the written results of the autopsy, and was in my office reading it. I needed help. I bowed my head to ask God for guidance, when a young man came into my office and introduced himself as Chuck Mariner, Deputy Attorney General for the State of Alaska. He was in town to represent the State of Alaska in court as the prosecuting Attorney for commercial fishery violations. I looked at him and said Chuck, you do not know it yet but you are an answer from God for help. Chuck answered, "I am kind of new about this kind of thing." I answered "What kind of thing?" "This being a Christian," Chuck said. It seems that Chuck had just recently made a decision to accept Christ as his savior. I then told him that I had an apparent homicide going and had just received written word regarding the autopsy verifying that the baby boy had indeed been killed from a powerful blow to the body, splitting his spleen and causing him to bleed to death internally.

I asked him to wait a minute and reached for the phone. I called Ann who was just across the hallway in our apartment and said we have a guest for lunch. Ann responded that lunch would be ready in 15 minutes. It is amazing how fast Christ can answer prayer. Chuck was realizing this as quickly as I was. As he did not have any cases this trip to town, but was down checking out the court and meeting the people he would be working with throughout the fishing season. This gave him time to help me with my homicide case.

After lunch we started through the case and what I had verified to that point. I reviewed the chronology and the details about the case with Chuck. The next step would be to re-interview all parties involved, attempting to establish exactly what happened to the little boy.

We also had to decide if we had enough to arrest Jackie Bronson. Chuck and I hashed and rehashed the case. I spent most of a day tracking and backtracking with all parties involved. And under advice from Chuck, I arrested the juvenile Jackie Bronson for killing the baby boy, and transported her to our holding cell behind the building our office was located in. Chuck went on to the airport in King Salmon to go on to Dillingham, where he would also be working commercial fishing cases.

The plan was to hold her for the night and then transport her to Anchorage the next morning. I had not been able to find anyone else to work as jailer that evening, so Ann was it, working as the woman jailer. After advising Jackie of her rights again, I went on with my interview one last time. Talking with her, I suggested that sometimes it is hard to understand what is wrong with a baby. Sometimes when they start fussing and will not stop, it can be frustrating. I noticed that Jackie was nodding with me as if she was agreeing with what I was saying. I looked at Jackie and asked, "Is that why you hit him?" She answered, "Yes, I had tried everything to please him and he would not shut up, I lost my temper and just hit him." I looked over at Ann and she almost fell off her chair. She told me later she had started to believe that she had nothing to do with it.

I was relieved to get Jackie's confession, as she looked and acted like a very young girl, meek and incapable of such a violent act against a baby. On the commercial airplane going to Anchorage the next day, the Alaska Airlines stewardess was going to give her a small metal toy knife. I had to prevent the exchange and wow . . . the look I received from the stewardess was a surprise. I was in full uniform, as we were required to be on a prisoner transport. The rest of the trip was uneventful. I had to go to Anchorage several times over the next two years to testify in this case.

Every time I came in to testify and work with the prosecutors I noticed there was an interesting change in progress. Jackie, who had appeared very young, rapidly took on a tougher and more mature image. She went from the meek, nice appearing young lady to a very hard looking street girl. When I went in for the final day of the trial to testify, the looks she gave me were like daggers. Life certainly is interesting. The broad array of cases I received was paving the road to the future. Jackie was finally found guilty.

Chuck, who became a good friend, helped me at the critical early stage in the field, but he was soon knee deep in commercial fishing cases, and my case was taken over by another attorney. Chuck did climb the ladder and became one the state's top attorneys. He argued several cases before the US Supreme Court.

For me the Mariners turned into much more than business acquaintances. A few years later I had to go to Kodiak Island for a four-day Harbor Master School. The flight plan was to fly to Anchorage then catch another flight into Kodiak. I had been in school for most of the week and caught the last flight out of Kodiak into Anchorage.

I was spending the night with the Mariners and going home to King Salmon the next morning. I received a call from Ann that my Mom, who had breast cancer, wanted desperately to talk to me. Mom's cancer had taken a turn for the worse and they had been trying for a couple of days to get in contact with me. A good part of the time I was not near a telephone. Mom and dad were staying with my sister, Patty so I called and she answered the phone. "Gary, mom is in very bad shape and she wants desperately to talk to you. She is too weak to come to the phone." The tears started coming down my face. Then I could hear some noise in the background, and Patty said, "Mom, what are you doing?" Then Patty said to me, "Gary, she made them bring her to the phone," and in a weak voice my mother said, "Gary do you still have your job?"

The tears continued to fall. "Yes Mom, I'm doing fine."

"Gary you are so far away and we have not been able to get hold of you. I have been afraid you would lose your job."

"That is ok Mom. I won those criminal cases where they were going to sue the city and they were so pleased that they also made me Harbor Master in addition to my other duties, and are paying me more now."

"Gary I am so relieved. I have been praying for you."

Still crying, I said, "Mom I love you and have been praying for you too." My mother had refused to die until she could talk to me and find out we were all right. She died a few hours later.

I will forever be grateful to the Mariners. If I had been at a hotel, they would have never been able to find me. A friend in need, is a friend in deed.

Chapter 23

Our experiences in Naknek continued to broaden when Ann got the opportunity to get into the commercial fishing business. A fisherman with a large skiff and enough wood to build an 8' x 12' cabin got sick and was unable to fish his license that year. The doctor filled out the affidavit and the Department of Fish and Game made the license transfer to Ann. Unbeknownst to us, this action taking place when it did made Ann the last person eligible to receive a limited entry fishing permit in the Bristol Bay commercial fishery for set netting (gill netting).

Two years later the state legislature set the limited entry program in progress. We met the requirements, and had several months to apply. We applied but could not find our copy of the original transfer so we were turned down. In the meantime, we were paying for the boat and the fishing equipment, which we had bought from the man who had transferred the permit to Ann. Even though it was looking like we were not going to get a permit, we honored the $5,000 agreement we had with Roger. We appealed and just before making our last payment, we received a letter from Department of Fish and Game turning down our appeal.

We could not find our copy of the permit transfer. We had gone through the entire file of our records for that year several times looking for it. After we received that final letter, we decided we would go through our records for that year just one more time. We sat down and prayed that we might find the only paper that the Department of Fish and Game would accept as proof of holding a commercial fishing license.

There is no possible way to explain what took place immediately after our brief prayer meeting. I opened the box holding those files and there was the yellow carbon copy of the fishing permit right on top of the files all by itself. This yellow carbon copy was the proof the Fish and Game required! Ann and I had gone through that box several times in the past two months and had not been able to find it. We sent off a copy of the transfer to Fish and Game and received the limited entry permit in the return mail. WOW! We did very well in the commercial fishing business, and several years later we sold that permit for $50,000.

Roger, the man Ann bought the cabin and boat from helped get us started that first year by running the skiff over to the campsite we had chosen to work from, at the point where Copenhagen Creek entered Bristol Bay. It was a couple hours travel by boat. Ann and the kids flew over with me and after several passes to make sure it was safe, I landed on the beach. When Roger arrived, he steered the boat right up on the beach. The tide had peaked at 18' while he was crossing the bay so he had no trouble since the high tide immersed all the dangerous sandbars in the bay. When the tide went out it left the boat high and dry. We started carrying the plywood and the 2 x 4's up the beach to the cabin site. We then went down and took the 50 fathom net (300 feet long) off the skiff and carried it up the beach, along with the camping gear, sleeping bags and groceries for a week. The last load to come up was the roll of roofing and the tools. We needed to get the cabin up and the furniture and beds built and moved in before an incoming storm. The cabin was barely completed with two bunk beds built, along with a table and benches as the rain arrived, accompanied by 20 mile per hour winds. We had beans and hamburgers that wet evening and boy was it good. We accomplished a great deal in setting up and I was able to fly Roger back to Naknek the next morning. The following day was the first day of a two-day regulated opening and we got the net out on the morning tide.

I was able to help Ann with that first set, which included helping her and the kids eat one six pound red salmon, the entire catch. Then I flew back to Naknek and to my work as an Alaskan State Trooper. Wow, what a weekend!

Ann and the kids were going to spend the rest of the opening there on the beach until the next afternoon, when I was going to pick them up in the airplane. Time sure passed slowly as I was anxious about leaving them alone on the beach. Ann had pointed out they were not alone as there was one other camp that also had one net out.

That next afternoon I was ecstatic as I flew across the bay to our fish camp, about 15 minutes out by air. Ann and the three kids came down to the beach when I circled and landed. Everyone was happy to greet me and I was glad to see they were all well, and also pleased by the six red salmon they had caught. We flew back to Naknek and I delivered my family home, and the fish to Whitney Fidalgo Cannery. We were now officially commercial fishermen.

That fishing season was the worst one in the region in several years. We caught a few hundred dollars worth of fish during the season, but we looked at it like a vacation home on a remote beach . . . well maybe a plywood shack, but it was waterproof . . . well maybe water resistant. But it really was wild at times and even exciting. One of the things that appealed most to Ann and I was being able to go beach combing by just walking down the beach, or by getting in our rubber boat and going up Copenhagen Creek about a mile or two where there were a couple of buildings where some fishermen 40 years before had set up a small salting operation. They would clean fish and salt them down as they packed them into kegs and take them back to sell in Seattle.

Some years when we were not getting many openings because of light runs of sockeye salmon returning to the bay, we had lots of opportunity to explore, or do some sport fishing. It was fairly easy to catch some nice kings for camp meat.

We also went to old abandoned canneries up the Kvichak River and spent hours exploring and catching a peek at the past. The thing that intrigued me was the lumber they had used. All the lumber was cut to exact size. A 2 x 6 was a true two inches by six inches. There were a lot of unplaned 2 x 6 timbers in one cannery, and Sitka spruce planks without a single knot up to 24' long. The history is incredible all through that country. Most surprising of all, there are no trees anywhere in the area. There is a layer of permafrost under the tundra so the timber had come from southeast Alaska.

Bristol Bay, Alaska has the very best sockeye or red salmon fishing in the world. Some of the old canneries had airstrips and some were only accessible by boat, but a few were accessible by boat and airplane. We spent hours in some of these facilities really experiencing the history of Bristol Bay.

The fun of exploring and discovering was done at our leisure, but the commercial fishing was serious business. While that first year was very poor, we were able to find out just what commercial fishing was all about. Everything we did on the beach that first year was all by hand, but we were learning just what we needed to handle lots of fish. We found that we had to be ready for the unexpected. Our cannery would put a boat tender over off our beach, but in times of heavy fish they would not always take our fish. The drift fleet would also deliver to our tender and when they were full they could not take any more fish, so we had to scramble. That is where our Cessna 180 came in mighty handy. We used several ways to deliver the fish by airplane. By using plastic garbage cans, we could keep the mess down a little. We would take every seat out of the airplane except the pilot's seat, and get in eight to 10 plastic garbage cans.

Later, we bought a smaller Piper PA-12, and used a big plastic bag that was fitted to the rear seat area. We would put hooks along the bottom of the windows and on the back of the pilot's seat, then fill 'er up!

No matter how we did it, though, there was always a mess. We could get around 1,000 lbs. of fish into the Cessna 180 and about 600 lbs in the PA-12 flying off the beach. Red salmon weighed from 5 to 7 lbs. each. A garbage can would hold around 100 lbs., and we could get in 10 plastic squared up cans, in the early model Cessna 180 I was flying. We were flying right off the beach, so the elevation was zero at sea level. We were using right around 900' of beach to get airborne, and there was another 300' that was usable, if the tide was out.

So enter another complication, this was not a fly at our leisure! We had a hot cargo, and for quality purposes it had to be delivered within only a few hours of coming out of the water. When we had to fly our fish instead of delivering to the big tender just off our beach, it was usually due to a weather problem. We'd get a south east wind blowing 45 to 70 miles per hour directly onto our runway on the beach, creating a crosswind. One day I was trying to get one more load of fish off the beach before losing my runway to the fast moving tide roaring in with a 70 mile an hour wind howling in off Bristol Bay. I taxied down away from Copenhagen Creek so I would be heading towards the creek, and then on towards town instead of away from it.

The actual runway section of the beach had a bluff 20' to 30' high straight up from the beach. The water line was getting higher all the time as the rising tide approached. High water this evening would be right to the bottom of the bluff so I was starting my take off 60' from the edge of the beach, with that 70 mph wind right on my wing tip. About half way through as I was getting up speed, the aircraft started skipping sideways toward the bluff. I shoved the yoke forward trying to glue the wheels to the beach, but it was not working. I had a full load of fish, and that wind was pushing me at an alarming rate right at the bank with my left wing tip getting closer and closer. I was past the point of being able to shut it down, now it was get off or crash! I felt my gut tighten up, but I was waiting until the last second, trying to get all the ground speed I possibly could so the aircraft would fly and not roll up in a tangled mess. I expected the wing tip to touch any second when I finally kicked hard right rudder, turning the nose of the aircraft directly into the wind, and out over the incoming tide. While pulling back on the wheel yoke with my left hand, trying to drag that heavy aircraft into the air, my other hand had a grip on the flap handle pulling full flaps, and praying at the same time that the landing gear would lift off the beach instead of doing a colossal ground loop into that chilling cold Bristol Bay water.

Bristol Bay
Fish waiting to go to market

That would have been spectacular but deadly. *PRAISE GOD!* My wing tip did not touch the bluff and my airplane struggled off the ground into that seventy-mile-per-hour headwind and no one on that beach really knew how close I came to meeting my maker face-to-face. Except Ann, who witnessed the whole thing, and immediately prayed I would not attempt to come back that evening. I didn't return until the next day. She spent the night in the small cabin with the wind howling all night, listening for the sound of an airplane engine.

Oh Lord, thank you seems so inadequate. I will attempt to use better judgment from this point forward.

Another time, again with a big southeast wind I had taken off with a big load of fish in the late afternoon with the tide still far enough down the beach I was able to quarter into the wind with no problems. I flew to Naknek and landed on their runway, which was directly into that southeast wind, delivered my load of fish and started back to the beach. As I expected, the tide was in and very high and there was virtually no beach to land on. The tie down area that we had hand carved out of the tundra just off the beach was full of tied down airplanes, eight of them. I flew up Copenhagen Creek and slowed the aircraft down as I headed back down into the wind. I came to my tie down ropes on the tundra at the end of the line of the other airplanes, and slowed my ground speed down to almost nothing, then circled around towards our fish camp. Mark, my son came out first with his crew behind. I pointed to the tie down area and four of them started down the beach towards it. As they arrived I went around again and started a very slow approach. I slowed my speed to a slow walk and lined up on the tie down ropes. As I got right over the tie down the aircraft ground speed was zero. I thought I would just stall it out and it would just settle down on the ground, but as I pulled back on the stick to stall the airplane, it flared out while it was still flying. I should have realized that, so I went around again.

This time when I was over the tie down I just used my throttle to adjust my elevation. As I eased the aircraft down to a foot above the ground there were two crew members on each side of the airplane and as I set the wheels down on the tundra they took a hold of the wing struts and slipped the rope through the tie down steel loop on the aircraft and tied it down there as I sat both wheels down with zero roll. The airplane was tied down.

Mark delivering another load of fish to tender.

So I shut off the engine. The landing was smoother than most helicopter landings I have been around. My wing tip was two feet from the end airplane.

There were four guys that had heard about all the fish we had flown off the beach from Copenhagen Creek last year, so they had brought their aircraft up from Seattle to join the flying circus and hopefully get rich flying fish to King Salmon. They all had their aircraft tied down and had been sitting out by the bluff and watched the whole show. After my landing and tie down, Mark, his crew and I all went up to the cookhouse as Ann had dinner ready. The Seattle guys all came over and said they had never seen anything like that before. And congratulated me on the great flying feat I had accomplished.

As they left and before my ego could soar too high, young Russ Gagel from the next camp to ours came over to our cookhouse. He complained about my reckless flying, which he felt had endangered his airplane that was tied down three feet from my right wing tip. I did not tell him that it was only two feet. Win some, lose some.

The Fish and Game had kept the fishing season open, as there were plenty of fish escaping up the river, so we were fishing wide open. I had succeeded in getting the last of the fish off the beach that we had caught on the incoming tide, so as the tide started going down we were fishing wide open. This is when fishing gets interesting on the beach. That big southeast wind was blowing all the fish right in towards shore and into our waiting nets. Our whole crew was on the beach picking fish as quickly as possible. We started out working in the water as deep as we could wade out. Things were wild in that it was hard to stay on your feet with the big waves crashing in on you, and there were fish running into your legs in the water. The net was going crazy with the whole cork line looking like it was smoking, with new fish hitting it constantly and fighting to get loose from the gill net.

Getting a rubber boat off that beach with the wind around 70 miles an hour, getting the upper end of a net cleared of fish and then dragging that net off the beach with the rubber boat with big rolling waves crashing onto the beach was extremely hard work. At least a couple of us would be in the water up to our chests as another big wave came in and then down to our knees as the wave went on up the beach. We were wearing hip boots underneath with full rubber raingear. After a short time we were wet all the way to the skin and our boots were filled, weighing us down as we sloshed about doing our work.

If we could get the net cleared, before low tide, then we could move it down the beach and back out into the water before low water for another very lucrative set through low water. We were looking at 4,000 fish in that 300' long net. Everyone on our crew was working for a percentage of the catch, so there was no goofing off. We were working mostly in the dark that first night of the extended season. Actually not in total darkness as it would get dusky about 12:30 a.m., then stay that way until about 3:00 a.m. when bright daylight came again. As soon as I had a couple of hundred feet of beach I was in the airplane and getting the plane down to the beach and loading it again with fish, and off I would go. In good fishing if there was no tender off the beach I had to fly from daylight to after dark.

If the tender was anchored off our beach I'd put a brailer net in the bottom of the open hull of our rubber boat. We would start loading fish, constantly moving the boat into deeper water so it would not "beach" on the sand. Then once the boat was full, I'd climb aboard sitting on top a mound of fish, start the outboard motor and haul them out to the tender. They would swing a boom out over our boat and lower the hook. I'd lace the brailer onto the hook and they would lift the load out of our boat. Then they would pause where we could still see the scale as the load was weighed. They liked the brails to be around 900 lbs., but sometimes they went as high as 1,500. This was an amazing load for a 14' Zodiac inflatable! Then back to the beach and start another load of fish. With great fishing like that we were lucky to get a couple of hours of sleep a day.

It was always hurry, hurry, hurry to get those fish off the beach while they were fresh. Our biggest year we put in a little over 300,000 lbs. of fish in the month and a half season. Without exception, everyone that fished with us said this was the hardest work they had ever done.

Chapter 24

Ann and I found fishing was a great way to raise our kids. They learned right away that the harder you worked, the more you made. I never had to get after any of our crew. If anyone was loafing, the crew let them know they were expected to carry their end of the load.

In Alaska, commercial fishing offers the possibilities of making a great deal of money quickly. Sometimes a single set can bring in thousands of dollars. This atmosphere has the same excitement and thrills that the old gold rush created. It also sets the table for some people to sometimes not act in responsible ways. One year in one of the local bars in Naknek, a fisherman was demonstrating that he had money to burn, so he took an ash tray and put in four $100 bills and lit a match to them. Then swatting away hands of those not quite as carried away as the man with money was, he proceeded to burn the four bills. I did not come in until 15 minutes later. This did happen! Irrational behavior is not always just an illusion.

Put these temptations in front of a large group; add a strike against the canneries to get more money per pound and things can get very volatile. Some fishermen cannot withstand the temptation of going fishing anyway, even though there is a strike and that is like pouring gasoline on a fire. When fishermen that do not support the strike start fishing, tempers flare quickly, and fights happen constantly. There is sabotage to boats and fishing gear, there are boats ramming each other and things are constantly in an uproar. I went through one of these strike years in Bristol Bay all by myself. I have been on both sides. This year I was the lone State trooper! There were some Fish and Game enforcement officers, but this was before they came under the Department of Public Safety. They were just as busy as I was, but always off in different areas.

Not only do the tempers flare from the fishermen, they also flare between the cannery workers at the canneries and the fishermen. Because the fishermen will not fish or let others fish, the millions of fish in the bay go up the rivers, never to be caught. There are no fish to process and the workers cannot collect the big wages they usually make in a good year, so tempers get out of hand and create enormous problems in the community.

In 1971, the commercial fishing season was about halfway through. It was a Sunday afternoon, and I was relaxing at home. I had on a pair of Levis and a new pair of loafers when I received a phone call from a bar two doors up, on the same side of the street. The bartender, was excited saying the Philippine crew from Nelbro Cannery were there throwing bottles from inside through the windows outside, and now they were outside throwing bottles into the bar back through the same windows. They had really torn up the place, breaking the windows and destroying many bottles of beer.

One of the guys had pulled a knife on a guy that had a motorcycle and stolen his motorbike at knifepoint. I was looking out the front window of our house as the bartender was speaking. I could see several guys that appeared to be of Philippine descent running down the street. I spoke to the bartender and said, "There are several guys running past our place and they seem to be led by a guy wearing a black jacket, would that be one of them?" He answered, "Yeah, that's them. Get him!" I grabbed my gun belt and put it on quickly, grabbed my jacket with my badge on it and ran out the door. I could see they were running down the street and into the Red Salmon cannery driveway.

As I started down the road after them in my State Trooper pickup they looked over their shoulders and the group of seven or eight men started jumping into the brush along the road. The two biggest, including the one wearing the black jacket turned to run around the rear of a warehouse going through a swamp. I slid the pickup to the edge of the road and jumped out in pursuit of those two and a third that had a 50 yard head start. They were going through the swamp. As I was catching up the smallest turned off into the brush, but I kept after the two bigger guys, including the one wearing the black jacket.

I caught up to them and as I was reaching out to grab them, I felt my gun belt come unhooked and drop down into the swamp. To make matters even worse, I could feel the mud and slop oozing between my toes inside my new loafers. Now I was losing my temper. I was able to grab them both in the next couple of steps and they both sat down in the swamp, and refused to get up. That was OK with me. I just grabbed each one by the ponytails they were wearing their hair in, and started for the pickup back through the swamp. They slid real well through all the goop. I stopped where I lost my gun belt and scooped it out of the muddy water, threw it over my shoulder and continued on. I came out right at the back of my pickup and stopped at the rear bumper, took my handcuffs out of their case in my gun belt and put one of the hands of the guy wearing the black jacket on the inside of the bumper and took the other guys hand around the outside of the bumper, handcuffing their hands together around and below the bumper. Then I picked the first one up and rolled him into the back of my pickup. When I got him in, he was bending over the tail gate reaching down with his hand cuffed to his friend's, which was on the inside of the bumper. I then picked up the other guy wearing the black jacket and flipped him into the back of the pickup next to his partner. Both were reaching down with one hand cuffed to the other guy around the back bumper of the pickup. I could see up on the main road where two more of the crew was heading back to the cannery after getting through the swamp from the brush. I turned to the two I had handcuffed and told them, "Now whatever you do, do not fall out of my pickup while I'm driving." It is amazing how they decided to co-operate.

As I went bouncing up the rough road I could look in the rear view mirror and see their legs occasionally, bounce up in the air where their rear ends disappeared over the tailgate. After catching the other two on the main road, I placed them under arrest and loaded them in back of the pickup and told them to keep their friends from falling out. Then we started back to the bar.

At the bar the owner came out, went around to the rear of the pickup so he could see their faces, and said they were the ones that were tearing the place up. "This guy here," he indicated a fisherman in the bar, "had another one of them pull a knife on him and steal his motorbike. Then they went on up the street." I suggested we go to the bar at the end of the street and look for his motorcycle. At the end of the street we found his motorbike outside the bar parked at the front door. As we approached the bar a man came out the door and the person who had the motorcycle taken from him said that was the guy who took it. I advised the man of his rights and he responded, "He was not going to hurt anyone, he just wanted to get away because they knew that the State Trooper had been called."

So I arrested him as well, and loaded them all up and went back to my jail. After getting everyone locked up and getting a jailer hired, I started putting together the paperwork. I received a call from Nelbro cannery, and they wanted to know what time the arraignment would be. The cannery boss said he would have all the rest of the crew there that had caused the problem also. The cannery boss also contacted the bar and was co-operating in getting everything put back together. There were a total of 14 from the cannery involved in the disturbance.

The only one that had serious charges brought against him was the man that stole the motorcycle at knifepoint. I transported him to Anchorage where he faced felony charges. When the State Trooper met me at the airplane to transport my prisoner, he said, "What in the world did you get into? We heard you had single handedly broken up a major riot, and locked up so many people from one cannery that they had to shut down for two days." I responded, saying, "I just went after the leaders of the riot and when I got them the others were easy," all the while grinning. Wow! How stories build their own head of steam.

The year they pulled me out of Naknek, I was replaced with several Troopers, as there was another strike year coming.

Chapter 25

South of Naknek was a large Bible camp located on the north shoreline of Lake Becharof. There were several large buildings that were used for the main kitchen, bunk houses, and meeting halls. The camp was built in the middle of the wilderness and was set up with a large generator for power, and kids came from all over the region including Naknek, Egigik, Lake Clark, Dillingham and many of the smaller villages throughout the area. Transportation to and from the camp was donated by local private pilots, which enabled the camp to keep the rates very inexpensive. I had the privilege of helping with the flying.

Our kids attended the camp and they all had a ball. There are all kinds of wildlife at the camp, including moose, caribou, and brown bear. The brown bears congregated along the lake where the streams came in during the salmon runs that came up the Egigik River from Bristol Bay into Lake Becharof, then further up the streams that flow into Lake Becharof to spawn.

People and brown bears get along well if they all stay out of each other's way. The campers and the bears were usually good neighbors, and the kids made enough noise so the bears wanted to stay out of their way.

Late in October that first year we were in Naknek, there was a wedding, where one of the local guys was marrying a young woman from Dillingham. I found out later that with lots of people coming in from out of town these types of celebrations could erupt into huge fights as the evening progressed. I had not been aware of the potential for problems. But I learned fast.

It was only 8:30 in the evening when Joe the bartender at Hatfield's Bar called, and he sounded tired, "Gary. this is a hell of a mess, the women are fighting with the men, and they are fighting with other women, and the men are fighting with the men . . . I am just getting tired of the whole mess and I can't get them to go. Could you come up and help me close up?"

Joe was a tough bartender. If he needed help closing this early in the evening, then he had some major trouble.

Looking at my watch, I was surprised to see it was only 8:30 p.m. Wearing a pair of Levies and a wool shirt, I strapped on my gun belt and put on my jacket with my badge on it, and went out to my Trooper's pickup. It was late October and it was cool outside, with snow on the ground, and temperatures in the mid 20's. I drove up to the end of Main Street and parked, just outside the front door of Hatfield's Bar. When I went in I was surprised to find the entire bar full, and a dozen of the tables full, somewhere between 70 and 80 people.

The jukebox was blaring music and there were half a dozen people dancing, but clearly there were no fights going on. I went down to the end of the bar where Joe was standing and asked if he still wanted to close the place. Joe did not hesitate and answered, "Gary, they just quit when I told them I was calling the State Trooper."

I went over to the jukebox and pulled the plug. All of a sudden you could hear a pin drop. I announced that at Joe's request the business was closed for the night. No one even made a move to head for the door. I had to identify the leader of the troublemakers.

Those three couples on the dance floor headed back to their tables, but that was the only movement. I went to the nearest table and said this place is closed, are you leaving or going to jail? One of them said they were going. I went to the next table and asked are you leaving or going to jail for trespassing? Again and again I went to every table and told them this place was closed, and asked are you leaving or going to jail for trespassing. Everyone at every table said they were going, but none of them made any move to leave.

I went over to the bar and started at one end going to each person telling them the bar was closed, are you leaving or going to jail? Everyone said they were leaving, but one of them. About half way down the bar I asked that same question to a big, broad shouldered man who looked about 45 years old, and he responded, "Go to hell!" I recognized him as being a convicted felon that had killed a man in a barroom fight with a pool ball 10 years before. He had spent several years in jail but was now out. The State Trooper I had replaced had warned me of potential trouble with him. I went on to the next man and asked the same question and he responded the same as the majority of the people at the bar. I got to the end of the bar with everyone going to leave but the problem guy that told me to go to hell. Everyone was waiting to see the fight!

I had found the head troublemaker, now I had to get him arrested and out of there. To lose this one would probably mean at least half a dozen on my back. I had to win, and quickly.

I started down the bar and as I came to the problem I told him it was time to go. He responded he was not going to go anywhere, so I said, "You are under arrest," and I put the sleeper hold on him from behind. He was sitting on a bar stool without a back on it, I did not tighten down, instead I pulled him backward off the bar stool and relaxed my hold until his tailbone connected with the floor, giving him a solid jolt, then I put the squeeze on his artery that goes to his brain, picking him off the floor by his head using my hip while dragging him to the door.

At the door I opened it with one hand and we went outside where I reached for my handcuffs, but he was reviving very rapidly in the icy evening breeze coming off Bristol Bay. We had to go around a snowdrift and I slipped losing my grip on him. He took off running around my pickup. On the third time around the pickup I was still about half way around it behind and not gaining, so I jumped into the back as I went behind the cab and dove off the other side tackling him and rolling both of us into a snow bank. I came up on top of him and grabbed my handcuffs. Seeing the handcuffs he relaxed and said why do I always get the handcuffs? After putting on the handcuffs I put him in the pickup securing him to the truck and noticed that several guys had followed us out. They saw the results. They went back in the bar and I followed them. Now everyone was putting on their coats and leaving the bar. I gave a great sigh of relief, as I had never heard about the good guy winning a fight with those odds present. Get the leader and the rest will follow. *Lord, thank you for taking care of me again.*

The Alaska Peninsula is completely different than the Glennallen-Copper River country, including the Wrangle Mountains. There are some mountains in the area but nothing like the Wrangles. I learned mountain flying in the Glennallen area, then on the Alaska Peninsula I learned flying in high winds, with big loads and low ceilings working on and off beaches that were not always hard, while commercial fishing.

On the Alaska Peninsula the bears, moose and caribou are considerably larger, or they were in the area I was traveling. Most of the hunting I did for our winter meat was south and west of Egigik.

Ann and I heard that there was a late run of silver salmon at Cinder River that started in late July, so I flew us down to look it over. We found an old cabin still standing, but with holes in all the walls and roof, but the cabin itself and the floor was solid. This was on the inside beach of a bay. The cabin had its own beach that we used for a runway. We decided to use this for a base camp to hunt out of while trying the commercial fishing for silver salmon. It was only a 55 minute flight in our Cessna from Naknek.

The day we were down checking out the cabin the wind was almost blowing as hard inside as it was outside. When we returned we brought a big roll of clear heavy plastic and wrapped the walls and roof, built a one wall outhouse, and were in business for a base camp. It was incredible what that plastic did in the way of weather proofing that cabin. Just using the little Coleman stove put out enough heat to keep the inside nice and toasty.

We were able to walk over to the outside beach for some good beachcombing. It seems that every trip we brought back several treasures such as glass balls from Japanese fishing floats, big plastic baskets, and other Items they used on their fishing boats. It was a constant reminder that they were using our waters for commercial fishing. We did not see any large game near camp, but we were able to watch a couple of foxes that came around and there were always geese flying by. It seemed like a land of plenty.

We sure were not getting rich with the fishing. We were averaging around 200 lbs, of fish a day, which required a trip a day to the cannery. But when you put the whole thing together it was a great vacation that was paying us to experience Alaska backcountry living. I used the extra trips to deliver fish to also take my winter supply of meat, as we were hunting when we were not fishing. Wow what a life! The run of silvers was pretty much over in 15 days.

I decided to take Karen and Beth, our two young daughters caribou hunting at the new camp. Karen our oldest daughter and I went down on the beach a couple of days to target-practice with a .222 Remington rifle.

We went out and found a small heard of caribou and were able to get within 50 yards. We could not find any rest for Karen to shoot off of so she fired one round offhand and I was amazed when she hit her mark. We were hunting winter meat, and Karen had hit a nice young bull. It did not go down and we still could not find a rest for her to lean against for a finishing shot, so I did the honors with a second shot. It was a good thing because Karen had hit the caribou in the foot. We dressed the animal, took care of the meat, and took it back to the cannery where they let us use their freezer. Those caribou were feeding on wild peas that grow along the beaches. They made very good eating.

Getting to tie down off beach

Chapter 26

Our Commercial fishing operation took place from the middle of June every year until late July. We have to be very mobile and ready to adapt to any situation. Our main fishing camp was located on the west bank of the Kvichak River right at Copenhagen Creek. There were no roads in the area of our fishing camp. The only way in or out is by airplane off the beach or boat via Bristol Bay.

The fishing district we are regulated under is the Naknek-Kvichak district. The Department of Fish and Game's job is to make sure that each river gets their minimum escapement of fish so that there is enough fish spawning to sustain, or build the run. At the same time they are to allow the harvest of as many excess fish as possible.

Sometimes the Naknek River gets its escapement early, so they will keep the Kvichak district closed and open Naknek only. Or they might close the Naknek River and open the Kvichak River. Or if there are no Kvichak fish at all they will open fishing only inside the Naknek River with no fishing permitted anywhere in the outer bay.

Or they will only allow fishing south of the Naknek River . . . or use any other combination to harvest excess fish from one river while making sure that all rivers obtain their minimum escapement.

If they are only changing the opening for a day or so we will just pick up and take fishing gear with no camp, or whatever it takes to get where the opening is and catch the fish.

Catching fish takes some experimenting. The beach fish generally follow the beach in very shallow water populating the water in the first 30 yards off the shore. As the tide moves on up the beach you generally do not catch fish again on that tide until the tide reaches high tide and goes out to where your net is again, located in that first 30 yards of water. Depending on our location and the weather we can move the net up or down the beach if there are not too many fish in the net. The net is 50 fathoms long (300 feet) and has a cork line attached along the top to keep the net floating, and there is a lead line attached to the bottom to keep the net right side up in the water. We attempt to remove all the fish possible during fishing.

When we are fishing the outgoing tide, we are out in the water in rubber gear picking fish as fast as we can, so as soon as the net is clear we can move it down into the water again. We call this swinging the net, by disconnecting the top of the net (highest on the beach) and dragging it to water line, hooking it to a skiff, and dragging it out into the water where it is attached to a buoy anchored in deeper water.

Having the airplane made it possible to quickly get from one beach net site location to another. One year they would not let us fish anywhere but south of the Naknek River. We knew that there was no one fishing down at the south line near Johnson Hill, so we threw one fifty fathom net into the plane along with anchoring lines, buoys, rubber gear and some sandwiches. We caught some fish, and the run was showing strength so they extended the opening. Fish and Game did this for three days, so we kept fishing, but I did fly back to our base camp at Copenhagen Creek and picked up our sleeping bags, Ann and the kids, a couple of tents and more supplies.

Word got around that we were catching fish, but we had those first sites at the marker staked out. I got up in the middle of the night and found a drifter that had made a set all the way around my net so it was impossible for the fish to get into my net. The fisherman was holding his net in place with his drift boat, which was in front of my net just 10 yards off the beach. With his engine running as he held his position, he was catching all the fish.

I went down to the waters edge yelling at him to get off the beach as what he was doing was against the law, and he yelled back, "No speaky, English!" I responded by picking up some rocks and he pulled off 50 yards or so. There was a lot of fish in his net.

The next day I contacted Fish and Game to report him, but it did no good. That night I caught three fish where I had been catching several hundred. He had covered up his commercial fishing number on his boat so I could not identify him. So I flew back to base camp and brought my rifle over to the beach.

There was a big sandy bluff behind the beach, so I set up a target on the bluff. And when he showed up late the next night coming in on the beach, I brought my rifle out and shot a hole in the target. He was wearing a yellow slicker and he dove into his wheelhouse on his boat with only his arm visible steering the boat. He yelled something at me and I yelled back, "No speaky, English!"

The outlaw fisherman did not come back.

We ended up staying there for two weeks, making a good year in what could have been a bust year. The canneries were not getting many fish so with higher fish prices we made pretty good income. The big drawback was that I had to fly all our fish to North Naknek. We got some heavy fog, and that made the flying pretty rough at times.

I would fly all the way to the mouth of the Naknek River right on the beach with all the strobes turned on. At the mouth of the Naknek I had to cross the river, so I would be right on the water, until I would come to a fishing boat, then I would have to fly around each boat I found. If I tried to go over the boat it would put me out of sight with the water because of the fog. Most of the boat masts only had a 15' to 20' maximum height but that fog was down to five to 10' off the water.

As soon as we got across the river we could usually get over the bluff and land in Naknek. That day, I could not get over the bluff without getting lost in the fog, so back down on the deck I went and I flew on down to New England cannery, about two miles, down the beach where they had a very low bluff that had a landing strip right on top of the bluff. That day I had to land there and wait an hour until there was room to get across to the Naknek landing strip. That's a lot of fooling around to get a load of fish to the market.

The normal years we never left our base camp at Copenhagen Creek, but being equipped to handle the unexpected really paid off for us over the years. We had built up our base camp since that first 8' x 12' cabin and it was centered around a camp cookhouse where the kitchen was located. It contained a large dining table with benches on two sides for meals and leisure time. There was also a boy's bunkhouse and a girl's bunkhouse, and as our kids got older those became a women's bunkhouse and a men's bunkhouse.

Then we built a shop to work on the equipment, and a laundry house with an old wringer washing machine. We also had a shower, and a steam bath, built the way the local natives did it. A hot burning wood stove with a big pot of hot water. As soon as the stove was roaring we would just put some water on the wood stove and create a cloud of steam.

We had a windmill mounted on top of the cookhouse. This windmill generated DC power into a big Caterpillar battery, from which we ran the direct current lights in the main cabin, and lights in each of the bunkhouses. Electric lights were a luxury on the beach, when we were fishing around the clock all our rubber gear was kept on a covered porch just outside the main cabin. It was a lot easier than lighting a gas lantern every time you came and went from the camp after dark.

We lived there about a month and a half every year. We enjoyed very comfortable Bristol Bay headquarters, not fancy but comfortable. Sometimes early in the season, right after we first arrived in the spring, or later during the last week or so that we were there, we had unwelcome visitors on the beach.

You could always tell after just a short walk on the beach. The Alaska brown bear leaves a huge footprint. We kept our garbage cleaned up and would burn it regularly on the beach. We were always careful to give them plenty of room. And they always gave us plenty of room.

Chapter 27

We woke up one morning to find that the wind was blowing pretty hard. A trip down the beach revealed that our big boat, a 32' aluminum stern-located cabin with twin inboard outdrives had been dragging its anchor and the boat was washing up onto the beach in the surf as the tide was going out. We did not have long to act; we had to get that boat off the beach as the tide was going out. We would need to use the boat on the afternoon tide. That afternoon's tide would not get high enough to float it.

I rallied my brother, Gregg and crewmember Ken Willard. We all put on full rubber gear. We went in the water trying to push it off the beach, but every time it looked like we might make it another big wave would come in pushing the boat higher. We all worked hard trying again and again. I jumped into the big boat and started the right engine with the prop all the way out of the water I lowered it until about half in and gave it a little throttle. This caused water to fly way back in a rooster tail, giving Ken and Gregg a shower but provided little help. Next I lowered the engine a little more it started to gently pull ahead, then a big wave passed below me and dropped the boat way down so that the prop hit the mud. Luckily it then came back into the water without breaking the prop. I was finally able to get the other engine going, and lowered it partially into the water and we slowly pushed off the beach. Both Ken and Gregg jumped aboard.

We went out and after two passes snagged our buoy farthest off the beach to moor the boat overnight. Now we had a new problem. The tide would not get this low for several hours for us to be able to walk off the boat, and we were all soaked to the skin. There was no food on the boat and we had not eaten breakfast yet. We talked it over, it was only 250 yards to the beach and we were all strong swimmers. I was the oldest at 40, with Gregg 13 years younger and Ken just a year into college at 19. We took off our boots, socks, and rubber gear. Wearing only a tee shirt, and Levis we prepared for the swim. Ken hit the water first in a flat dive with Gregg right behind him and I followed closely. Ken's lead got longer as Gregg and I followed. A little over half way I noticed that I was falling farther behind and was starting to experience some of the same feelings I had gone through up on the high Sierra Nevada Mountains during that blizzard. Although I forced myself to keep swimming, everything seemed in slow motion. I was just approaching the shallows where the waves would hesitate, then start forward in a rush causing a slight under tow that normally would not have bothered me, but now my swimming strokes did not have the strength and power. I was being sucked under, and was having trouble taking in air without salt water getting into my mouth. I realized I was getting close to being able to touch the bottom, but took on some more water, and now I knew if I could not get a breath I was done. *Oh GOD, help!* I reached down as far as I could with my left foot and *Praise God* I touched the bottom! But just barely! I did not have much strength left, but was able to push off slightly and my head bobbed to the surface. I was just barely able to get a quick breath, and was sucked under again.

I went right back down and this time I was able to get my foot solid on the bottom, so I got my head out of the water and was able to get rid of some of the water I had swallowed, and suck in fresh air. What an incredible feeling, it was re-entering the world of the living. Finally I was able to keep my feet under me and walk. I finally made it through the surf, but it was difficult. Gregg was still there on the beach, but he was having some of the same problems I was having. Ken went on up to the guys bunk house as he was also feeling hypothermic.

I had not even thought of hypothermia as it was summer time and we were in shallow water, yet the icy waters of Bristol Bay almost claimed three more victims. I had heard similar stories in the past, but never thought it could happen to me, or us. *In Christ I can do anything, but alone I can do nothing.*

Chapter 28

I received a call from the village of Nondalton, Alaska, located 10 miles up the Kvichak River and 35 miles North of Naknek. Jeremy Williams, one of the leaders of the community wanted to talk to me about their school teacher, who he thought might be molesting some of the young boys in the community. I told him I would charter a flight the following morning. This type of a case always left me in a bad mood. I felt like I was being sucked into a cesspool.

One of the air taxi services dropped me off at the airstrip in Nondalton at 10:00 a.m. and would come back to get me at 1:00 p.m. It was a short walk into the village and the Williams' house. When I arrived. I sat down with Norma and Jeremy. Their two boys were attending the one teacher school. They started first by telling me that the previous year their teacher, Tom Mahoney had been nominated for the teacher of the year in the state of Alaska and had in fact won that honor. Winning that achievement had put him in competition for the teacher of the year in the nation, and he also won that title. Almost every evening he would have some of the young boys over to his house for the evening. It was not unusual for one to three of them to stay the night. There were very seldom any girls there.

I asked what kind of a teacher he was, and they said he appeared to be very good. Their boys did well in school. I asked if they had talked to their boys about their teacher, and what he did when they were over at his house? They said that they had talked to their boys and they were concerned that the teacher had molested them. It seems that he had them pull their pants down and touched their private parts.

Jeremy requested that I go and talk to another family. He said that his boys were coming home for lunch in about 45 minutes, so I got directions to the neighbor's house and went to talk to them. It was much the same story at the neighbor's house. The story was that Tom Mahoney was not interested in little girls, as he did not have the same attraction towards the daughters that he had for their boys.

Going back to the Williams' house I was able to talk to their boys and I had no doubt that those boys had in fact been molested. Before going to meet the airplane I talked to several other families and they confirmed the other stories. Because of the titles won by the teacher this was going to be a very high profile case and I needed to get it wrapped up airtight with no mistakes.

As soon as I got back to Naknek, I called the Anchorage State Trooper office to alert them as to what was going on. The next morning I was back in Nondalton conducting more interviews. After I had talked to most of the school age kids, and all their parents, I scheduled an appointment with the teacher, Tom Mahoney for right after school. When I went in he seemed very apprehensive. There is no way he could not know what was going on. He greeted me with a polite handshake, and invited me in. I introduced myself to him and informed him I was here in the village conducting an investigation about charges against him. I then told him I needed to advise him that he had the right to remain silent, he did not have to say anything, he had the right to an attorney and to have him present while being talked to, and if he could not afford an attorney one would be appointed by the State of Alaska. I then asked him, with those rights in mind do you wish to talk to me now? As usual I was amazed when he stated yes, I will talk to you now.

I have found that I seem to do better in these situations if I establish a bit of trust in our conversation, and the best way to do that is to tell the person I understand the difficult situation you are in and I try to put myself in his or her shoes. I truly feel sorry when a person has let his behavior get out-of-hand, while at the same time knowing that Christ is the place he should turn for answers. I gave Tom Mahoney all the dignity he would allow me to give him. And then he started telling me what has been going on between him and his students, going into great detail. The story got very graphic.

By the time we had finished there was a very good case against him, and it had all come from his own mouth. So I went back to the office and laid it all out on paper.

The next day, a Saturday, he flew into Naknek and came into my office without calling or at my request. He just wanted to talk to me again. So again I advised him of his rights and he started. I had put all the things together, lined out in my notes and now I was able to go over and polish the story with Tom Mahoney's guidance. We were also able to get his signature so it read as a confession. *This opportunity had to be provided by Christ.*

I sent in all my paperwork and there was instant reaction from the Attorney General's office and the Alaska school board in charge of our local school district. Tom Mahoney was relieved from his position.

Because of his Teacher of the Year award from the State of Alaska, and also his National Teacher of the Year award, they were keeping the situation very hush hush. But there was a huge problem. We had a very tight case, especially with the confession, but they wanted to keep it quiet and use a form of plea bargaining to make everything go away. I did not realize what was going on and I was demanding, "He did the crime, so he should do the time." As you might guess, I am not a big fan of plea bargaining.

The defendant's attorneys came forward with a plan that Mahoney would not contest the revoking of his teaching certificate if he did not have to spend the time in jail. My bottom line was that Tom Mahoney would never be able to get another teaching job anywhere in United States of America. I was assured that he would not ever be teaching again. This case took a year and a half to finally come to its conclusion.

I am still wondering if we really won? The reason for the plea bargain was to keep some of those in power from being embarrassed.

Chapter 29

It was a cold, stormy November afternoon and I was visiting with Dan O'hara, a good friend in Naknek. We were in the hallway of the district court just down from our residence in the same building. We had a room rented down stairs that we used for church services, and Dan was our pastor. He also was a commercial fisherman and lived his faith. It was the Wednesday before Thanksgiving and a couple, Jim and Lora Stevens came up to us looking for information.

They had just flown in from Anchorage and were on their way home a couple of more hours on down the Alaska Peninsula to a very small settlement where a few of the motorcycle gang known as the Brothers had taken up residence. The weather had shut down all hope of reaching their destination this afternoon and probably for the next couple of days. They were just glad to have made it to Naknek. Dan called his wife and was taking the Stevens' home with him for dinner that evening, and then they were coming back for Wednesday evening prayer services in the room downstairs.

We all came together for the services at 7:00 p.m. with Guy and Shirley Morgan and their kids also there. The rest of our small church was out of town or getting ready for their Thanksgiving Day dinner. Dan was also the caretaker of New England Cannery and he invited the Stevens to stay with him.

Dan, Guy and I are all pilots, and when we began exchanging stories, flying and airplanes went right to the front of the group and that is when we found that he was having some problems with his airplane and needed his wings recovered.

Jim was wondering if anyone locally did airplane repairs. Guy cleared his throat. He was a certified engine and air frame mechanic, and spent a good part of the winter working on airplanes, and the summer commercial fishing.

The next day Jim and Guy went to check out Jim's airplane and got things ready to go to work on it. We were all getting together for a potluck dinner that afternoon and Jim and Lora joined in and we all sat down to a huge feast and good time.

Jim and Guy worked long hours and were able to get the airplane airworthy again before the weekend was over. This was the second experience I had with the Brothers motorcycle gang, and I must say the results were quite different than the first meeting. But the third experience was approaching and it was a hair-raiser.

I'd been hearing rumors of a transfer and as fall approached it became a certainty. This time it was back to the Anchorage area. They were bringing two of us back into the area to either debush us, or to beef up and give the new recruits the benefit of a little experience. It ended up being some of both.

Anchorage was much the same as the last time I was working the area four years before. The main difference was that the city was growing rapidly. The good thing about being back was again I would be working under Corporal Art English, and Sergeant Scott Gilmore. The one thing you could depend on was that both would back you to the limit, as long as you were on the right trail, and if you requested anything they would bust their tails to help you.

Labor Day the entire State Trooper force was working as this was a huge get out of the city day, and for those that live outside the city, it was a big go to the city day. I was working the highway south of Anchorage, through the Fort Richardson gate to the army base, and on to Eagle River. There was a new Trooper working Eagle River and farther south, half way to Palmer.

Trooper Patterson was working the east side of the unincorporated portion of Anchorage. He was a Trooper about the same age as I, and very solid; one you could always count on to back you up at any cost. That day we had the luxury of an eye in the sky, Lieutenant O'brien who was flying a small Cessna 140. It was the lieutenant's son, a newly commissioned State Trooper working Eagle River, the area east of me.

The night before, temperatures got down into the upper 20's, and the next day was beautiful sunshine with temperatures in the mid-40's. The leaves on the trees were turning to various shades of gold, yellow, and brown. It was one of those picture-book days that happen rarely.

I was approximately three miles east from the main gate of Fort Richardson when the dispatcher came on the air and radioed Trooper Patterson and myself that a citizen had just called in that 12 motorcycles from the Brothers motorcycle gang were heading east out of Anchorage on the main highway towards Fort Richardson. Several bikes were riding double and there was one three-wheeler in the rear, with two men aboard, and the one riding shotgun had a double barrel with the barrels sawn off very short.

The highway was only two lanes wide, with one lane eastbound and the other westbound, and bracketed by wide shoulders. There was a heavy stream of traffic bumper-to-bumper heading out of Anchorage averaging 40 miles per hour, while the traffic coming into Anchorage was not quite as heavy.

Almost immediately, I met the line of motorcycles with the three-wheeler in the back. I noticed that the passenger riding on the three-wheeler appeared to be carrying a shotgun. I turned on the red lights and the siren and brought my line of traffic to a halt trying to get turned around. The line of traffic out of anchorage slowed and I was able to complete the turn around and start after the motorcycles. I had several vehicles to get around, and I was on the radio giving my position. I was going to attempt to stop, the three-wheel bike with the shotgun. I called Anchorage dispatcher and reported I was now behind the group of motorcycles and they were all pulling over. My position was right behind the three-wheeler, and indeed the passenger did have a shotgun with two sawed off barrels. He was holding the shotgun up and he broke open the shotgun letting me see down the barrels from the rear of the shotgun as we were all coming to a stop. He was showing me at this time both barrels were empty.

All the motorcycles pulled over and the riders and their passengers dismounted. I pulled in behind them telling the dispatcher we are stopped three miles east of the Fort Rich gate. They were coming back so I dropped the microphone and went to meet the motorcycle gang. One of them was wearing dirty levis and a tee shirt with a small hole in the bottom front. He was agitated and wanted to know why I stopped them. I said that I wanted to check the shotgun they were carrying. He walked right up to me and gave me a shove. "You son of a bitch I just got out of jail and I am not going back." I told him he was under arrest for assault. Then the whole group spread out and started to surround me.

I was ready for this as that is exactly what they had done to me in Glennallen. As they started to move around me I backed up onto the highway pulling my revolver pointing it straight up in the air. I made the statement to the whole group I am afraid for my life as I backed out further onto the highway. The traffic had to swerve out and across the centerline to avoid hitting me. There was no way for any of them to get around me without getting hit by the bumper-to-bumper traffic still doing 40 miles per hour. It was interesting as the vehicles could see what was happening they missed me but stayed close as possible to keep them from getting around behind me. When one of the gang members on my left tried to get out around me and three vehicles in a row swerved at him after going around me, they were doing their part in keeping any of the Brothers from coming around behind me. I was also paying attention to the airplane circling, as it was Lt. O'brien. He would be putting the word out that I had drawn my weapon and was facing down the whole gang.

Lt. O'brien heard the dispatcher alert Troopers Gunkel and Patterson, so he headed that way. When I pulled over the motorcycle gang, Trooper Patterson was coming back to assist. Lt. O'brien arrived overhead as I was getting out of my patrol vehicle. At that same time, Lt. O'Brien heard his son stopping a vehicle on a regular traffic stop, a few miles on towards Eagle River. His son could have been the first one to arrive and help, but for some reason had not responded. So Lt. O'brien started looking for a place to land. There were tank trails down each side of the highway but they were like a roller coaster, an impossible place to land his airplane.

When Trooper Patterson heard that I was pulling the Brothers motorcycle gang over, he started that way, with red lights and siren, but could not make much headway because of the traffic. Then when he heard the report that, "Trooper Gunkel had drawn his weapon," he started running people off the road in an attempt to reach and assist me. But he was still 10 miles away.

The Brothers gang member to the left of the guy I had arrested, said, "Officer, what is the problem?" I told him I have arrested this man for assault and he is going to jail! He turned around and grabbed the belligerent gang member by the arm and the gang member on the other side of the bad guy did the same. And they said, "Now what?" I was amazed, but said, "Now put the handcuffs on him." So they turned him around with his hands out behind him. I gave them the handcuffs and they cuffed him. Then I had them put him in my patrol vehicle. I told them I also wanted to see the shotgun to check the barrel length, but after searching my vehicle I could not find any kind of a ruler. Anchorage dispatcher called again. I picked up the mike and Anchorage said they had Fort Rich on the phone and they are prepared to send help if I needed it. I reported I had a sawed off shotgun, and I needed some sort of a ruler to check the length of the barrels. The dispatcher came back on the phone that the Military Police were responding with the requested equipment.

The Military Police arrived with three vehicles containing four men per vehicle, bringing me a tape measure. We measured the barrels of the shotgun and found they were 17 1/16th inches long. The shotgun was legal, so I released it to the rest of the Brothers. They decided to put away the shotgun rather than parade it so everyone could see what they were packing. Then I transported my one prisoner back to jail.

Can you imagine what those people driving down that highway thought when they saw a lone State Trooper standing in the middle of their traffic lane with weapon drawn facing a motorcycle gang?

No matter what the odds, Christ has always taken care of me and provided me with what I needed to get the job done. Was I afraid? Let's just say I was very concerned. Do you know it takes less than three seconds to load that shotgun? It is amazing the doors that will open and close with a little faith.

Chapter 30

We rented a three-bedroom mobile home that was set up in a large mobile home park in Anchorage. We were not planning on staying there more than a year or so, it was in the fall of 1972 and we were glad to get a winterized place that would withstand those cold Anchorage winters and keep us warm and comfortable.

Our Cessna 180 was tied down at Merrill Field. The winter was just average, and the large city living was not really our preference, but we made the most of it. I did enjoy the big city law enforcement, though. The Anchorage State Trooper post was now a much larger detachment than it had been during my Anchorage Police days there, so it was pretty much a large city type shift work. I even got two full days off every week. That is the first time I enjoyed that luxury since the last time I was in Anchorage, right after getting out of the State Trooper academy four years before.

As the only trooper, in a bush post, my shift would start sometime in the morning and continue until I was done. By the end of the week I had run up 50 to 70 hours of work, so I would take a few hours off here and there, but never enough to get the two days I was supposed to get each week. Then when the State decided that we would get paid for overtime we were supposed to turn in all the overtime hours we had worked but had not been paid for. I had kept my trooper daily logs, but the overtime hours I had worked would have equaled or in some cases exceeded my regular hours, so I decided to just forget them. I considered myself on a salary and I gave the state a good month's work for a month's pay. I was amazed what some State Troopers turned in for overtime hours.

Shortly after the Christmas Holidays I put in for my annual leave to be from the first of June for two weeks. This was denied and I could not find out why. I was unhappy about this since that was the time period I needed to be off to go commercial fishing with Ann in Bristol Bay. Corporal Art English asked me to come in and talk to him when I had time.

The next day I went in and Art asked me to sit down. He was careful to ask if I had been thinking of leaving the State Troopers. And when I explained I would much prefer to raise my family in a smaller town, he then asked me if I would be interested in going to the small first class city of Seldovia, Alaska and serve as the Chief of Police. At that time to get police powers the community had to be a first class city.

I was very interested . . .

Chapter 31

Art began his proposal; "Let me give you the background on Seldovia. First, my father is the mayor of Seldovia. He is 71 years old and is very strong on law enforcement. They have not had good law enforcement there since Alaska was still a territory. At that time they had a federal marshal stationed there and everything was under control as he was strict on enforcing the laws of the United States of America. But someone caught him out the road towards the mill and beat him severely with a tire Iron. He did not die but was just a vegetable after that.

"They have had some very bad police chiefs since then. My dad finally ran for mayor so he could get a good Chief of Police, but he had a tremendous problem in accomplishing this as there are only 600 people in Seldovia and they cannot afford to pay very much. They finally got someone who would do something. He put a man in jail and the man kicked the door of the jail open and the chief told him not to come out or he would shoot him. The man started out and the chief shot him in the leg."

Art continued, "As you might expect, the city lost a big civil suit and are still paying on it. I have been looking for a long time for a man that had law enforcement training and experience and enough backbone to clean up the town.

"A year ago, the last Chief of Police started with good intentions, but I am sure you have heard the expression if you can't beat them then join them? He got a couple of girls, and started a gambling ring and rented out prostitutes. We had to run him out of town.

"They have a local bad guy that has intimidated most of the rest, by beating people up.

"One area we can help you with is housing in the old hospital. The new doctor uses the second floor for his office, and there is a nice apartment down stairs that has three bedrooms that provides free housing. There is room out back for a garden and you could have chickens if you want. I guess the main thing we can offer you is a great living style, if you can clean up the town.

"Commercial salmon fishing is the main occupation during the summer, and king crab fishing all winter long. These guys fishing crab are handling 700 lb. crab pots and are in good shape. They are used to no laws being enforced and it will be a chore to get things under control."

I told Art I would talk to my wife, but I was very interested. I was used to enforcing the laws where none have been enforced before and Art was aware of that. He told me I was one of the few people he would want to send there. His dad had tried to do it himself and people just laughed at him. At his age, Art was afraid he'd get hurt.

Seldovia sits on the southern tip of the Kenai Peninsula across Katchemak Bay from Homer. It is beyond the existing road system, with the village of Seldovia right on the waterfront and surrounding tiny Seldovia Bay. The water is crystal clear with a good part of the town sitting right on the water. The forest is beautiful and there is a modern boat harbor, well protected that has fresh water and electricity available for moorages. There is a 2,000' airstrip right at the edge of town, one lodge, a restaurant and bar, and a large modern grocery store; There are three other bars in the town of 600 people, with a lot of booze consumed. And of course there are drugs, and rumor had it that the bully was bringing in the drugs.

There is a road system around Seldovia and out to Jakalof bay where a lumber mill is located. There is a modern school for grades kindergarten through 12, with a swimming pool and a large gymnasium administered by the Kenai Peninsula Borough.

Seldovia is right out near the end of the Kenai Peninsula. On our next days off Ann and I flew to Homer, turned left and flew out across the end of famous Homer Spit, past the boat harbor and the big dock where the ferry ties up, and across Katchemak Bay to Kenai Peninsula, and up to Seldovia Bay. We circled over the town of Seldovia, seeing the waterway coming in from the bay and winding through town and into a large lagoon surrounding both ends of the 2,000' airstrip. There was a large parking area and the road went back into Seldovia about a half mile away.

We landed at the airport and walked into town. We had never seen such a beautiful little community. Walking into town we passed a boardwalk with houses built on pilings over the water on one side and into a hillside on the other. Past the boardwalk and down main street along the water front we went by the boat harbor, then a bar, then a fish processing plant, another bar and then a short roadway to the city offices, and out at the end the city dock where the State Ferry tied up to load and unload.

We went into the city offices and met Elaine Giles, the City Manager. Elaine was a very efficient woman. She called Jack English who came right down. Jack took us up to the hospital and showed us the apartment we would live in, the school, the layout of the town and then to the outside beach.

Jack pointed the road to Jakalof bay and took us by the church, which was mission operated. We stopped and Jack introduced us to the missionary pastor. Then we went down to the post office. Jack's wife, Susan, was the Postmaster, and in the same building Susan had a store that carried just about everything but groceries. Jack and Susan took us inside and answered all our questions. We went back to the city offices and Jack showed me the Chief of Police office. It was very small, but adequate.

"Well, are you ready to come down?" Ann, Elaine, and Jack were all looking at me. I knew that Ann was ready; you could not help but fall in love with this place. It was just what we wanted. I told them that the only thing that concerned me was making enough for a good living. If we came, I would be first of all the Chief of Police. That would take priority over everything I did. I would enforce the law, fairly and impartially. But I would be looking for other things to do. I explained that we fish commercially in Bristol Bay. We leave around the third week of June and return about the same time in July. Would that work as my vacation? Jack and Elaine both nodded their heads in the affirmative. Jack again asked eagerly, "When are you coming?"

"I have to give the State Troopers two weeks' notice, but then as soon as we can get moved. I should be ready to go to work in three or four weeks."

Another move but this time we were paying the moving expenses. As per usual the excitement of meeting new people helped overcome the sadness of leaving old friends. I was going to miss the State Troopers, but was grateful for the training and all the experiences gained while working around the state, and especially the friends gained.

We rented a moving truck with a 14' van and got everything loaded. We left in the middle of the night, as we had to arrive at the ferry terminal in Homer by 11:00 a.m. in order to get loaded for the trip across the bay to Seldovia. The boat ride only took a couple of hours, and we were there.

Elaine gave us the keys and we started unloading that afternoon and evening. It took another couple of days to get everything moved in and the rental truck on the ferry and back across to Homer and then to Anchorage, then get our airplane from Anchorage.

Chapter 32

Jack told me about a man named Sparky. He grew up in the community with no father. Since Sparky was a little boy he'd never had any discipline. No one ever said no to him. When someone tried, Sparky would throw a temper tantrum. At first those around him thought it was cute. But the older he got the uglier things became whenever he'd lose his temper and anyone that got in his way got trampled. He was the town bully.

When I became the Chief of Police in Seldovia, Sparky was in his mid-30's. I saw for myself the vicious results of his temper. There was a place in town where they showed some movies at a small restaurant called Mike's. Sparky was involved in running the place.

Our friends, Dale and Carolyn Greiner had flown down to Seldovia from their home in Eagle River to spend a couple of days with Ann and I in this new paradise we had discovered. We had just finished dinner and were sitting back and catching up with the three months or so that had gone by since the last time we had gotten together when I received a call that a big fight had occurred at Mike's place. Sparky had beaten up a man and a woman using a Tabasco bottle in his fist. Every time he would hit them the top of the bottle would leave a circular cut from the top edge of the bottle. The guy had around 40 cuts and the woman about 25 of these cuts, of which at least half of them required closing with a stitch or two. The doctor was out of town.

When I received the call, I asked Dale if he wanted to come along, He said no way are you going to leave me out of this. We interviewed the victims, but no one else that was present would say anything. I begged those two victims to press charges against Sparky. I had the

Tabasco bottle he used as a weapon, but they were so terrified of him that no one would testify in court.

Next, I questioned Sparky, but he listened to my advising him of his rights and he refused to answer any of my questions.

Dale had been quiet the whole time, but I could sense that he shared the same feelings I did. During the whole investigation, Dale was the strong quiet one. Everyone present was wondering who he was. Dale got a kick out of that, saying they think I am from the Secret Service. I never told anyone that he was just a good friend and hunting buddy.

As a registered nurse, Ann often helped with situations like this when no one else was available. I called her and she came down. She could not do the stitches, but closed the larger cuts with tape and butterfly bandages. The couple had cuts on their faces, sides of their heads, tops and backs of their heads. There were also a few cuts on their hands and bare arms where they had tried to protect themselves. And there was blood everywhere. Apparently the man was beat up first, and when no one else would stop Sparky, the woman tried to stop him. So he turned on her and gave her a savage beating also, striking her head, arms and hands. The man left after Ann got through bandaging his and her wounds. He had received almost twice as many cuts from that Tabasco bottle as she had.

The woman was terrified of Sparky. She was afraid that he would come to her house after she went home, and asked if she could stay at the doctor's office for the night. She would not sign a complaint against Sparky because she thought he might come after her and kill her. Ann ended staying with her upstairs in the doctor's clinic for the rest of the night.

I could not believe that others had stood by and not tried to stop it. And why didn't someone call me while it was going on? This beating had apparently taken twenty minutes or so.

I had run into a dead end with him this time. Maybe he will start behaving, and there will not be a next time. Yeah, and maybe the rivers will start running uphill!

I had to gain the respect and trust of the people of that town. They had seen Sparky fight and win lots of fights, winning with horrible behavior, which had terrified the people in Seldovia. This would not be the last time I met up with Sparky.

Chapter 33

At 12:10 a.m. the phone rang! It had started snowing lightly just before dark and now there was an accumulation of four inches. "There has been an accident on Main Street in front of the shopping center. A man on a snow machine ran under a semi-trailer and he looks to be hurt bad."

I responded and found that a person had come along Main Street on a snow machine where there was a semi-trailer parked against a loading ramp door, just off the side of the street. The snow machine angled to the left and ran right into the semi-trailer striking it just behind the front set of dual wheels. The bottom of the trailer had sheared off the snow machine windshield and the top part of the cowling over the engine. It appeared that the driver rolled off at the last second, and escaped under the trailer, not hitting anything solid. He was lucky.

To cause that kind of damage the snow machine had to be traveling 40 miles per hour or more. At the time the snow machine driver appeared to be intoxicated. I arrested him for operating a motor vehicle while under the influence.

I received another call on a frosty Sunday morning just after daylight. A woman about 30 was found lying along the shoulder of the road in a residential area. I hurried to the location and found she was not breathing. The woman who had found her and called lived right there. We carried her into her house. I sent her son to find the doctor. There was no indication of trauma, her flesh was cold, and I began CPR, trying to get her breathing. After clearing her mouth I breathed through her mouth, and pumped her lungs until the doctor arrived. He checked the victim and announced that she was gone, it had been too long since she had quit breathing.

Later in the day a check at her favorite bar showed she had been there until closing and had left by herself. The only thing that was fuzzy was when closing time had occurred. One other person had said that everyone including the victim had left the bar at 15 minutes after midnight.

Everyone present at the bar reinforced the fact that she had left alone and was very intoxicated. Doctor Larry Reynolds had responded to where I had found her. It appeared that she had gotten tired and laid down and went to sleep, dying of what appeared to be exposure to the cold and intoxication. The autopsy showed nothing contrary to what I had found.

I went to the mayor to discuss what I had learned about the town. "Jack, I have been here a little over two months and I just wanted to check in with you to let you know what is going on. The biggest problem is booze and some drugs. Things usually do not get out of hand until late, after the legal closing hour of the bars at 11:00 p.m. That is one of the problems; the bars are not closing if there are customers around regardless of the hour. They just close their door, and lock it only letting their customers out when they are ready to leave. They keep right on serving drinks behind the locked doors."

The bar in the building where the shopping center is located was turning into another problem. I stopped by the secondhand store, which is located on the south end of the shopping center right next to the bar. I found the small repair and secondhand shop where the proprietor also lives in his store was being harassed by the bar owner and some of his customers. There was a door from the bar into the secondhand store that was locked with a double door. They both have front entrances on to the main street as well.

Late in the evening as the alcohol takes effect, the bartender and some of his customers open the bar's side of the double door and bang on the second-hand door yelling threats to the old man like 'open this door or we are going to kick it in, and kick your ass.' He was afraid that they were going to force their way into his residence and he was going to get beat up. I told him that if they forced their way into his residence he could take whatever action was necessary to protect himself, but first call me. "The next time they start banging on your door and making threats, just call me. I will take care of the problem."

I went to the bar owner and warned that forcing the door open and breaking into the store and residence when it was closed was a felony crime, and I would lock up everyone involved. The bar owner said that it was just some of his customers fooling around. They would leave the old man alone.

"So Jack, as you can see most of our problems are going on late in the evening after the bars are supposed to be closed.

"Then, there is Sparky and his followers. He is a tinderbox waiting to explode. He could go off any time. If we had gotten someone to testify after he attacked that couple with a bottle, a conviction would have been easy. But the whole town is terrified of him.

"I am going to increase my bar checks and late night patrol. As the after-hours crowd gets accustomed to me enforcing the law, they will start obeying those laws that they do not like."

Jack responded, "Gary, you are doing a good job, I am behind you a hundred percent."

Chapter 34

Our family had no problems blending in with the community. Karen, our oldest was in junior high school, and Beth was just one year behind Karen. Mark would not start kindergarten for two more years. We fit right into the local church.

Our kids were always involved in the school's different sports programs, swimming, and basketball. Our whole family attended these events, and we traveled to many of the away games, and swimming meets. Every away game required a ferry trip of an hour to an hour and a half, or an airplane trip to get there and the same on the way home. We all had a great time, and this helped to keep our family close.

It was requested that I do some basketball refereeing. After agreeing, I found out how bad a referee I was. After awhile I decided no more, then the weather turned bad and a visiting high school team was able to get to town but the qualified referees were not able to get here, so I said OK and was calling the boy's varsity game. This was a fast moving team and the game was close.

About half way through the third quarter with our local team two points behind, the out of town team, Ninilchik was pressing and things were moving very fast. Right in front of me, a Ninilchik defender was trying to steal the ball and he was not quite fast enough. So he doubled his fist and hit the ball handler in the face, causing him to lose control of the ball and the opposing offender grabbed the ball and headed down the court for a layup.

Immediately after observing the blow to the face, I blew the whistle calling a flagrant personal foul and ejected him from the game. The young man I ejected was in the clear by the time I was able to blow the whistle. The visiting coach went ballistic and the whole gymnasium, erupted in wild yelling, which was all directed at me. I went over to tell the other official what had happened and the visiting coach was all over me. I told him what I had observed and I tried to walk away. He obviously did not see what I had seen, and was right in front of me. I tried to get away from him, but he would not let me go. He was forcing me to eject him from the game. I finally did, which included ejecting him from the gymnasium, as required by the rules.

Not only did he not see it, apparently no one else in the gym had seen the blow to the face. This was a very uncomfortable situation, but we were able to get everything under control and resume the game. Seldovia was eventually the winner.

I had forgotten about the video camera that one of the Seldovia senior boys was recording the whole game with. But the boy's coach did not forget it. As soon as the game was over the coaches and the principal sat down and reviewed the game and found the foul I had called. It was very clear, where after missing a chance to steal the ball, the visiting boy apparently frustrated at being beaten by the Seldovia boy doubled his fist and threw a punch right into the boy's face. The injured player then dropped the ball, allowing the visiting boy the chance to pick up the ball and break for the opposite basket.

I was feeling the weight of public opinion after the game, so as I was leaving the school I was surprised and relieved when the Seldovia coach, Rex Edwards came up to me and explained that he and the principal, Tom Overman, and the Ninilchik, basketball coach had all viewed the tape of the basketball game.

Rex said the tape clearly showed that I had been 100% correct in calling the flagrant foul, and administering the rules. The Ninilchik coach had to catch a plane right after they had viewed the tape, and he requested that I please accept his apology. Then Rex went on to explain the coach really was upset with his actions as he had been dealing with attitude on his team, and now he had to go to his team and explain his own behavior.

He also said he would deal with his player who had committed the foul. The coach had asked his player if he had thrown a punch to the face of the Seldovia player, and he denied it. Now, after seeing the truth, he was going to take care of the young man. Rex then restated, "The visiting coach was really sorry for his behavior."

My background in basketball started when I participated in adult basketball leagues after graduating from high school. First in the mountains around Truckee, California where we had our own adult league, but we ended up traveling to many desert communities scattered around Reno, and Carson City Nevada. Then I continued to play when I was in the Alaska State Troopers, stationed in Glennallen, Bristol Bay and in Seldovia. The quality of our basketball was not always that high, and the enthusiasm made for some very rough games, with lots of bruises and abrasions. I was accepted, and earned respect because I played hard and accepted their fouls by just playing harder.

Seldovia was no different. It was a small town with four basketball teams. Three of the largest bars in town sponsored teams, and the church members made up the fourth team. Our league was over in February and we invited a couple teams from the much larger towns of Soldotna, and Kenai to come to our tournament in March. The excitement over this tournament rivaled the March madness of the huge NCAA tournament . . . at least in our town. Ann and I embraced this as another family event, along with the other families in our church.

We lured these teams to town with the enormous king crab feed after the tournament. Some of the guys did bring along families, and the crab fishermen in town furnished the crab. We never did beat those two teams, as they were a group of all-stars from a much bigger community, but we did have a lot of fun trying. Basketball went a long ways towards unifying the community, when it came to law enforcement. The people saw that I was human, as they witnessed my mistakes and triumphs.

The other side of the community also got their shots at me and felt the physical response. This helped winning their respect as well, which I needed in order to gain their trust. It is impossible to win in enforcing the law, unless the citizens in the community want law and order

Chapter 35

Our two daughters, Karen and Beth were on the girls high school basketball team. When there was a two week road trip that ended in Glennallen for two nights of basketball. Ann and I decided we would like to go, as I had spent two years as a State Trooper in Glennallen and we had lots of friends in the area. I went to see City Business Manager Elaine Giles and Mayor English. They put their stamp of approval on our going for five days.

We were having a great time, when I received a call from Jack English that there had been a problem at the bar in the shopping center and the secondhand shop next door. Late in the evening a man in the bar had kicked in the locked door between the bar and the secondhand store where the owner also lived. The intruder, a local deck hand working on a crab boat had confronted the old man in his store and residence, telling him. "Old man, I am going to kick your ass." The storeowner had a pistol and told the intruder to get out. The intruder started after the storeowner, who shot the intruder in the chest knocking him to the floor. Then the old man told the intruder to get up and get out, or he would shoot him again. He got to his feet and was able to get out to the sidewalk in front of the store, where he fell down again. They called the doctor who hurried down and called for a medical evacuation. The man did not survive the wound.

I told Jack I would get back there as quickly as possible. Jack said, "No reason to hurry, the state is taking care of the problem and there will be no arrest. It was self-defense." I told him we would be leaving for home early the next morning.

The ride home was long. It is a little over 400 miles from Glennallen, and no freeways. We had to pick up a few things in Anchorage and then rush to catch the ferry the next morning in Homer. The long ride home gave me time to think more on what was going on in Seldovia. Those guys in the bar apparently must have figured with me out of town it was time to run that old man off. Well that backfired on them. Now there is one fewer of them than before.

Back in town I went to see Jack right away. He said that shooting that intruder was really hard on old George. He was having a hard time handling it, so he ended up leaving town. I felt badly that I was away when he may have called, but I never had the opportunity to talk with him again.

A month went by without any problems and I thought the shooting might help solve the staying open late problem, but now that George was gone that problem got worse. On a Tuesday evening I noticed that the lights were on in the bar when I drove by on the way to another call. By the time I was through handling a family disturbance, it was near 1:00 a.m. in the morning when I went back by the bar. The lights were still on.

Along the front of the bar were big glass windows that went from three feet above the floor, to a few inches from the ceiling. They had painted the bottom of the windows up to about eight feet, so you could not see in.

I pulled into one of the parking spaces in front of the bar and tried the door. It was locked. I walked back to my patrol vehicle and stepped up on my bumper and could not quite see into the bar, so I stepped on the front fender, and with my height of 6'4" I had a clear view of the bar along the south wall of the room. There were a half a dozen guys sitting at the bar. And all had drinks in front of them. I got down and went to the front door and knocked loudly. The bartender asked who it was, I answered, "Gary Gunkel, Chief of Police, open the door!" The bartender replied, "We are closed, go away."

I walked back to my vehicle and stepped up on the front fender again and watched the bartender serve a can of beer to one of the people at the bar. I went back and knocked again and the bartender answered,

"What do you want now?" "Open the door." The bartender replied, "No, we are closed." So I stepped back, raised my left foot, and slammed it into the door right beside the door knob. This split the door frame and door where the latch and dead bolt was installed and knocked the door open as splinters and little pieces of wood flew!

I walked over to the bar and collected the last can of beer I had watched being served and other drinks sitting on the bar for evidence. I then advised the bartender that he would be charged with serving beverages containing alcohol after hours. The bartender and his customers were all very surprised, at my entrance into the bar. The customers left the bar while I collected all the information I needed to put together the complaint and accompanying report.

After advising the bartender of his rights I asked him the hours he was able to operate. He told me he knew that he was supposed to close at 11:00 p.m., but what authority did I have to kick open his door?

"I was driving by your place and saw your lights on, so I pulled into the space just outside that window, and stepped on my car to see in. You served a can of beer, which gave me probable cause to believe a state statute was being violated. When you refused twice to open your door when requested, I opened it myself."

My actions really got the attention of the bar owners in town. Because of all the problems arising from those in bars consuming too much alcohol well after the state 11:00 p.m. closing time, there had been auto accidents caused by drunk drivers, an intoxicated woman had frozen to death walking home, a snow mobile hitting a parked semi-trailer, a drunk breaking into a residence resulting in a shooting death and fights breaking out late in the evening. I had been patrolling and doing bar checks in the evenings and that is when I found that it was common practice for bars to stay open as long as any customers were around. I had started reminding the bars of the State mandated closing hour. The bars did not like the prospect of shorter operating hours, so they had been using different ways to stay open late. The bar owners decided to take it to the City

Council, two of the city council members were bar owners. Now enters the world of politics.

The Mayor requested me to attend the next City Council meeting. I was there with a smile. Mayor English asked me to address the closing hours issue, so I took center stage and read the state statute, addressing the hours that any business that had a license to serve beverages containing alcohol could serve them between the hours of 9:00 a.m. until 11:00 p.m. each day.

One of the crab fishermen attending the meeting stated that he did not get in from fishing until late in the evening, so after eating dinner he was not free until late and the bars were closing when he arrived. Isn't there something we could do about that?

"I do not make the laws, but I do have to enforce them. If there are bad laws out there I will work with you to change them, but until it changes I took an oath to enforce them. We have been having problems in Seldovia with intoxicated people endangering themselves and others, so I am doing my best to solve some of these problems, and right now enforcing the hours alcohol is not served looks like the best solution."

Jack warned me later that the problem was not going away, that the bar owners were not happy with me kicking open that door, and shortening their hours. I responded, "That is exactly the problem. This is a small town, with a lot of bars. There is a limit to the number of customers available, so their solution is to keep the bars open longer so each customer can drink more."

Then Jack said "And that is the problem!"

Chapter 36

A week later it had started snowing in the early afternoon with just a few flakes drifting down. Then as it was getting dark, it started snowing harder, until by 10:00 p.m. there was 10 inches on the ground. I left home to patrol around town, but there was little going on.

I went out to the airport to check the airplanes and then back to town and down to the boat harbor. I walked through checking the boats and all appeared well. As I came up the floats and over to my vehicle I could hear what sounded like a snow machine, down at the other end of town and beyond the city dock, offices and the fish and crab processing plant. I started that way and met the snow machine right at the big shopping center. There were two guys on it and when they saw me they accelerated and took off at a high rate of speed.

I turned around and started after them. They went past the road out to Jakalof Bay, but turned left at the next block away from the boat harbor and then back again towards me only a block to my left, I followed and got behind them and followed about a block behind. They then made another right hand turn onto the Jakalof Bay road and went out past the old dump site. They were doing 45 miles per hour and were driving all over the road.

As they were approaching the road to the outside beach, I was 50 yards back. The road swung slowly to the right and as the driver was leaning into the turn, the passenger was leaning the wrong way, away from the turn. With all the fresh snow there was a rooster tail of snow coming from the belt of the snow machine. The passenger lost his balance throwing his weight back to the left, grabbing the driver and throwing him off balance. The snow machine began to fishtail to the left sharply, sliding broadside with a wall of snow going into the air, then hitting a bump throwing both the driver and the passenger off the snow machine onto the roadway. The snow machine lost its speed in the deep, soft snow, righted itself and came to a stop. The driver and passenger both rolled a little beyond it in the deep snow.

I brought my patrol vehicle to a stop, and got out with my big three-cell flashlight. I had on a down coat and a pair of Levis with light boots. Both guys appeared to be all right. They landed in the deep snow and did not hit anything hard. Both were about my height but 50 to 75 lbs. heavier than I was. I had seen them around town, but had not met them. They were deckhands for one of the crab boats and were in good shape. They handle big seven foot crab pots weighing 700 to 800 lbs. each, and appeared to be 25 to 30 years old. I asked if they were all right, and they said they were fine.

I asked the driver if I could see his operators license and he got it out. By now I could tell his voice was slurred. They were snow from one end to the other. He handed me his driver's license, and it was valid. I could smell beer and asked how many beers he had, and he answered five or six. His balance was unsteady. I told him he was under arrest for drunk driving, and reached over and took his left arm just above his elbow to guide him towards, the patrol car. He took a swing at my head with his right fist, which I blocked with my left arm. I still had the flashlight in my gloved hand and his hand struck my left wrist causing the flashlight to sail off into the snow.

I grabbed him around his head and spun him around over my right hip to put on the sleeper hold. It held for a few seconds, but all the soft snow was like grease, and he slipped right out of it. I tried again with the same results. I switched hips and put him on the ground using my left hip, but slipped in the snow going down right beside him. He jumped on top of me and I rolled grabbing his left leg and he went over on his chest with me on top. It was a wrestling match, and he started hollering for his friend to help him. When I was able to get his hands behind his back, and was reaching for the handcuffs, his friend came up behind me and grabbed me around the neck and started dragging me backwards off of his friend. As we got to the edge of the road the driver started yelling "Get his gun, get his gun!" The driver had gotten to his feet and was heading towards us and I was still being dragged backwards. I had to make a decision quickly whether to pull my weapon, or get rid of it. I did not want this to turn into a shooting match, but if they got it, that could be the end of me. I decided to get rid of my weapon, so I got it out of my holster and reached over and left it under the snow at the bottom of a clump of grass.

The driver came up and hit me in the face a couple of times, then they both got up, and when they saw the holster was empty, they started for their snow machine. I looked for my flashlight and found it. Both bad guys left, and were on their way back to town on their snow machine. I went over to the clump of grass and pulled out my .357 Smith & Wesson revolver, got all the snow off, unloaded it, cleaned it up and reloaded it.

I had to get those guys and put them both, in jail. I needed help and the principal of the school, Tom Overman had said he would help if I needed it. I went to find him. He will keep the other guy off my back, until I get him cuffed. I found Tom at home, and after seeing my black eye and blood from my split eyebrow splattered over my face and jacket, Tom suggested we also get Rex, the boy's basketball coach. We went by and picked up Rex. I had no idea where these guys lived but Tom thought he knew. We went by where Tom thought they lived and there was their snow machine with fresh tracks in the snow where they had just parked beside their house.

We went to their front door, and knocked. The passenger, who had dragged me off the driver, opened the door. When he saw me he tried to close the door, but I shoved it open and pushed him up against the wall telling him he was under arrest for assaulting a police officer. Then I saw the guy I had arrested earlier for drunk driving across the room, so I left this guy and intercepted the driver who was on his way out the back door, taking him down. I looked over my shoulder and saw Tom take the guy that had answered the door, to the floor as he tried to come after me.

It went fast, and the only lumps and bumps were my black eye and split eyebrow from the original encounter. Now all we had to do was transport them to jail. As I took Tom and Rex home, I thanked them. If I had not been able to arrested the men that evening, word would have gotten out and it would have been a long time if ever that I could get things under control in Seldovia. Instead, word would travel fast that the citizens of this community will not stand for a lawless atmosphere. When their police department is outnumbered, the community comes to their aid and there is no hiding. I no longer felt like the Lone Ranger.

The next morning was busy getting ready for the arraignment before the Justice of the Peace. Both Kevin Baker and Roger Johnson entered pleas of not guilty. Also entering a not guilty plea was the bar owner whose door I had kicked in and charged for serving alcoholic beverages after hours.

A couple of days later, Jack called me and we got together for a meeting. Jack said the Assistant Attorney General, Jerry Masterson, working out of Kenai, had contacted him. The attorney representing Kevin Baker and Roger Johnson had contacted him and said that David Burnett, the bar owner had also asked that he represent him on the other case of serving alcohol after hours. The intent of those accused was to win the criminal case, then to sue me and the City of Seldovia.

Jerry Masterson, the Assistant Attorney General suggested that a good strategy would be to plea bargain, and accept a plea of guilty, then reduce the sentences to little or nothing, in exchange for an agreement of no law suit. "What do you think of that?" (I thought, here we go again, politics, big time). The bar crowd is out to turn around these cases and they were pulling a power play. By forcing a plea bargain, and getting out with no penalty, that sets up a big civil case against the city and me. The backlash for that would mean terminating me.

"Jack, these two cases will decide who wins in Seldovia, those that want the old lawless ways, or law and order."

"Gary, I realize that, but I do not think we have a choice. We do not have enough votes on the City Council to override them. I am going to have to bring it before a council meeting to get direction."

The City Council meeting went the way Jack had described. We lost by one vote, so Jack had to advise the prosecutor, Jerry Masterson, to go ahead with a plea bargain. The following week I had to fly to the town of Kenai for the formal arraignment and the plea bargain. In the pre-court hearing, Jerry was telling me that his main office in Kenai handled all the criminal cases for the Soldotna PD, Kenai PD, Ninilchik PD, Homer PD, and our town, Seldovia PD, as well as the State Troopers cases all over the Kenai Borough. He had to use plea bargains in order to get through the huge caseloads he had to handle. This was his way of apologizing for not going to court on these cases. I was instructed to not say anything unless I was asked a question by the judge.

Chapter 37

The judge came in and called the court to order and asked the clerk for the first case. We were first on his calendar, and the defendants were at the other table with their attorney. The Assistant Attorney General made a motion for a plea bargain. The judge asked if the defendants were present, and their attorney said they were. Then he asked if the police officer was present, and he said I was. The judge then asked if the police officer would come forward and be sworn in. So I stepped forward and the bailiff had me raise my right hand, "Will you tell the truth, the whole truth, and nothing but the truth, so help you God?" I answered, yes.

The judge started by asking me how long I had been in law enforcement? "Two years as a police officer for the city of Anchorage, five years as an Alaska State Trooper, and a year as the Chief of Police for the City of Seldovia."

"What training have you had?"

I responded, "I went through the police academy for the city of Anchorage, and graduated, also I have been through the State Trooper Academy in Sitka, Alaska, and graduated. I have been through several in-service training courses, including Rape Sensitivity and Riot Control."

"Have you ever been sued?"

"No sir."

"Concerning the charges of serving drinks after hours, tell me what happened."

I looked at Jerry Masterson and hesitated. Jerry said go ahead. So I went ahead. "We have been having problems with the bars in town staying open two and three hours after the state mandated closing time of 11:00 p.m. This has caused some serious problems, in one case a woman stayed way beyond closing and was so intoxicated when she left the bar for her house only three blocks away, she fell and froze to death on the way home." I became encouraged as the judge was letting me fill in some background, and not just the case before him. "Another case some of the customers in one of the bars got intoxicated an hour and a half after the state closing time and broke into a secondhand store through a connecting door of the next door business. When confronted by the owner, of the secondhand store, the intruder stated he was going to beat up the owner, which resulted in a shooting fatality.

"When I put pressure on the bars to close, they would lock their doors and refuse to open the door for me, but freely let their customers come and go keeping their doors locked."

"How did you solve the problem?" This judge really wanted to know what happened. So I went into more detail and put a little more emotion into my testimony.

"The bar located in the shopping center had windows on the street front with a sidewalk along the front of the building, with parking spaces along the street front. I was out late on a family disturbance call when I noticed the lights on in the bar way after the state closing time. After taking care of the family disturbance I went back to the bar. This bar had windows along the front of the store that were painted solid up to the height of eight feet. I tried the door, but it would not open, so I knocked. Someone inside asked who is it and I answered, Gary Gunkel, the Chief of Police. The same person inside answered 'Go away, we are closed.'"

The judge continued to ask me the details of the case trying to determine if I had probable cause to use force to enter the bar. "I went back to my patrol vehicle and stepped up on the bumper but could not quite see into the bar, so I stepped up on the front fender and I could see the full length of the bar along the south wall. There were at least six people sitting at the bar with drinks in front of them. I went back to the door and knocked again and the same person asked who was there, I again answered and was told to go away. I went back to my vehicle."

Then the judge asked, "Was your vehicle parked in an area open to public parking?"

I answered, "Yes sir, it was." Then I continued. "I again stepped up on my fender of my vehicle and could see the same people sitting at the bar, and watched the bartender serve a can of beer. So I went to the door and said open the door, but again I was told to go away, so I kicked open the door, went in, and collected the evidence."

The judge looked at the Assistant Attorney General and asked if there was another case he wanted to plea bargain, and he said, "Yes Your Honor, the Kevin Baker and the Roger Johnson case. They were the driver and the passenger of the snow machine the Chief of Police arrested."

The judge asked me to explain what happened. He was playing prosecutor, then defense attorney, and was checking to see if I had a solid case or if there would be any problems getting evidence I needed into the case. This was very unusual for a judge to ask all the details of a case in a plea bargain. I thought it had been all cut and dried, and politics had taken over and that I was slated to end up on the outside of this one. In all my years in law enforcement I had never seen anything like this happen. I answered the judge by giving him step-by-step, and blow-by-blow of the entire case of events for the evening.

At the part where the suspects headed back to town the judge again, asked, "Then what did you do?"

"I found my flashlight where it had disappeared in the snow, retrieved my pistol, and removed the snow from it, and started back to town to get help."

"Who did you get to help you?"

"I got the principal of the school, Tom Overman, and Tom, after seeing my face thought it might be a good idea to get the boys basketball coach, Rex Edwards." The Judge seemed impressed with the quality of the help I had secured.

The judge asked if I had collected any evidence, and I replied I had photos taken of my bloody face and clothes, and black eye. I also had the can of beer, and other drinks I had seen the bartender serve in the other case.

The judge asked if there was any additional information from the prosecutor or the defense attorney. When they both said no, the judge said there would be no plea bargain as all three of these men are going to court. That is the only time that I had ever seen a plea bargain denied. The trial was to be tried in Homer.

I am not a politician, and needless to say my confidence in the legal system had taken a nosedive with the maneuvering taking place. But that judge restored my confidence in the criminal justice system. I had not realized the influence that judges had over attorneys that practiced in the same area the judge was seated in. All of a sudden the prosecutor from the Attorney General's office, Jerry Masterson became very interested in the three cases in Seldovia, Alaska.

Jerry entered charges for two assault-and-battery, two resisting-arrest, one driving while under influence, and two escape charges. The serving alcohol after hours case received six charges of serving drinks containing alcohol after legal hours. Jerry did an outstanding job in presenting the cases, bringing attention to the fact that the principal, and the boy's coach came forward to help the police chief when problems arose in affecting the arrest.

The jury was out for two and a half hours, then returned guilty decisions on all thirteen charges. I was blown away by the results. I had done everything I could do and those against law enforcement had done some politicking and power plays and had reversed the tables on me. *Then Christ took over and we went to court and won convictions on all cases filed! Christ tells us to not be lukewarm in what we do, but do it as if we were doing it for Christ.*

I had done everything I could and felt it was not good enough. I was on the brink of being sued, then fired for enforcing the law, but with Christ in control we can accomplish anything. By getting to court to try these cases, the guilty verdicts wiped out all the accusations against me and gave me hope for the future in Seldovia.

My next objective was to get through to the kids in town and give them more incentive to obey the law, and to understand what going to court was all about. I met with the principal and presented the idea to get the high school and junior high kids together for a pretend, crime, arrest and trial. We would use kids to act out the rolls of criminals, policemen, victims, judge, attorneys, jury and the court bailiff.

St. Augustine volcano erupting from beach

197

St. Augustine Volcano not erupting

Tom thought it was a great idea, so we put together a committee to make it happen. The teachers put together the main characters to fill the rolls needed, and I put together the crime we enacted, and the arrest was accomplished by affidavit for warrant, search warrant, and arrest warrant.

We did this over two days. The first day we did the crime, and the arrest and an arraignment. Then the following day we chose attorneys, selected a jury, had a trial and sentenced the convicted prisoner.

Wow, what a job to harness all that energy and get the message through. We ended with a runaway jury. Those sitting on the jury felt sorry for Joey, so they ended up finding him not guilty and wanting to know if they could find Mr. Hilts, the 6th grade teacher who was playing Prosecutor, guilty instead. My oldest daughter, Karen was on the jury, and she turned out to be the leader causing the rebellion. Everyone had a great time, but I am not sure how much was learned by the exercise.

As it was there was no one to sentence. Karen took care of that part of the program. It was a good thing they could not get Mr. Hilts, as I am sure he would have gotten at least 10 years in jail.

Chapter 38

It was a beautiful morning in April and Max Embree, who was now our church pastor and I were in my new plane (well, new after the Cessna 180), a Piper PA-12 just taking off from Seldovia. We had borrowed the high school video camera and were on our way to Saint Augustine Island to video the volcano on the little island that had erupted the week before. I also had my 35mm camera.

We took off to the east, and as we gained altitude we made a slow circle around to the west, gaining slowly but steadily as we came around following the shoreline back over Seldovia sitting protected in the timber scattered along the shoreline in Seldovia Bay, a beautiful sight. Then we continued along the shoreline for about six miles, then as the tip of the peninsula curved around to the left we were going out over open water as we started off across the head of Cook Inlet. It was 70 miles to Mount Augustine, which was an island about 12 miles off the Alaska Peninsula. We were flying at 6,000 feet with a 10 mile an hour wind out of the southeast.

We could see Mt. Augustine across the water, but the weather seemed a little murky over on the Alaska Peninsula side. As we got closer we could see that something was going on over there. There seemed to be a cloud right over the island, then about half way there the cloud took shape and we could see that the volcano was actually erupting with a dark ugly ash boiling out of the top of the volcano, and tailing off to the northwest.

The closer we got, the higher the dark, boiling cloud rose into the sky. We could not see how high the cloud was but later heard that a passing, jet airliner measured the cloud at 45,000 feet. The island is about a mile across with the volcano rising approximately 1,500 feet right out of the middle of the Island.

Staying on the upwind side of the island we flew to within 100 yards of the eruption coming right out of the top of the volcano. We could see rocks as big as 18" in diameter, and on down to small golf ball size coming out with tremendous energy. All the rocks and small boulders looked like they were being shot out of a giant cannon, and then would disappear into the rolling cloud mass overhead.

We flew around so we could see the downwind side of the volcano, and observed what appeared to be lava going into Cook Inlet, with lots of steam. The southeast side of the island had a nice sandy beach so we landed and got out. It was impossible to take your eyes off the volcano. I took my camera and shot several photos. Max shot some footage of video, then asked if he could use my 35 MM camera, and went over and using the airplane in the foreground and the erupting volcano in the background, he shot the most popular photo of the trip.

My vocabulary is inadequate to describe what I saw that day, and the feeling that has remained ever since witnessing the all mighty power displayed by our Creator. I know that God is in control, and with that demonstration I knew without doubt he manages this world and everything in it. And as in the past when I find myself in the presence of God I grow very quiet with awe. When I am able to get myself out of the way and let God take over and work through me, incredible things do happen. Max was also very quiet for awhile.

The video camera was one of the first put on the market. And shortly after they came out they were replaced with a different size that was never compatible with the tape size I had. I finally threw them out. I did submit several of our photos to National Geographic and they published three of them along with a short story. Max took two of those with the airplane in the foreground and the erupting volcano in the background so our flight was recorded.

We later found out that a heat flash accompanied the original eruption, scorching fir trees on the main land 12 miles away. That would have caused some major problems with my airplane, like igniting the fabric. I also later found that it was a foolish thing to do, flying so close to the erupting mountain, but God was in control and He apparently has other plans for Max and me in this life.

As Chief of Police, I had pretty well gotten the rebel rousers under control in town, but now had to concentrate on the younger generation in high school and below. My plans were to give them the opportunity to choose an attractive higher way, rather than following the trail of booze and drugs that was so prevalent in the region.

Pastor Max thought it would be a good idea to start a series of meetings for the younger boys in the church, with me leading it. While I had taught some Sunday school classes, this was different. So Max included himself in the plans. First of all, the meetings were held at a vacant building owned by the city of Seldovia, timed to start right after school, one day a week. This age group included my young son Mark, as well as pastor Max's sons James and Dan. We called it a club. We were not having it at the church, because space was a bit of a problem, and we wanted outreach to get other kids in the community involved.

We would have a short devotional and a snack time. Then the sky and our imagination was the limit for the projects that followed. Some of the more popular projects were building and flying of paper airplanes. We would build them for speed and accurate flight, airplanes that turned to the right, airplanes that turned to the left, and airplanes that would go the farthest in one flight.

Other airplanes were set up to always climb. When you flew one of those airplanes they would take off and go up until they stalled out then fall until they had speed to climb again. It was fun building them, because you never knew what they were going to do next.

Boats were also popular. We designed and built many sailboats. This always took a couple of meeting days, keeping the design and construction simple, then another day painting the boats. The less detail, the better they sailed. We had boats with one, two, or three masts. Right across the street from where we met was the boat harbor. On the last day of the boat project we would go over to the boat harbor to test the boats, and have boat races.

The wooden and rubber inner tube guns were also a giant success. We made and shot rubber bands cut out of inner tubes, usually making the barrel long enough to loop two rubbers together. Most of the guns used clothes pin release mounted on top. To get more range we drilled a hole through the pinching part of the close pin and put in a nail that was cut off just beyond the upper lip of the clothespin. That metal pin allowed more tension so the rubber would go farther.

The last day of the project we would have a big shoot out with every hit sitting down one of the participants. I always thought of it as the shootout at OK Corral. There was lots of enthusiasm with the boys and the adults. We wanted to show that you could have fun, and at the same time recognize the love and power of Jesus Christ.

Not long after we arrived in Seldovia the people decided the church should become independent. The missionary in town worked for the mission, and the property belonged to the mission. There was a three-bedroom apartment built onto the one meeting room that could seat approximately thirty people. We contacted the mission at Glennallen and asked for help to set up an independent church. They came down on a weekend and we completed all the paperwork for the state of Alaska, our statement of what we believed in, and elected a church board setting up the way we operate. It amazed those that came to help that we were able to put it all together over one weekend.

We had been operating for a year or so and the building had become way too small. So, we started a building program. We connected onto the side of the existing structure using the old meeting room as the foyer and entrance of the church. The new construction was two stories, 40' by 60'. We did not hire anyone, we built the building ourselves. Pastor Max was the key person in the building program.

I had just bought an old D8 Caterpillar dozer with a cable blade. We needed to grade an area that was mostly rock. We had moved quite a bit of dirt and rock when the right final drive went out. I knew pretty much nothing about working on bulldozers, but Max was well educated in what makes them go, and during the rehabilitation of that D8 we not only got it going, but I learned all about them as well. Pastor Max also turned out to be a very good operator.

Max had found a small portable sawmill just out of town and received permission to use it. He located some seasoned cottonwood logs, and cut them into siding and planned them into finished siding for the interior of the main meeting room of the church.

A large church from the Seattle area sent up half a dozen kids from their youth group to help us on our construction project. Two of the young girls from Seattle stayed with us. With our two high school daughters and the two girls from Seattle our house became a very lively place. There are always lots of kids around. Pastor Max was able to harness this young enthusiasm and again progress on the church went forward. School started and the kids went back to Seattle and our kids went back to school. We had the building closed in, but finishing the interior went slowly. We wired the place, plumbed it and started on the sheetrock. It seemed we were working forever and little was getting done.

Then Pastor Max got another Idea. I was working with our local youth group. We'd meet at the church on Wednesday evenings at 7:00 p.m. and work until 10:00. We had six to eight people, which I broke into three different crews. We were hanging sheetrock and getting started with the taping and finishing.

At first I was frustrated, and had the feeling that I was accomplishing nothing. I would go from one crew to the next putting out fires. It seemed that nothing was getting done. I felt I could have gotten much more done by myself. Then, after three weeks, things really started moving ahead. The kids started seeing the results of their work and took pride in their accomplishments. This got the attention of the adults seeing the progress the kids were making, so they started showing up. Now we were up to six or so crews and progress was really moving forward. Pastor Max began installing the cottonwood siding, then the carpet. We were getting close to the holidays when things came together. The church was really a work of love.

Everyone in the community felt the pride of accomplishment in the beautiful building that was built and finished as a complete community project. Pastor Max used the Church as a testimony as to what Christ and the community could do working together.

The shop teacher at school was a big help in the building program, as he had opened up the shop for Pastor Max to store the freshly cut cottonwood siding to dry for several months, then Max used school equipment to finish the cottonwood siding.

The shop teacher rarely attended church, but was involved with community projects, and was very impressed with the youth group's part in the building program. Most of the kids were in his shop classes in school. The shop teacher, and Principal Overman were greatly impressed with the new skills of the youth in the community, and they persuaded the school district to back the Seldovia shop program to buy a lot and build a home to be auctioned off in our community.

This project was to be accomplished in one school year. The kids were excited about the project, and took a lively interest in taking the new school shop class. The boys and especially the girls were enthusiastic, so they all pitched in to help with the building program, which moved along very well and kept the kids busy with an occasional overtime day or two.

During that period of time I was amazed at the lack of enforcement problems in the community. It was incredible to see everyone in the area come together, first, in building the church that had gathered momentum as it went, and then the school picking up the ball and running with the building of the three bedroom home in one school year.

Then I was even more delighted when the school district decided to carry the program a second year. The impact on law enforcement was incredible. By giving the kids something to do, their attitudes changed. I did not have to look far to see the difference as my two teenage daughters were very much involved in the building projects.

In the past, alcohol consumption amongst the high school age group had been a huge problem in Seldovia. The influence of the building programs at the church, then with the local school district, carried on over a period of three years. This went a long way to help in breaking the bad habits.

But alone it was not enough to change the tradition of party, booze and sex. Some of the parents from the church drafted other parents from the community, and together they came up with an alternative event to compete with the high school prom and party time that followed.

Local fisherman, Gordon Giles the father of teenage children and who owned a late model 98' commercial fishing boat, offered his boat for transportation. This opened the doors to many possibilities for trips out of Seldovia. It required a boat ride of an hour and a half to Homer and connection to the Alaska Highway system, or a 20 minute airplane ride to Homer.

The organizers then went to the kids to see what they wanted to do. The kids wanted to go roller skating, in Kenai and eat at a restaurant. It was a two plus hour drive from Homer to Kenai, so they made reservations for a dinner at a fancy eating place in Kenai, and booked an all night party at the roller rink in Kenai. They then reserved room for a big breakfast at another restaurant in Homer, finishing with the trip back across the bay to Seldovia.

This trip was so appealing to the high school kids that they cancelled the Junior Prom, as all the kids were going on the alternative trip to Kenai.

The boat trip to and from Homer was also such a big hit with the kids that they wanted a trip on Gordon's boat the following year.

This was set up again on Junior Prom night. They left Seldovia Bay, and instead of turning towards Homer they headed on out to the very tip of the Kenai Peninsula and entered a bay on the outside of the Kenai Peninsula where an old saw mill had operated for several years. All the meals were prepared on the boat, with skiffs used to explore the beaches and old mill in the bay. Again, the Junior Prom was cancelled, but no one seemed to mind as everyone enjoyed the time.

Chapter 39

It was 9:30 in the evening when I received a call from a woman that was obviously distressed. She asked that I come quickly. I could hear an angry male voice in the background. She gave me her address and I left immediately for her residence across the slough. Her residence was an older mobile home and as I got out of my vehicle and approached the front door I could hear a heated argument going on inside. I knocked and the woman opened the door with a rush.

Her husband, not happy with my arrival, asked what I was doing there? I explained that I was called and how could I help? Swearing at me he turned and started down the hall. I quickly asked his wife if he owned a gun? She said no, and hesitated, then said he did have a pistol. I started down the hallway and we were both startled as we met at the first doorway to the right. He was just coming out and had a Smith & Wesson revolver in his right hand holding it waist high pointed at my stomach. I quickly reached for the revolver with my left hand, but I was a little high and ended up grabbing the revolver just behind the cylinder just as he was squeezing the trigger, causing the hammer to strike my flesh in the web between my thumb and first finger. There was a startled expression on his face as the pistol didn't fire, the hammer hitting my hand instead of the primer of the round in the chamber.

I hung on to his hand and the pistol jerking him towards me as I started to spin to my left bringing him across my extended right leg and throwing him to the floor then coming down on top of him as I twisted the pistol out of his hand. He gave up at that point as I pulled the handcuffs out of their case on my belt.

Only by the grace of God, did I walk away from that domestic violence call.

One of our late summer chores was putting together our winter meat supply. Most of this was caribou and moose meat. When living in Seldovia we discovered a good supply of silver salmon. By taking the road to the mill in Jakaloff Bay, then continuing along inland, their logging road began to parallel along a small river (more of a creek) that was going the wrong way. This river that entered the ocean on the outside of the peninsula is called Rocky River. If you followed the river on down to salt water, there was an old abandoned sawmill located on a small inland bay. At that time the road came to an end where the mill in Jakaloff bay had logged a couple of miles short of the old abandoned mill.

This was one of our explore Alaska destinations. Making the hike down to that old mill into an area that no one had occupied for many years was exciting, but at the same time kind of sad as Americans of past times had dreams, and great hopes, and this abandoned mill was the result of some of those who had lived here before.

The river goes through an area that is very wet with standing water, and we needed rubber boots. I saw otter tracks, and in one area a beaver lodge and fresh cutting on trees as they were getting their winter food supply ready. When we approached the little inland bay a flight of ducks took off from our end and circled down to the other end where they landed as we watched. What an incredible setting, for a home.

As we got on down to the bay and the sawmill we found the saw carriage was still there complete with a five foot diameter saw blade. Someone had spent a lot of time and money setting up that mill and the camp living areas. There were different hand tools in the area of the mill, but in the living quarters there were no personal items or furniture.

It was indeed a trip into the past. There was a narrow waterway out of the bay that I followed down a short way, but did not follow it to the outside beach. On the way back the afternoon sun was shining down on the sawmill site, and I was able to watch Mark, Beth, and Karen follow their Mom looking for new discoveries. We made the hike down there a couple of times, but it was a hard trip with kids. There was no trail, so it was a matter of picking your way here and there.

We found, that Rocky River had a good run of silver salmon. We loaded our pickup with tent, sleeping bags, a propane burner with a small propane tank, a pressure cooker, and a smoker.

We would get there early the first day, and catch what we planned to can. Then we got the fish ready to go in smoker, and smoked the fish all night in a cold smoke. Then in the morning we would load them into one quart glass canning jars leaving room for one tablespoon of brown sugar and a slice of lemon. Ann would cook the salmon in the pressure cooker while I would go fishing for more salmon to eat and freeze for later in the winter. This was our favorite time of the year.

I met George Hamm, a fisherman in town who was a boat builder. He was fishing a 32' fishing boat for shrimp. I mentioned that I wanted a little skiff to try the halibut fishing in the area. George said to buy three, 4' x 8' x ¾" sheets of plywood, a quart of glue, a couple of pounds of two inch wood screws, two 1" x 4" strips 16' long, a gallon of primer and another gallon of enamel and we will build you a 16' skiff in a day. I did, and George did. I was there to help all the time and occasionally George would let me hold something for him, but he really did it all. I did get to help with the painting, and the second coat went on the following day.

I have built a few houses but I have never seen a man work with wood like George. He is a master craftsman of which I have never seen his equal. George took it as an insult if he was called a carpenter. He refused to cover a frame building interior wall without first leveling it and then squaring it.

George had always wanted an old fashioned bathtub with four legs built out of wood, and he finally built one. It was an incredible work of art. He used different light and dark hardwoods glued together then, sculpted it out so that it was one solid piece of hardwood. He used a clear resin finish. Dorie, George's wife enjoyed the bathtub, that held the water in, and I enjoyed the 16' skiff that kept the water out.

I put together a 1,000' running line out of quarter inch nylon rope and coiled it in a galvanized washtub. Then I bought 50 stainless steel snaps and put a 12 inch leader and a halibut hook on each snap. I bought another wash tub and used it as a circular hook rack.

I had an anchor line for each end of the running line, with a buoy on the end. I went just out of the mouth of the bay and anchored out the first end of the buoy line and one end of the halibut line, then started the outboard and start laying the halibut line attaching the baited halibut hooks every 40' as I was laying it right out of the washtub. It would take me from 15 to 20 minutes to get the line baited and set, then back to the boat harbor.

The next day I went back out to find the end of the running line that was down current from the running tide, pulled the anchor buoy line and start working back up the line re-baiting each hook, removing any small bottom fish I had caught, and Whoopee, a halibut on. I had felt a little gentle tugging on the line but when the boat come into sight the halibut shied off to the right. I gently guided the fish over to the side, and it took several tries until he calmed down. Then I got out my .38 special and shot him in the head. Halibut are primitive and can literally beat a boat apart if brought on board while still alive.

There was a little water splashed then I was able to ease him into the boat. A 40 lb. halibut! That day I caught another 25 lb. fish, and right at the other end of the line I pulled in another 10 lb. halibut. That was a good day. I usually fished two running lines so I was always moving one to try other places. This kept things lively, and taught me a lot about the bottom of the bay, where the deep channels were located.

I did my halibut fishing in the late summer and early fall. The biggest halibut I caught weighed 90 lb. That was a lot of meat and almost filled that 16' skiff. It was really good eating.

We did not take many boat trips out of the bay, as it could get rough in a hurry out there and a 16' open skiff is not very big. But for use around Seldovia Bay it was great. My halibut fishing was usually within three miles of the mouth of Seldovia Bay.

It was a couple of miles to the head of Seldovia Bay where a small creek entered. Pink salmon ran up the small river in early spring, and there were always a few trout around. This place was a fisherman's dream come true,

Late one afternoon, I was at the school talking to Tom Overman. Ann had been trying to catch up with me as there was trouble brewing in town. Sparky had been at the Lodge and was stirring the pot. He was cussing out a man and woman who were eating there.

I got there as quickly as possible. I noticed as I drove up there were a lot of vehicles in the parking area. I hurried in, entering the dining area. Every table was full and everything seemed normal. I walked to the far end of the dining room where the bar was. A quick look around the bar showed that most of the chairs were full, everything was quiet, but there seemed to be tension in the air. I walked to the end of the bar, and the bartender came over to me. I asked him what was going on and he nodded to a table where a couple were sitting in the dining room, and said that Sparky was yelling and cussing at them, until just before I came in. He said that Sparky was down at the other end of the bar.

I started down the bar and the room quieted down even more. I spotted Sparky, He was watching me and then darting a glance at the table in the dining room, then back to me then at the bartender. His eyes were like a wild man's, and he looked like a trapped animal. I was still 25' away when he came off his bar stool, lowered his head and came at me in a run with his head down like a battering ram and roaring like a crazy man. People were scrambling to get out of the way with chairs scraping, and a woman started to scream.

As Sparky approached he was gaining speed, so I started falling over backwards and as he struck me I was rolling with the blow reaching up grabbing the front of his jacket and hanging on while I kicked my right foot up into his lower stomach accelerating his lower body on over the top of me with force. I had a good grip on his jacket and did not lose it as he crashed to the floor beyond me landing on his back, shoulders and head, pulling me right on over landing on top of him.

The shock of crashing into the floor left a dazed look on his face, as I released the hold on his jacket and grabbed his right wrist with my right hand and my handcuffs with my left hand. He started to struggle, but then relaxed saying, "OK, do not handcuff me, and I will go peacefully." I hesitated then looking at his gang members closing in I thought it may be to my advantage to just get him out of here as quickly as possible.

So on his promise, I got up off of Sparky and brought him to his feet and started for the door. His friends parted as we headed out. I opened the door and we went out into the entrance way to the building, as his followers came into the entrance way I looked back and Sparky hit me in the eye splitting my eyebrow and splattering blood over my white T shirt. I grabbed him and threw him against the building as he was throwing his left hand at the same target. He hit a glancing blow on the same eye splattering the blood across my face, but I took most of the force of the blow with my shoulder.

As Sparky bounced off the wall I grabbed him with a head lock as I twisted and turned it into a sleeper hold, then threw him over my hip taking him to the floor. I put on the handcuffs while I was watching his friends, and then I came to my feet. I reached down to get him up and he refused to get up. I looked at his friends and told them I need their help getting him to my pickup. They refused. Looking at them I stated that if anyone touched us they were going to jail also.

Then looking at Sparky I told him, you could walk or go feet first, your choice. He started swearing at me, so I walked around to his feet where he was laying and picked up both feet and started dragging him down the walkway towards the truck. Every four to six feet, there were one or two steps down and his head would bounce on each step, as he was completely relaxed. His friends came running shouting, "Police brutality! Police brutality!" I looked back up at the Lodge and 10 or 12 people had come out to see what the uproar was about outside. My left eyebrow was bleeding profusely, so I wiped it with my forearm smearing the blood. I must have looked like a wild man with blood all over me. More people came crowding out of the bar and restaurant.

I again picked up Sparky's feet and made it to my truck, where I opened the door and put him inside. It had become obvious that if anyone came to help Sparky, the people from the community were going to back me up.

The first piece of evidence collected was a photo of me, blood, black eye and all. The town was no longer afraid of Sparky. They saw a single policeman arrest him and take him to jail. Even with his gang present. He was just a guy with a bad temper. He also had to obey the law. It would be awhile before he got out of jail this time.

Chapter 40

There was four inches of snow on frozen ground and it was starting to rain. The temperature was right at freezing and coating everything with ice. The rain, with solid ice under it was very difficult to walk on. My four-wheel drive was all over the place until I put the chains on the front. I had to go to Homer, so drove out to the airport and got my PA-12 ready to go. The ice had melted off the airplane before the rain started, so there was no problem flying.

It was just getting around on the ground with the water standing on ice that was the problem. I soon found that when the plane started wandering all I had to do was give it just a little gas, and the prop pulled the airplane along in a straight line, keeping the tail wheel directly behind the nose of the airplane. There was no wind so being very careful I taxied out to the runway, did my run up at an idle, gave it full throttle and took off without any problems. I flew across Katchemak Bay to Homer.

The weather was a little warmer so there was no ice on the runway in Homer. After landing and getting my car we kept in Homer, I got the short list of shopping done and was on my way back to Seldovia. There was a severe weather alert for Seldovia with the ice and water still in place on the runway.

I lined up landing to the west. There is a waterway coming in from Seldovia Bay into town that approaches the west end of the runway and flows along the north side and is mostly north of the runway but it also goes around the east end of the runway. That puts water at both ends of the runway.

I slowed the PA 12 down on the approach and stalled it out just off the runway so it settled down very gently on the ice-covered runway with a half inch of water. The airplane seemed to squirt ahead actually gaining speed. My ground speed at touchdown was 39 miles per hour and it was taking forever to slow down. I tried the brakes and there was no change, I kept going at an alarming rate and the end of the runway was coming up fast. I tried touching the left brake with no results, so I locked the left wheel with the brake and the airplane started a very gradual left turn, but was not turning enough to get off the runway before going over the edge into the water.

Now I had to do something in a hurry or I would be in the slough! I immediately kicked full left rudder and gave it a burst of throttle sending a blast of air along the fuselage, hitting the rudder and causing the tail to swing out to my right so now I was sliding sideways, then another short blast of throttle and I was now sliding completely backwards. Right at the west end of the runway I straightened the rudder and moved the throttle forward slowing my backward slide then giving it more throttle and reversing my backward slide so that at last I was moving away from the water at the west end of the runway and on to safety.

As you might guess, I felt an enormous relief after going through that fiasco. How would I ever explain how I came to taxi backwards, into the Seldovia slough.

Chapter 41

I had picked up a book about modern day cattle ranching. It told of the problems of normal day-to-day ranch life. The rancher in this book was living with lots of wildlife in and around his ranch. It was not an easy way of life but the life style was very appealing to both Ann and I. After finishing the book I gave it to Ann to read and waited for her to finish the book to get her reaction.

We had looked at getting into that business for several years, but never could come close to getting a place that would make a living. It was late fall with winter coming on, and things were peaceful in Seldovia. The kids had gone to bed and Ann and I were sitting near the wood stove with a nice crackling fire going, taking comfort in knowing the wood shed was full. Ann had not said anything and I was anxious to get her take on the book.

I said, "You know, it's funny how we used to be interested in cattle ranching and the outdoor life style of living in the mountains, and now we are far removed from all that. I wonder why we changed." Ann was quiet for a while, and at first I thought she might have dozed off. I looked over and saw Ann was very much awake. She responded slowly with, "Did we really change?" I said, "That is the same thing I have been thinking. Reading that book put old ideas back in my head. Why don't we pray about this, and see what the Lord has in mind for us?"

The fishing season in Bristol Bay was supposed to be a huge one that year. Four years before a big surge up the river late in the year was predicted to pay off big time. Most all of the late spawning fish got up the river after the majority of fishermen had quit. So the survival rate was high with those that had returned.

The last few years I had taken over the garbage pickup for the City of Seldovia,. I had bought their newly acquired garbage truck and had become a public utility maintaining the local dump site with the old D8 Dozer, and running the local garbage service with a used six yard dump truck I had purchased.

The Kenai Borough had advertised and put out for bid the closing of the current dump site, the construction of four miles of road and opening a new garbage dump, with a contract to keep the road open and maintain the new dump. I won the contract, and work was scheduled to start in the summer. We had built a scenic log cabin right across from the entrance to the small boat harbor. We carried health food and some bulk foods. The storefront was also our office for the disposal business, store and other fun things, as well as a comfortable place to sit and visit.

We had a wood stove right across from the main door with old barn wood on that partition and the giant 5' saw blade as a heat reflector behind the stove that we'd found a couple of years earlier. There were two rocking chairs near the wood stove. Life in Seldovia was becoming very comfortable for the Gunkel family.

Chapter 42

While living at Lake Tahoe when we first got married, Ann and I had spent lots of time outdoors, hunting, fishing, skiing and running our sled dogs. We always cut our own fire wood, and had bought five acres 15 miles from Truckee, California with our nearest neighbor living at Hobart Mills, four miles from the nearest plowed road. That made the winters very interesting.

We really enjoyed our time working together with our two little daughters, carving a home out of the wilderness, developing a spring for year round water, and traveling the racing circuit with our sled dogs. Some of our friends were cattle ranchers, so we also had some insight into what ranching was all about.

We traveled to races in California, Nevada, Oregon, Utah, Colorado and Arizona, and raced our teams of Irish Setters against several breeds of huskies, seldom losing. It seemed the tougher the conditions the greater our margin of victory. Most of the races were tied in with winter carnivals, so every weekend was like a holiday. We drew lots of attention because we were using Irish Setters as sled dogs, and beating the huskies.

On the way to one of our races we were driving out across Nevada through a remote area when I had a flat tire. Our dog box was on top our pickup, with our racing sleds on top. Ann was getting the dogs out a couple at a time as I started changing the tire. A man drove up in a late model pickup and asked if he could help. He asked if our dogs were sled dogs, and was very interested.

The rancher said that he raced horses and did a lot of traveling to horse-races. We had exchanged a few racing stories and I asked if he was able to do well racing horses. He sighed and said that his horses were just fast enough to keep him broke. I laughed, and thought about it a minute. I responded that was a very accurate description of our operation also. We did just well enough to reach for the next level. At that time Alaska was a dream. Then the flat was fixed and we were on the road again.

Chapter 43

That was in the 1960's, and it was in 1979 in Seldovia, Alaska when my thoughts had been directed back to ranching in the high country. Well, Lord, if that is what you have in mind for us, you will have to provide.

Spring arrived along with another commercial fishing season. Our crew consisted of Ann, our oldest daughter Karen in her second year of collage, daughter Beth a senior in high school, our son Mark, going into the sixth grade and myself. Also fishing with us, my younger brother Gregg, There were two more guys, high school and collage age, on our crew that year as well. We would be in Bristol Bay for a month or so, which takes a lot of supplies, and groceries.

We started just after Christmas buying supplies for the coming fishing season. The first thing was to order fishing gear through the cannery, which includes hip boots and full rubber gear, special fish gloves for the whole crew, and another summer's supply of picking hooks, new nets, hanging twine, one more cork line, and a couple of new lead lines.

We ordered another Ranger track vehicle, and parts for the old Ranger to rebuild its final drive. We also ordered lumber to build a shop off the back of the girl's bunkhouse so we could get out of the weather to work on equipment. Wow, what a luxury that will be.

I took the airplane in to change the tail wheel and tail wheel spring. We would be using the airplane to haul fish, and this is the first year with the smaller Piper PA-12 working off the beach. It needed a stiffer spring and bigger wheel for the big loads in that soft sand.

Then we planned the groceries. I got the feeling that we were attempting to buy out Anchorage. Every year about that time I wondered how we could catch enough fish to pay for all the supplies we needed.

With the expectation of lots of fish we arrived early that year. We got to the beach in early June and moved all our supplies across the bay and, settled into camp. That first day we started hanging nets. The next morning out goes the first net to see what might be around. We hope to catch a fish or two for the table. Bristol Bay sockeye salmon caught right out of salt water are incredibly fine eating.

As we opened camp and started getting everything operational there was excitement in everything we did. The anticipation of a big year was in the air. Every year there is some of that excitement around, but that year also had a cloud that could dampen the whole fishing season. The Bristol Bay Fishermen's Association was talking strike against the Canneries and cash buyers. This meant when the Fish and Game Department starts their regulated season in late June, the fishermen will tie up their boats and quit fishing until the buyers agree to a higher price for the fish.

That first day provided three 5 lb. salmon, which made a great meal, and we were off.

We started delivering fish the middle of June with every tide showing more strength. As the camp was set up, the outhouse got a new hole, which is not an easy job because of the permafrost. The early building projects were finished, the nets re-hung about the same time as the windmill set in motion driving its 12 volt alternator, recharging the batteries for camp lights. Every year we had to relocate where we dug the refrigerator into the permafrost. We have to set up a drain so the melting water had a place to go.

There was a small fresh water lake 300 yards behind camp that we used for doing the camp laundry. Water was pumped into two water storage tanks that held a little over a hundred gallons on top of the A-frame house roof and furnished water with pressure for our wringer washing machine, and dish washing area in the kitchen.

The camp shower was set right next to the steam bath in the wash building. We used a 55 gallon drum with a GI issue drum heater that worked with a slow drip system of stove oil. We could get hot water for the whole camp to shower by heating with the fifty-five gallon heater twice. That allowed approximately 10 gallons of hot water each. It was enough to get wet, and then turn off the water while soaping down, then turning on the water just long enough to rinse off.

The crew members were the water police. They saw to it that everyone got an equal and fair share of the shower water, but no more. The last one in line sometimes got a little more, but sometimes got a little less. If it turned out less you would hear it for a half mile down the beach.

Chapter 44

The last week of June starts the regulated commercial salmon fishing season, which means that you cannot fish unless the Fish and Game announces they are having an opening. And it was official, the Fishing Association was striking for a higher price per pound. And all their fishermen will anchor their boats until all the canneries agree to pay the price they demanded. One of the smaller canneries agreed to pay the price, but the Association would not let their fishermen go fishing, until all the rest of the canneries agreed to the price also.

Now the Gunkel camp had to sit down and decide what to do. Do we follow the rest of the herd and sit down to wait for a break in ranks of the fishermen, or scab-fish and deliver to the canneries?

The last strike year I was the only law enforcement officer in the Naknek-Kvichak district in Bristol Bay. A strike was not something to take lightly. It could be dangerous. What really burned me was there was a cash buyer that would accept and pay what the Association was demanding, not after further negotiations, and the Association still insisted that no one could fish until all the rest had come on board.

There would be a lot of fish go up the river before we ever got the chance to fish. The Association refuses to take set-net fishermen into their Association, but insists that we do not break rank with them. Therefore, we had no say on whether to fish or not fish.

We had just received short notice from the Department of Fish and Game of an opening in the Kvichak district in Bristol Bay where we were. If we fished, even though there are no roads into our area, everyone would know we were fishing. Others here on our beach would not be happy . . . but our crew said, "LETS FISH."

This opening started an hour after low water, so we loaded a fifty-fathom net onto each ranger to take down the beach to layout when the tide gets to the low level. We had a meal an hour before they let us start fishing. We were seeing lots of fish all the way down the beach in the shallow water. The fish were fining in the shallow pools and were out in the bay waiting for the tide to change while we were waiting for the opening. Walking out into the bay at the area our net was going into the bay, red salmon would swirl around running into our legs. As soon as we can hook our D-ring on our cork line into our outer buoy (3:00 pm.) this area will explode with the fish going crazy. Right now they are just waiting for the tide to change directions and then they will go charging on up the bay and into the river. Looking up and down the beach, we were still the only fishermen on the beach. It felt lonely down there.

The tide changed and the fish started milling, and at 3:00 p.m. we laid out our nets having to drag them out in the water to get to our outside buoy and we immediately started catching fish. We were trying to keep our nets picked as fast as possible because we wanted to swing our nets up the beach, at least to the middle set. We had our rubber Zodiacs out with a brailer spread inside each hull so that we can pick fish directly into the brailer. As soon as we had our first load we sent the Zodiac back to the beach and began hauling the fish up the beach to load into the airplane for delivery. Our first delivery was for 937 pounds of red salmon, which I flew into the King Salmon airport.

High tide, small catch

Hurrying back, we put the Zodiac back into the water and cut the cork line loose from the outer buoy hooking onto the lower end of the cork line to drag it back to the water line. It was already filling up again. We moved the boat in as far as it would still float, and then secured the cork line to a Ranger. Next the crew assisted the Ranger in dragging the net and newly caught fish up the beach. At first I was wondering if we were going to make it, but we finely were able to complete the swing, hooking the cork line to our upper buoy, then back to picking and franticly throwing the new fish into the boat. Everyone was in the surf again picking fish as they were slamming into the net and our legs as we were in water knee to waist high deep.

The object was to catch as many fish as possible, but also get the fish out of the net quickly to keep moving the net with the tide. Most fish were in the shallow water, but the tides in Bristol Bay change from 12' for a little tide up to 23'. Our beach was pretty flat allowing the water line to move up and down along the beach gradually, approximately 900', on every tide. This happened twice a day.

When there are too many fish we cannot swing the net as it loads up faster than we can pick the fish. When that happens, we just leave the net until the tide goes on up the beach, and back down to the waterline where the net is set. We catch some fish while it is in the deep water, but most fish are running in the shallower water. We were working two or three nets, with eight to 10 in our crew. With each opening we were on the beach almost the entire time, with short time-outs for meal breaks.

There were a lot of fish in the bay for this opening and we were doing very well. Because of the short opening, we were milking this tide for every fish. About three hours before the end of the opening, Fish and Game announced an extension. We had an extension! Everyone jumped up cheering. We had just finished swinging both nets too the high set. That gave Ann time to fix a meal while we finished delivering our fish that were on the beach. We had about two hours to eat and grab some sleep before the tide reached the top and then started down again. Looking up and down the beach, we remained the only crew fishing.

There were still a lot of fish in the bay as this extension was winding down. Again, Fish and Game extended the opening. This time there were a few groans and someone said Whoopee? I responded, "Ok, you guys are getting rich, remember? You have all winter to sleep."

The King Salmon airport was US Air Force on one side with a squadron of new F-16 fighter jets, and the commercial airport on the other side. Alaska Airlines and other commercial enterprises were operating out of the civilian side. I landed and taxied to a warehouse next to Alaska Airlines. I contacted the cash buyer, and he rolled a cart out to load our fish. So, within 25 to 30 minutes, delivery was complete and we were on the beach again, to collect another load of fish.

We did not have a tender on our beach during the strike. When there was no tender I flew around the clock. During the three hours it was dark we made markers on the beach for the runway by using a number 10 tin can, putting a roll of toilet paper in it, filling it with stove oil, and then lighting it on fire. It was spooky because they did not give much light only marking the edge of the landing area. The first pass I would come in low making a pass letting the crew know I was going to land, so our crew could make sure the runway was clear, Then I would come in slow with the nose high feeling for the runway (beach) with the tail wheel.

I would prefer delivering by boat to a tender as we could move a lot more fish a shorter distance in a shorter time. But without the airplane we would have had lots of down time, and no way to get our fish to our cash buyer in King Salmon. When the Fishermen's Association refused to let us participate by joining their Association, we went out and found our own buyer that would pay what the Fishermen's Association was demanding. That way we made no big splash, but quietly went on about our business fishing and keeping out of everyone's way. After the strike was over we resumed fishing for the cannery.

Everyone on our crew was working for a percentage of the catch. After the evening meal they would do the math to keep track of how much they were making. We were excited on how our season was shaping up, but the toll on all of us was also building. It seemed like we were always tired.

As I started writing this book I asked my younger brother Gregg for his recollections working as a member of our crew. Gregg wrote . . .

"For me this was the most exhausting work I had ever done. And I, theoretically, was in the prime of my life. The physical labor of picking fish made my hands arthritic. Every nick or cracked cuticle was an avenue for minor infection from the fish slime. My back ached from the bending over and the lifting.

"There were very few nice days that summer. We endured lots of rain and drizzle. Picking at night by lantern in the rain was pretty bleak, and those night picks were typically after only two or three hours of sleep.

"We lived in levis, t-shirts, sweat shirts and rain gear. Although we would rotate our clothing, hoping it would dry out in the damp bunkhouse shacks where we slept, it seemed as if we were always wet. And the constant 50-60 degree temperatures during the rainy spells meant that unless you were well-nourished, you were cold.

"Ann was our savior! With the food she prepared, we ate well, and she did her best to keep us in clean clothes.

"The spirit of excitement and adventure kept us electrified. Since we were fishing as scabs during the strike, it seemed like we were constantly on our guard.

"The morning we went out and found that one 50 fathom-shackle of net going dry with what appeared to be every hole in the net containing a fish. A literal carpet of thousands of five and six lb. sockeye was awe-inspiring. I remember my heart stopped in excitement, and then the magnitude of what I was looking at brought the reality of a very long day lying ahead of me".

That big tide was incredible. I had never seen anything like it before or since. The night before, our crew was wearing out as we had been fishing none stop for several days, so we set the net to the middle set and went to bed getting almost six hours sleep.

I got up early and went down to the beach and saw an incredible sight. The far end of the net was still in the water, and there was fish boiling all around it. The net was laying in a curve and was a mat of solid fish almost three feet high. When I got down there it looked like a giant carpet. I got the rest of the crew up and we all went down to the beach. We could not find a single hole in the net without a fish in it. I asked in trepidation, "How are we going to get all those fish picked and off the beach before the tide gets back in?" Ann answered, "One at a time!" There were thousands of fish in that net. The strike settled within a day or so after our big set and we went on to harvest 305,000 lbs. of fish for the season.

The fishing continued with lots of fish for the next week, then started slowing down, and finally it was over. The overall catch for the season, was well above average. For us, that translated into thousands of dollars for each of our crew for three weeks work. It was the highest poundage of fish we ever caught in one season's fishing.

Chapter 45

We closed fish camp and left Bristol Bay and returned home to Seldovia. We put our ranch plans into motion. I turned in my resignation as Chief of Police, and we flew to Martinez, California to leave our children with Ann's parents while we went looking for a mountain ranch to develop.

Ann and I started traveling northeast through California, Nevada, and eastern Oregon finding some very interesting country, but none that met our expectations. I had corresponded with a realtor in Lewiston, Idaho who was excited about showing us a property east of Lewiston. I called in late afternoon about fifty miles out of Lewiston, and made arrangements to meet him the next morning to look at the property.

We spent the evening mixing with the local people, and discovering that the difference between Lewiston, Idaho and Clarkston, Washington was which side of the Snake River you lived on. Then we went out to eat at Taco Time in Clarkston, across the street from our motel. After all the road traveling the last few days it felt good to walk, even if it was just across the street.

The next morning we met Perry in his office and headed east out of Lewiston towards the property with Perry talking of the positive things about this place. Perry did say that he had not been able to contact the owner, but he would show us the property anyway. We stopped at a gas station where he tried to call one more time, and found the property had sold yesterday. Disappointed, he took us out for lunch, and we headed back to Lewiston. Perry then said he had one more place for sale in which we might be interested.

We went back to Lewiston, at 700' elevation, crossed the river into Clarkston and drove down the river to a town called Asotin. We followed the road up Asotin Creek, crossed the creek and started winding up the side of a ridge emerging from the deep canyon. It was mid-August and the temperature was over 100 degrees. There were no trees after we left the creek and everything was brown as we climbed out of the canyon coming out along the top with brown fields of harvested wheat and barley. We passed a few scattered farmhouses framed by trees, and a church with a small cluster of more houses. The road kept gaining altitude as we worked our way up and across the large ridge of harvested fields. Now we could see timber up across the ridge. We passed one more house near the timber. As we rounded a group of pine trees a half mile farther there was a stock pond with a couple of large apple trees, and a small road that turned off to the right. Just beyond the trees was another pond and a driveway that curved back past the pond then away to the left. The road circled the low farm field and then went into the bottom of the draw with pine trees scattered along the bottom of the draw. A big rooster pheasant took off near the dry creek bed. Finally, we passed over a cattle guard crossing and turned up a draw by a spring where a stock watering trough filled a hundred yards further up the hill. On the far side of the draw sat a large Barn that was old and leaning decidedly, crying for attention.

The road crossed through what in by gone years had been a corral, then started up the far side where an old cabin sat in a state of disrepair next to an old rusted-out wood stove. We got out of Perry's vehicle to look around. We saw an old outhouse, with a wood shed out back. In the draw below the house was a big chicken house that was in much better shape. There was a great pile of chicken manure in the chicken house. This property was known locally as the old Charlie Knight place. Everyone knew of the spring.

We got back into Perry's vehicle and rode up the road 150 yards to the edge of the farm field and stopped to open the gate. As we started across the harvested barley field I saw a group of four legal bucks spring up and move away from us. They moved right along the drive we were following.

The road continued up across the field that sat on a smaller ridge and then down into the timbered draw a couple of hundred yards, and back up out of the bottom. There were springs along the road. Near the first spring we saw two large grouse, one of which ran off into the grass on the side of the road and the second thundered into the air. The bottom of each draw was filled with lots of pine trees, brush, and fir trees. The road continued up the far side of the draw to the farm field and then on across a second field. Soon a third draw that was twice as deep as the last one filled with a lot of timber. From here the road descended to the bottom of the draw and continued for half a mile or so. Towards the end of the road the field opened up to about 50 yards across. Right in the middle there was a small fir tree and some tall grass. As we approached the field, a big cow elk jumped out of her bed followed by that year's calf. This was in the middle of the afternoon. I was sold!

The ranch consisted of a total of 750 acres, with 450 acres tillable, located at 4,000' elevation, in the Blue Mountains. To me this was about as close to heaven as you could get.

We wanted to be in the mountains, with firewood available. We wanted to be in good hunting country. We needed to be in an area that was serviced by a school bus, and we wanted to be able to generate some income from the property that would work in with our commercial fishing operation in Alaska.

We also would prefer being serviced by electricity. It took a couple of days to confirm that yes, the school bus would come to the Charlie Knight driveway, or the end of the snow-plowed road depending when the county snow plows get the road way cleared. And yes, the County would clear the road to just beyond the Charlie Knight driveway, but it might be four or five days after the storm as this area is low priority. And yes, as soon as the Clear Water Power Company replaced a few poles they would hook power up to our ranch.

We bought the property, and rented a small house in Asotin located along the Snake River to live in until we could get our new home established on the ranch. Now the race was on to get moved down from Alaska, get a home built, and move in before the snow season arrived.

Back in Alaska, Gordon Giles, the owner of the Tejin Two, a 98' commercial fishing boat, offered to move all our personnel belongings to Seattle, Washington. Gordon was taking his boat down to install new equipment.

I loaded Ann on the Tejin Two, with all our belongings, and away they went. I had sold our house in Seldovia and the garbage business. I tied up the loose ends and took off for Seattle in the PA-12. I got there a day early and put the airplane in a shop to get a new exhaust system installed, and bought a new 4-wheel drive Chevy pickup. The next day I met Ann and the Tejin Two. Also rendezvousing with the Tejin was daughter Karen in her vehicle, daughter Beth with little brother Mark in her vehicle, and Ann's parents in their vehicle. Ann's parents and our children had all traveled from California to meet us at the boat harbor in Seattle and travel with us to our new home.

We rented a U-Haul trailer, loaded our things in all the vehicles, and started across the State of Washington in a caravan to our temporary place in Asotin.

Chapter 46

Two of the first people we met in our new hometown were Gerald and Marilyn Hodson, and their boys. We met them at a church evening service at the fairgrounds in Asotin. Gerald had a large farm about six miles from our new home in the mountains. The Hodson's were instant friends, with Gerald becoming my teacher and consultant in farming.

Up on the ranch, we excavated into the side of a hill providing for a full daylight basement to be placed under a new 20' X 60' mobile home. Next we laid out and installed a septic tank and leach field. Then had a crane lift both sides of our new trailer onto the new basement, hooking up the electric, water from our spring, and septic system.

During the pauses, as we waited and assembled all the pieces, we were busy filling the old woodshed. One of our projects had been to install a wood furnace in the basement and a wood stove in the family room, just off the dining area, and would have plenty of wood to keep warm. Then the gravel trucks finally arrived to haul three inches of road base to upgrade the entire driveway of 500 yards, where it went from the main road across the cattle guard and by the old barn. They were hauling material from a local gravel pit. This provided us a year-round roadway, assuming we could keep the snow clear enough to get through the winter.

We located a D4 cat with a dozer blade in good condition. The price was right and now our living year round on the ranch looked possible. The hours spent on that little tractor, was measured in high yields of accomplishments around the ranch.

The late summer and early fall were jamb packed with things to get done. Our wood cutting project also allowed a little reconnaissance into the different hot spots for hunting deer and elk. I never passed up the chance to get out in early and last daylight, when the wildlife was most active.

As fall approached I was surprised at the interest and activity of the local hunting community in the Clarkston-Asotin community. Starting about two weeks before the hunting season early hunting party arrivals came from all over the state setting up hunting camps. There was an incredible amount of hunting pressure throughout the region. This got me to thinking that these animals are pushed so hard that they needed a refuge somewhere. My property seemed to afford just such a refuge.

By May 1, 1980 the airplane was still not finished. I had brought it in to the aircraft hangar to get the Piper PA-12 rebuilt, adding extensive modifications. These included installing a set of flaps in the wings to get better stability at slow speeds, install PA-18 landing gear to support larger wheels for those soft landing surfaces, and wing-tip gas tanks. PA-18 fuel gauges were installed to provide a positive reading at a glance, allowing for longer flying range for the aircraft, and finally, enlarging the baggage area behind the rear seat of the aircraft.

We had already been buying and shipping supplies and equipment to Alaska for the upcoming season that June. We had just a little over a month before we would be departing in the aircraft. Amazingly, everything got purchased and delivered to our cannery in Seattle in time for shipment to Alaska. It is nice to know it will be waiting when we arrive in Bristol Bay. All of a sudden it was time for Mark and I to load our airplane and head north with our personal gear and some travel supplies. We took off from Lewiston at 2:30 p.m. and landed for the night in Penticton, BC Canada. This leg of the trip would be a shakedown flight checking out the airplane. I was really impressed with the stability of the PA-12. It is not very fast but is good for short field work. We went over the entire airplane, and could find nothing wrong.

We fueled up before going to bed, took off from Penticton at 5:00 a.m. and flew to Prince George, BC, refueled and headed north into the Trench which continued up somewhere into the Yukon Territory for the night.

The next day we again took off early and got into Alaska by midmorning. We refueled somewhere around Anchorage and continued over to Bristol Bay, landing on the beach at our Copenhagen Creek fish camp in late afternoon. After unloading the airplane and opening up the main cabin we flew back to Naknek and the cannery. Mark and I loaded supplies from the cannery into the airplane and returned going south away from the fish camp, down to Johnson Hill to check the Johnson Hill marker to see if anyone was fishing the end site. It remained unoccupied and provided an alternative fishing location.

It had been a long three days, so we turned around and headed north directly over the water to our fish camp on the west side, and were back on the ground 45 minutes later. We went to bed early so that we could get up and return back across the water to Naknek to meet Ann who was flying into King Salmon Airport. We got out a 40 hp outboard that was giving us problems the previous summer to get some work done on it. We loaded the outboard into the PA-12 and taxied the plane back to the west end of the beach, and turned around to make our take off roll to the east.

I checked the airplane and everything looked ok. There was a 10 mph wind out of the southeast. I conducted a run up checking both magnetos with no problems. I pushed the throttle forward to full power and as the PA12 started rolling I pushed the elevator forward lifting the tail wheel out of the sand and the plane accelerated gaining speed. I lowered the tail wheel almost onto the beach while with my right hand I gave the airplane full flaps and the PA-12 leaped into the air. I immediately feathered the flaps back allowing a smooth roll and lift off, then stepping gently on the right rudder allowing a touch of right aileron which caused a gentle right turn out over the water. As we gained altitude slowly I turned the plane straight for Naknek and King Salmon, en-route straight across the water.

Just as I was relaxing the engine went from full power, to no power. *Oh Lord, Please Help Me!* I immediately started a turn to my left realizing I had a 10 mile tailwind in trying to get back to the beach. The same time I started a turn to the left I pulled the carburetor heat knob with negative results in attempting to restart the engine. I was running on my right main fuel tank, so I opened the left main tank, left wing tip tank, and the right wing tank so that all fuel tanks were open. I only had a couple hundred feet altitude so to maintain as much altitude as possible I had to drop my nose a little. Right then the prop was wind milling, but when that stopped I would really lose altitude. I could not fly directly back to the point of ground by Copenhagen Creek or I would lose 10 miles an hour of lift flowing over the wings that the tail wind would take away. I found that by using a slight drag of my left wing I was kind of skidding back to my left towards dry ground, but I had to get across Copenhagen Creek to land on dry land. To go down in Bristol Bay is disaster because of the frigid water. I tried turning a little more down wind, and the airplane felt solid. Dragging that wing seemed to help in avoiding a complete stall where the airplane would quit flying and fall out of the sky.

The prop quit turning, but I was too far away from dry land at 30 feet elevation. There is no way I can make it. The route of flight I was forced to take because of that tail wind was paralleling the creek and we were going into the water any second whenever the wings quit flying. Out of desperation, I tried lowering the nose and turning to cross the creek, and that is where I ran out of ALTITUDE, AIR SPEED, and IDEAS!

As the airplane stalled, it fell off on the left wing and rolled over into a flat spin with the heaviest end, the engine, leading the way upside down. I could tell because the world I could see out of the windshield was spinning around. I do not know how it happened but the left wing tip struck the ground first ripping the leading edge attach point loose and folding the wing back along the side of the fuselage. That reversed the spin to the right when the right wing tip struck the ground ripping the right wing loose from the leading edge attach point and folding the second wing back along the other side of the fuselage. We struck the ground hard, nose first, slamming my head forward into the dash of the airplane. Mark who was sitting on the outboard engine without a seat belt came forward head first striking me in the lower right back breaking three of my ribs and knocking the door open and falling out onto the ground unconscious.

I crawled out of the airplane noticing we struck the damp ground six feet from the water's edge skidding forward, there was steam coming from the engine so I went over to move Mark and found his arm pined to the ground with the wing strut on it. Mark woke up. I lifted up enough the front of the airplane to get the weight off of his arm and get him free.

Looking at the airplane it looked like someone had just leaned each wing against the side of the airplane and left them.

The very next thing we did was to get on our hands and knees and thank our ALL MIGHTY GOD for sparing our lives! GOD was right there with us on that beach, and we could feel his presence.

If you look back to our last hour of flight, and the next twenty minutes of planned flight, any other time for that engine to quit, would have resulted in our death in the waters of Bristol Bay. GOD kept that airplane in the air when I was not able to. He allowed for the impossible to happen, delivering both Mark and I safely.

For me, this commercial fishing season was a time to realize that I did not have to do it all. As I recovered from my injuries I was forced to watch while Mark, our 16-year-old son took over and ran the whole show, doing an outstanding job. There were not as many fish as the year before, but a large increase in price per pound allowed us to replace the airplane with a larger and more powerful Maul M-6 aircraft.

Chapter 47

We got home in time to get ready for the harvest of our 400 acres planted in barley. Then before we knew it we were through harvest season, and swimming in the Snake River, getting some of the yard work done around the house, repairing fencing and getting ready for the coming fall hunting season.

While visiting with our neighbor, French Weiss out at our mail box, I mentioned the pressure and stress on the local deer herds last year, and that I was thinking of closing our ranch to deer hunting for the entire deer season. French thought that was a great idea and that he would join with me and close all his ground that adjoined our place. Wow, that would cover several drainages and make a huge difference. Instead of just our 750 acres that would involve around 3,000 acres of prime hunting ground.

We both went to work putting up signs. I found that the signs alone did not work. It also required lots of hours patrolling. For a while this was a nuisance. But as I started paying attention to the land I could see it was working! We kept the No Deer Hunting policy going for three years. And every year the deer herds grew, with some larger bucks starting to show up. And this was happening with little impact to existing crops.

I am a dedicated hunter and to have to discipline myself that even I could not hunt deer on my own property was difficult. I was able to see the result of high hunting pressure and now I was witnessing the recovery of the deer population with reduced hunting pressure. Our goal was to get the population back up while also helping to control the population through harvest. We were reassured as we were having some impact on the local population of deer.

Our good friend Gerald Hodson and his family was a big part of our hunting gatherings, and outings. Rod Marshall, one of the hunting organizers for our hunts also became a close friend. He had recently graduated from Seattle Pacific, a Bible college, and on his way to becoming a pastor. I believe our love for hunting and the outdoors drew us together. Rod and I were always the first out, and the last ones to return.

Rod gave me a call one February evening asking if I would be interested in a hunting trip to Wyoming. The primary goal of our hunt would be deer and antelope. Rod had found a company that had hunting rights for several large ranches, in a high desert setting near Douglas, Wyoming. Rod said he had gone to the Seattle Outdoor show and an expedition outfit was selling hunting trips onto land they had privately leased for hunting. They had a promotion going on that they were giving away a free hunt for two. "Rod said I filled out the card and dropped it into the jar and I got a call telling me I had won a free hunting trip for two. Want to go hunting?"

Rod left Seattle and drove over to Gerald's house in Cloverland. Gerald had to finish his fall seeding so he could not go with us. We were driving straight through to Wyoming, so we could check in at the check station the next afternoon in Douglas. We left early driving Highway 12 from Lewiston, Idaho through Lolo Pass, and then on through Montana for breakfast in Therigan, Wyoming early the next morning.

We arrived in Douglas in early afternoon and found a sporting goods store to purchase hunting license and tags. We paid close attention to the deer heads mounted in the store. This was usually a good indication of how big the deer get in an area. I was feeling disappointment because I did not see any mounts that I considered to be a trophy. We asked around and found a taxidermy shop knowing that this is where we might find the really big bucks.

There were a couple of good bucks in the taxidermy shop, but again none like I was hoping to find. We headed out to check-in and get our hunting assignments for hunting the next morning. We had a couple hours of daylight so we went into that area to see what was there. The roads were all very well kept. They were dirt roads but very sound and well maintained. The roads went into and around to different oil wells of which some were pumping and others were not. The secondary roads were not quite as groomed but also well maintained. The area was set in a small range of hills 1,500' to 2,000' high with very few trees, light vegetation, and an occasional animal, or more.

We went back to our base camp at the motel in Douglas. This provided us a base without all the labor and time camping would require. It gave us more time for hunting. After a good night's sleep we ate a big early breakfast, and headed for the hills. Rod and I were in a hunters' dream with as many days as it takes to hunt, hunt, and hunt. I still had that nagging feeling that there were not any trophy-class bucks in this area. But I was determined to make the most of it, as there were plenty of animals to choose from. The trick was to see the animals first before they saw us, doing lots of glassing with our binoculars and riflescopes.

We saw animals shortly after getting out of town but did not start hunting until reaching the ranch, oil well property. We worked around and through the property and Rod had his eye on a four-point buck that seemed a little larger and a little wider. I thought it to be about 25" wide. We were watching this lone buck. He seemed to read Rods mind as he turned and started running away to our right.

Rod then made the decision he would be happy with that buck so he took up the challenge and put a round in the chamber and went to work getting the rifle sights lined up on the running buck. I watched as he squeezed off a round and that buck folded up and skidded to a halt. If Rod had time he seldom missed.

We were able to get the buck cleaned, skinned and quartered then loaded into the back of Rods vehicle. So off to the meat processor we went to get Rod's deer processed. After dropping the meat off, we headed back to the oilfields for a late afternoon hunt. We had spotted some antelope that looked promising. We relocated the antelope herd and Rod got a nice buck, again with one shot over 300 yards out.

Shortly after getting Rod's antelope meat processed, I shot a nice buck antelope with exceptionally wide horns. We took care of the meat, and got new hunting assignments, and then sat down to a late dinner where we made new plans for the next day's hunt. We were going into a new area that was a considerable farther distance away from Douglas and a different type of country.

Rod decided to leave his rifle in the motel as he had filled his tags. We left town early, heading for an old homestead that was located in a very remote area. We followed the only road in, where the main road ended. As we pulled off the main road, there was a distinct change in the road. Now there were lots of rocks and patches of sandy areas. There was some rim rock type rock structure in the hill area, and this was now turning into what looked to me more like high desert deer country. The road wove in and around a long ridge and gradually across it. We started down the far side gradually working downhill and deeper into the area.

There were no trees where we were, but there was scattered brush, which was about six feet high. We could see two or three hundred yards down the hill and even farther looking down the far side of the ridge. As we drove around a rock out-cropping, we could see beyond where the road entered the top of a small draw. Near the draw, an old building was located about 350 yards down the draw. We could see several deer around the draw that appeared to be feeding.

Now this was more like I expected. Rod shut off the vehicle and we were glassing the whole area. There were four bucks in one area and then a little below the building there were a few does. We sat there and watched as the deer watched us. At first the does started moving across the draw and up through the rim rock and on over the ridge. The bucks, which were a little closer to us, started moving also. The first two smaller bucks were followed by a three-point, and then a small four-point followed through the rim rock and over the ridge. Rod said, "Let's go on down and check this out."

We got back in the vehicle and Rod drove on over to the draw and picked his way down to the building. We got out and Rod said, "Do you see what I see?" We both went over to the building and found the building was made out of Petrified logs. The doorway and windows were just openings and there was no roof. The building was 15' x 25'. I had found a small piece of petrified wood before, but here is a full house made of petrified logs. The ground was gravel with lots of dirt in it all around the building site. This building has been here a long time. Wow, and here we are deer hunting!

I walked around back of the old house and on up onto the ridge, a short way. Dear Heavenly Father, Lord you know what is happening, we are hunting for a trophy, dear Father please just show me the biggest buck around here.

I started back to the house saying to Rod, "lets go hunting." We started over the ridge following the same trail the bucks had gone. We were through the rim rock and starting around the big ridge. Rod and I were walking together and I was watching the area just a couple hundred yards above us. There was a line of rock with a few larger bushes that provided shade, making what I thought was good deer cover. There was not much in front of us, only a big sandy area with no cover. All of a sudden Rod said, "Buck, b-b-big buck! B-B-biggg Buck!" I kept looking up the hill asking where is he? Rod said, "RIGHT IN FRONT OF US!" Rod had seen that huge buck raise right out of the sand in front of us. When I finally looked in the right direction, there he was, just 60 yards away. The animal was huge! He had big square light-brown rear quarters. As I watched he traveled around a big rock to his right, then back to our left around a low bush, his powerful rear legs driving him forward. Looking up from his rear to the back of his head, I could see his antlers going out past his ears and shoulder a good seven inches. I was trying to line up the crosshairs, but he was all over the place. When I finally was able to target and squeeze off a shot I knew I had missed. I put another round in the chamber and had to hurry off another shot before he dove into a low area of the hillside out of sight. We ran forward about 100 yards and when we saw the buck reappear he was now about 350 yards out. He was not running but was covering lots of ground in a hurry. I was breathing hard so dropped down on my rear end trying to get in a solid shooting position. After a few more shots he was out of range.

As I sat there I remembered my words "Dear Father Please just show me the biggest buck around here." I know now exactly what happened. My Heavenly Father did exactly as I had prayed. He showed me the biggest buck around here, and wow he was big!

Through Christ I can do anything. Without him I can do nothing!

I did not tell Rod about my prayer or the almost immediate answer to my prayer. I sat there in awe with what I had just witnessed.

We spent the rest of the day attempting to find the range of hills that the big buck seemed to disappear into. I was pretty much subdued and quiet from my experience that afternoon. I had decided that the next morning I would take the first legal buck we came across and we would head for home.

We got a buck shortly after daybreak, and packed up and started down the road for home. After a few hours I was finally able to share my prayer with Rod, and the remarkable answer, that he had witnessed.

Chapter 48

One afternoon while driving home from Clarkston, I turned right going up Asotin Creek Road. After going around the first little swerve I could see a sheriff's patrol vehicle off on the left side of the road, about 250 yards ahead with a radar gun pointing my direction. I was traveling 40 miles per hour, so I slowed immediately to 25 miles per hour just before reaching the 25 mile speed limit sign that was about 100 yards before the patrol vehicle.

As I was approaching the patrol vehicle the deputy inside turned on his red and blue lights and stopped me. He gave me a citation for driving 40 miles per hour in a 25-mile zone. I went on home and ran into Gerald Hodson and mentioned the incident. Gerald said that the local City of Asotin traffic court had a bad reputation. Apparently they had stepped on lots of toes locally.

I went back down the hill to Asotin to check and see what the actual speed limit was in the area where I'd been written up. The speed limit was 55 miles per hour, and did not change until reaching the 25 miles per hour sign just in front of where the patrol vehicle was parked, working radar.

I went into the city office and entered a plea of not guilty for the citation I had been issued. The City Clerk was upset because of my not guilty plea. She went on to explain that the trials were expensive. The trial was set so I went ahead and collected my evidence, which included photos proving it was not a 25 mph speed zone where the deputy had issued the speeding ticket.

The day of the trial arrived. They had a makeshift courtroom put together, in a rear office. The judge arrived and the City Attorney with Deputy Sheriff Roger Kepper. The judge called the court to order and asked for the defendant to come forward and sit in a chair in front of the desk, which I did. There was a group of people gathered around behind me, and they were all standing. The judge told me to give my name and for whom I worked for last. "My name is Gary Gunkel and my employer for the last seven years has been the City of Seldovia."

"Go ahead," the judge said, "and tell me your story." I did not say anything. Again the judge told me to tell my story. And when I did not say anything the judge with an angry voice told me to tell him what happened! So I went ahead and laid out the facts as to what had occurred. I explained to the judge why I was not driving 40 miles an hour in the 25 mph zone.

The judge asked the deputy what he had seen. Deputy Kepper stated he saw the defendant doing 40 miles an hour in a 25 mile zone. The Judge stated "that is good enough for me," then looked straight at me. I then requested that we go to the scene so he could see what we were talking about. The judge responded, "That was not necessary. You are guilty!"

"Judge you asked me who my last employer was and I told you the city of Seldovia. I did not tell you that for those seven years, I was their Chief of Police. Then the five years before that I was an Alaska State Trooper. And before that, I was a police officer for the city of Anchorage for two years. Your actions were strategized to intimidate me, by sitting me down, then surrounding me with standing people, and forcing me to give my side of the story without hearing the so called case against me.

"First of all you violated all kinds of my rights. I am presumed not guilty until proven guilty. I do not have to say anything in court until there is a case made that I have done something wrong. I have the right to cross-examine anyone that testifies against me. I was not given the opportunity to question your witness. I will not be paying any fine you might charge me. I am outraged at what has just taken place. You can lock me up! But be assured, I will be going over to the courthouse to file an appeal against you. I am appalled and ashamed at the glimpse of your legal system you have just shown these people."

I got up and went to the courthouse and contacted a deputy prosecuting attorney in his office and asked for the RCW (Revised Code of Washington) on appealing a City of Asotin traffic case. When asked, I told him about the traffic court. He said wait a minute and called the city office. He urged me to go back over to the city office and talk with the City Attorney. I did and he requested that I please give him a day, and he would be talking to the judge. He felt sure all charges would be dropped against me. The next day I was notified all charges were dropped.

The City Clerk made it a point to tell me that I should run for County Sheriff. She said it would not take you long to get things right.

We had just completed a poor fishing year, and now were on our way home. Chuck Fred, a neighbor and friend, had been commercial fishing with us in Alaska, was flying home with me in the airplane. Ann and the rest of the crew had flown home on a commercial airlines the same day we left King Salmon. It took Chuck and I three days in our little airplane.

We had been pushing dark trying to get out of Canada and were now lining up on the runway in Oroville, Washington for a landing. We landed in the last daylight, and now we were tying down our airplane. For some reason a hamburger just did not seem as good in Canada as it did the USA.

It was a mile or maybe a little farther to our dinner, but stretching our legs after the flight felt good. We had both been in that airplane for the most part of two days, so a good hamburger was the reward for our walk to town. The walk back helped to settle dinner and got us ready for bed. We got our sleeping bags and sleeping mats out and spread them out, one under each wing. It had started to rain lightly. We talked about the commercial fishing season and the slow fishing of this season compared to the last year. We got into our sleeping bags and settled in for the night. We both decided that it was not the

257

end of the world. Chuck had taken his vacation to go fishing, but now it was back to work for him. I told Chuck that I was looking for something to do after harvest this year. I knew law enforcement but we'd see what comes along.

We packed up the next morning and landed in Lewiston four hours later. Ann and Judy drove down from the ranch to meet us and haul the rest of our load home. At home, Ann told me she had heard that the sheriff position was up for election this fall. But to run for that office I would have to turn in an application before 5 p.m. the following day. When we left Alaska I had already served in law enforcement for 14 years, and I had become sick and tired of handling drunks, and domestic violence cases. I was not excited in getting involved in all this again. But I did need a job. At this time I did not have any idea about the current law enforcement problems in Asotin County. I did not know the issues and frequency of drunkenness at the Asotin County Fair, and other events. Right now I had a little less than a day and a half to make up my mind.

Ann and I went again to visit Marilyn and Gerald Hodson to see what their thoughts were on the subject. Gerald was an elected member of the school board, and belonged to several community organizations. They both were enthused at the idea of me running for sheriff. They pretty much stayed away from the County Fair. In a recent fair a young high school girl had disappeared and had not been heard from since. Marilyn said that several of the last fairs had erupted in full-blown riots. After leaving the Hodsons' I went down to the County Auditor's office by late afternoon to find everything they had about the sheriff's position, and to pick up papers to enter the race. I had not yet decided to jump in, but kept my options open.

The next day we did lots of praying about the sheriff thing. Our exploration uncovered some big problems in law enforcement involving drug abuse. What was going on? Nothing appeared to be happening within the sheriff's office! This got my interest up. By walking into the sheriff's office I learned that the sheriff only comes in once a month to pick up his paycheck. No one in the office knew me from Adam. What is going on here? Why are they giving out this type of information? It had been reported the current sheriff had serious heart problems, and was not making appointments. There were lots of unanswered questions and my interest was starting to boil. I also received reports that some deputies had refused to enforce the law because of their own fear! Now this was turning into a challenge. I remembered the problems with the City of Asotin criminal justice system from my own experience six months earlier.

Early afternoon on the last day I went down to file the papers. The clerk taking the papers said that I needed to declare what party I belonged to and I did not know. I started counting back the last three elections and whom I had voted for. I had voted Republican a few more times than Democrat so I put down Republican. When I did the clerk started laughing, and when I asked why, she said she was sorry for laughing, but the last time a Republican had won Sheriff in Asotin County was 1917. That really surprised me. I did not realize that by far the biggest political party in Asotin County was Democrat. That just shows how much attention I paid to politics. But I had just gotten the ball rolling, and now was time to get involved!

My plan was simple and extremely effective. First I start gaining the respect of the people by giving them 24-hour coverage with the same amount of people. Never before has Asotin County had 24-hour coverage. How do we do it? The Sheriff must be a working Sheriff. We will remove the booze from the hands of the kids, and get the drugs off the streets.

There wasn't much time and I needed to get yard signs ordered, start building ten 4' x 8' signs, and get brochures put together. Our strategy became talk to as many people as possible, both by group and through door-to-door visits. I would always leave them with something positive about why I would make a good sheriff, and always ask for their vote.

This turned into a great learning tool. As I was making my way through one neighborhood, people were telling me about a deputy that lived there that always took his vehicle home. At that time it was the policy.

When this deputy was scheduled to go to work he would call in stating he was in-service. Then answering with his hand held radio, taking calls the same as others did in their patrol vehicles. Lots of times he would not even put his uniform on, or even leave home for several hours. This information came from four different people in the neighborhood of the offending deputies. It appears that two different deputies would often use this method of covering their shift while never leaving home.

While my door-to-door campaigning traveled to the community along the highway above Swallows Park, I started hearing stories about the youth, high school and college age kids who were gathering in the parks and along the green belt where the bike paths go along the river. The homes on the hill could see what was going on in the park and green belt. As the weather started getting warmer and the days longer, the younger groups started bringing in coolers loaded with beer, and other cold beverages. The warmer it got the more the beer flowed, then the complaints begin to include topless, full nudity, and a few complaints of open-sex taking place in the park. The mothers with small children, and families filed complaints, but could not get the sheriff deputies to respond.

Ann and I went to a Republican meeting at the Clarkston City Hall to introduce ourselves and make ourselves available to answer questions. With my introduction I went up in front of the gathering. I was asked what I would do if I received a complaint that lots of beer was being consumed in Swallows Park, and there was nudity, and even open sex. What would I do? I answered that I would fairly and impartially enforce the law. Do you mean that you would go down there with hundreds of young people that are drunk and try to enforce the law? "Yes I would!"

"You have to understand I called the Sheriff's Department and tried to get them to go down to Swallows Park and they refused to do what I demanded them to do. I insisted they enforce the law as that is what they were hired to do. They refused to go down there. They were afraid! Do you mean you would go down there?"

I must have looked perplexed. I raised both hands up and Ann interrupted me saying, "I am here to tell you he would go down there." The whole room burst out laughing as Ann drove our point home.

The man asking the questions, Don Katsenburger, became an ardent backer and a close friend. Don hit the nail squarely on the head. To get the problems back under control all that needs to be done is to enforce existing law.

The Asotin County Fair had another volatile spot known as the Snake Pit. The street dance erupted into an annual riot for three out of the last four years. A quick check of traffic accidents in Asotin County over the four-year term of the previous Sheriff revealed that there had been 24 deaths on the county roads and 23 of them were alcohol related, mostly teenagers. I believed that a lot of those problems could be changed by eliminating drinking in public and putting a stop to keggers. We can do it, and will do it!

The primary election was in early fall. I was running against Clarkston PD Head Investigator, Lonni Grimm. I won the Republican nomination.

The current Sheriff, Herb Reeves was retiring as he had major health problems. Chief Deputy Brooks, Asotin County Sheriff department won the Democratic nomination big against four other candidates.

I knew I would need a solid Chief Deputy to help me tackle what was shaping up as a major undertaking. One name kept coming forward with nothing but good things being said about him. He had been in law enforcement for several years and had stood out as a man of integrity wherever he went. I called and made an appointment to meet with Ron Laverne and his wife. When we got together I told them of my background in law enforcement and what I had so far planned on accomplishing. I pointed out, as Ron was aware, of the shortage of manpower we had in Asotin County, which was due to the shortage of funds to operate in all county offices, not just the sheriff's office.

During the evening we discovered that the Laverne's and the Gunkel's both placed Jesus Christ number one in their lives. I told Ron of my plans to reorganize the Sheriff's Posse, into one group of reserve officers, that we would train and qualify them to meet the state reserve officer qualifications. That would leave those in the Posse still doing search and rescue, and fire fighting in outlying areas.

Then we talked about the fact that Asotin County had no jail, and had to beg jail space from neighboring counties, taking prisoners as far as Spokane County, two and a half hours one way. The city of Clarkston did have a six bed jail that the state had condemned. I felt that with the help of the county commissioners, especially Commissioner Bernie McCabe and Commissioner Neil Ausman we had a chance to get a new county jail.

Ron Agreed to join me as Chief Deputy if I got elected, and to work as a team in bringing fair and impartial law enforcement to Asotin County. Then it was time for me to get back to door-to-door.

Chapter 49

Election night was November 2, 1982. I started picking up campaign signs in down town Clarkston with my pickup about mid afternoon. I had put a lot of time and effort into this election. Getting out and doing some hard work felt good instead of sitting around being nervous. I got home just before seven with most of the signs gathered up. And listened to the election returns. Whoopee! We won.

Then the work really began. I received an invitation to the Washington Sheriff's Association, and the Washington Police Chief's and Sheriff's Association, held in Tri-Cities just a week and a half after the election.

I had gone into the Sheriff's Office and asked some questions I had not felt easy asking before. I had found that the Asotin County Sheriff's Department did not have an Operations and Procedures Manual. The department was union, so without the manual it would be impossible to apply any discipline. That meant that there was no dress code, or protocol in dealing with a high-speed chase. The only way to set limits was through following an Operations and Procedure Manual.

When I registered for the three-day meeting I requested several procedure manuals from other sheriff departments. Ann and I were not disappointed with the meeting and the wealth of information gathered at the meeting. I found that I would need to attend a two-week refresher course to be certified as a police officer in the state of Washington. Washington accepted the two academies, training and curricula from Alaska, and the refresher course would be in the last part of January.

I called Ron Laverne as soon as I got back, and we spent hours pouring through the policy and procedure manuals selecting one, and then working through each policy and procedure selecting the wording that we both liked and that would work best for our community. Sometimes we ended up combining several together and rewriting them. It took us most of the time before Christmas getting what we agreed was a good manual to start with.

On December 27th, 1982 at 2 p.m. I was notified to come to the Asotin County Courthouse, where the Asotin County Auditor, LaDora Smith would swear in the latest winners of the fall elections.

Raising my right hand, "I Gary Gunkel, do solemnly swear that I will support the Constitution and laws of the United States and the organic act and laws of the State of Washington, and that I will faithfully and impartially perform and discharge the duties of the office of Asotin County Sheriff according to the law, to the best of my ability."

And I added. "So help me GOD!"

The administering of the oath of office would take effect on January 1, 1983 and my duties would last four years. Taking that oath of office was a very sobering experience for me. I felt the responsibility settling in. I started this project because I needed a job, but then found a huge challenge developing. I felt confident and up to the challenge.

Chapter 50

January 1, 1983 I knocked on Sheriff Herb Reeve's residence in Clarkston, Washington and picked up his sheriff's patrol vehicle and keys to the sheriff's office. Then I was off to my first day on the job in the basement of the courthouse in Asotin, Washington.

My first official duty as Sheriff is to write a directive instructing all deputies to bring their patrol vehicles to the Sheriff's Office where the patrol vehicle would remain at the end of each day's shift. Each shift was to begin at the Sheriff's Office. I spent the next two hours reading mail, I left for the day as it was a holiday, and the only person working was a deputy out on patrol.

I did find out that two deputies had quit shortly after I was elected sheriff, so we were short-handed to begin with.

The first day in the office Chief Deputy Laverne spent with all deputies going through the new Operation and Procedure Manual, line-by-line, so everyone knew the protocol for being a member of the Asotin County Sheriff's Office.

We met with the entire staff and thanked those still remaining for staying on with us. We talked about some of the accusations that were floating around and said we were aware of the past but were now looking forward only to what lies in the future. If you want to help us clean up some of the problems around here, we can use the help. We lost another deputy.

The next day Chief Deputy Laverne conducted the same process with the office staff. We received some repercussions from the employee's union, but we were within our rights, and made a few small changes to keep the peace.

I went to our Civil Service Board and they only had two names on their list. They already had started advertizing and testing, and would have a new list in a month.

The head man, Jeff Molder in the local Army Engineer's Office, called and came in to talk to me. When he arrived he wanted to know if I had meant what I had said while campaigning about stopping the beer parties and drunks along the green belt and park along the river. I told him that was the plan. As soon as it started getting warm we would be there. Jeff said he would help by getting money from the Army Engineers for an additional man for me during the summer. He would get the paperwork in now, to get me an extra man to work the area starting May 1 through September 31. Just having a man in uniform in the park area to greet the visitors, with the no alcohol allowed signs should go a long way to solve the problem. We hoped it would only take a few tickets to avoid further problems.

Once we put the man down there I was sure the Lewiston Morning Tribune would stop by to visit with me. It never hurts to get a little free advertising.

During the campaign for sheriff I had been asked how I was going to solve the burglary and theft problems in the county. There had been lots of stolen property reports. I responded that I would be calling on the citizens to give us a call. There are over 16,000 pairs of eyes in this county and no one intentionally does something in front of an officer. So we need help from you! If you see something suspicious, give us a call.

Lorry McCroskey, a local contractor, had contacted me volunteering to head up a block watch program. And we were just getting it off the ground.

Lorry and I worked together organizing the first couple of block watches and then he took over and it took off like wildfire. The Block Watch was our eyes and ears, and with all the calls generated we started making cases and getting some bad guys put in jail. The community was getting involved.

One of our deputies discovered a local businessman that had a group of thieves working for him. He would tell them what he wanted and they would go out and steal it for him. This had been going on for quite awhile and it was difficult putting together a case. We were getting close though. The problem was that the public were all scared of him, and afraid of retaliation. No one had been able to get him. But we did, we finally were able to gain the confidence of one of his young thieves and accomplices, which helped to earn Walter Adams a two-year stay in Walla Walla State Prison. I owed a special thanks that went to deputy Tom White for doing a very good job on that investigation.

At a reorganization meeting with the Asotin County Sheriff's Posse, we were surprised by a big turnout. There were thirty plus guys who came, but not all wanted to become part of the reserve officers training program I had been promoting. Up until now the primary job of the Sheriff's Posse had been fire fighting in the backcountry, and search and rescue. But there was also interest in the reserve officer training. We had already contacted the State Training Center and had established the required training programs, with the correct amount of hours in each of the different topics.

We were establishing volunteer support. The Prosecuting Attorney would teach about probable cause, and the other do's and don'ts of putting together criminal cases. Local juvenile authoritie instructors would teach procedures for arresting and handling juveniles. We used in-house instructors for teaching traffic investigation, handling prisoners, and many other day-to-day duties of deputy sheriffs.

The Search and Rescue group and rural fire fighter groups of the Sheriff's Posse trained and adopted a new and revised procedures manual. Most of the fires we respond to are assisting local farmers fighting fires in fields in and around rural ranches. Using small slip tanks in the back of pickups, and lightweight 4-wheel drive vehicles. We were not an initial response fire department. We also had a small tanker used to get water to hard to reach area's assisting local ranchers. The much larger county fire department was better equipped, and trained to handle large fires.

We ended up training a class of fourteen men to be the first academy of reserve deputies. The class committed to just under a year and a half, for two to three hour classes, one night a week. After conducting background checks of the posse members entering the academy, Ron Laverne agreed to run the academy. He lined up the instructors, kept all records necessary, and I would help by making my time available whenever I was needed.

We were excited about volunteers that were accredited by the State, and properly trained. This was another way to get help.

Chapter 51

An early Monday morning in February began when two women and a man came into my office telling me of a dance to be held at the Asotin County Recreation Center, located in Clarkston Heights. It was scheduled for Friday, February 18th, and they said that they were part of a group that had formed to combat the wild, drunken parties that started at high school dances in our community. "We heard you say you could stop that type of behavior."

That was the start of several reports that came in the following week. I notified Chief Deputy Ron about the dance and we went ahead and planned to provide our presence at the dance.

We decided to make three regular officers available on-call, and we would deploy a duty deputy for the event. We would also provide three Posse members. We went ahead and rented three school buses in advance if we needed to transport the arrested kids from the recreation center to the Sheriff's office in Asotin. We had to get these kids' attention before any more of them ended up dead! Thursday the 17th I was hearing rumors that they knew we were aware of dance, and so we risked cancelling two of the school busses.

Then we received positive word at 10 in the morning on the Friday that the kids all knew we were coming to the dance to bust them if they were drinking and that we were bringing along a school bus to take them to jail. Ron and I talked it over and decided with them knowing we were coming, we decided to cancel the third school bus. We decided to have our team come in early and show up at the dance to impress them that we meant business. Friday evening we were getting ready to leave the office when State Patrolman, Rod Schmidet called the Sheriff's office on his radio saying, "Where is the Sheriff? There are drunken kids all over the place." Then he radioed in that he was stopping a 1975 Chevrolet in which the driver appears to be intoxicated. A couple of minutes later he arrested a 17 year old boy and two passengers and charged them with illegal consumption of an illegal beverage. "Tell the Sheriff I am a half block from the Recreation Center and there are drunks everywhere."

"OK, let's go!" We left the Sheriff's Office, in three patrol vehicles.

The Recreation Center was located at the end of a road where it opened into a large parking lot in front of the building. We passed by State Patrolman Rod Schmidet who was just getting ready to leave for the city holding cell. Rod had three prisoners he was taking to the Clarkston City Police Department. We turned up the road to the Recreation Center, positioning our vehicles so that they blocked all exits from the parking lot.

There was a line of young people who were entering a door where a security guard stood. Just inside the door the young people going to the dance were paying for tickets and going into the dance where a local band was playing. Stopping and talking to people in line going in, almost all of the participants had the odor of alcohol about them. It was obvious they had been drinking alcohol before arriving, and most were under the legal age for consuming such beverages. Several people in the line were apparently feeling the effect of the alcohol as they were unsteady on their feet, and their voices slurred.

Now what do I do? I was told that everyone attending would be drinking. Even when they understood we were coming, they came anyway under the influence. And some of the students were still consuming alcoholic beverages.

By this time I do not have the manpower to process hundreds of juveniles or equipment to transport them, but the dance is being held on county property, and the law is being violated right here. I cannot just leave. Liability could be a problem.

The band was just finishing a song so I went to the leader of the band and told him the dance was over. He turned his back on me and started another song. I went over to the amplifier and pulled the plug. That got his attention, so he came over and started complaining. I told him the dance was over. The law is being violated here with minors possessing and consuming. The dance is over.

In the parking lot vehicles had started lining up to leave. So we started checking drivers to make sure that each driver was not impaired by alcohol. We did not have to search any of the vehicles. We just told them that it was against the law for a minor to possess any beer or any beverage containing alcohol. The young people ended up pouring out case after case of beer in the parking lot. The kids were really well behaved when someone let them know exactly how far they could go. We ended up arresting five young people, for various charges, including damaging public property and minor consuming.

I was not prepared for Monday and Tuesday. The phone started ringing early and never quit. I was not able to get away from the phone. Our office staff kept score with the good guy calls at 85% with the bad guy calls running at 15%.

After the dance I found out that Principal Curtis Bowers of Clarkston High School stopped sponsoring dances because of drinking problems, littering, and damage outside of buildings where the dances were being held. They had previously used Clarkston High School and then switched to the Recreation Center, where this dance was held.

I contacted the Clarkston High School asking for them to start sponsoring dances again. I feel strongly that you have to give the kids social activities, with proper guidance, or they will create their own activities without proper guidance. Keeping things under control is easy. Do not assume you cannot keep alcoholic beverages out of the hands of minors! If you need any further assistance just let me know.

Within two weeks after getting elected Sheriff, I received a call from a person living just a few blocks from the police department. I went by to visit them and they asked, "When you were campaigning you came by and said you would work on the drug problem in our county. Is that true?"

"Yes, do you have a problem in your neighborhood inside the city?"

"Yes I do, that house right there, pointing to a house near where he lived. "We see people coming to the door, see them talk, watch them roll a cigarette and light it, exchange money for something in a baggie, and leave."

"Have you talked to the Clarkston Police department about this?"

"Yes, but they do nothing about it. We have called while it is happening and they never come."

I asked, "Is there anyone else in your neighborhood complaining?" He pointed out two other houses close by. I told him that I would talk to the two other people and then contact the Chief of Police and if there were no response I would do the investigation myself.

I received similar reports from the neighbors and early the next morning I called Clarkston Chief of Police, Andy Anderson and told him I had received a phone call reporting drug sales in his city by three different people. Their complaint was that nothing ever happened. He told me that he would look into the problem, so I thanked him.

I waited a week then called the complainant back and he reported that he had heard nothing. So I waited another week and called again. There still had been no word from the Clarkston Police Department.

It was obvious that the upper echelon of the Clarkston Police Department was not interested in working drug cases. This had been the problem for the last couple of years. Talking to the Idaho State drug people in their office in Lewiston, the local drug dealers in the valley were driving out of Idaho into Clarkston or Asotin to do their drug deals. They were doing this because neither the Asotin County Sheriff's Department nor the Clarkston Police Department was working drugs. They freely reported that you could do drug deals over in Asotin County and never get busted. We planned on changing that!

I knew what was involved in obtaining a search warrant. In Alaska in my early years in law enforcement I received extensive training while attending both the Anchorage Police Department Academy, and two years later, at the Alaska State Troopers Academy. At that time we were required to do all our own misdemeanor complaints on every arrest. Under certain circumstances we had to fill out the affidavit for a search warrant and, then the actual search warrant. This was especially needed for probable cause (information to make a reasonable person believe that someone had done something illegal).

This type drug case was difficult to put together without getting someone to make a buy of drugs from the suspect. Without evidence identifying the material being sold as an illegal drug there is insufficient evidence to make a case and we would lose.

We have changed.
Different sheriff, different men, different uniforms.

During the investigation we put together all the probable cause we could scratch up. We used many observations of drug deals going down as probable cause. The single observation of the witness walking by the suspect's residence and smelling what she identified as marijuana being smoked by those making the sale, ties it all together and tips the probable cause our way. It was late afternoon when we got together with the Prosecuting Attorney, who put the affidavit for search warrant and the search warrant together. I took these documents to the District Court Judge, and was sworn in and witnessed the judge sign the search warrant.

Taking these documents with me I picked up Chief Deputy Ron, and another deputy and we drove to the residence of the Clarkston Chief of Police where I knocked on his front door. His wife answered the door and got him out of bed. I told the Chief that I had come into the City of Clarkston and worked the drug case that I had called him about. I have just gotten a search warrant and we are going to execute the search warrant. If you would like to come along you are welcome to do so. He thanked me and called his head investigator. When we were all together, we went to the suspect's house. I was not out to get the Chief of Police, I was trying to recruit his department's help.

When we arrived at the suspect's house, the place was a total mess, with dirty clothes piled everywhere. We did find marijuana in a bedroom, but not a large amount. We placed the woman living there under arrest for possession of marijuana, a misdemeanor. We transported her to the City of Clarkston holding cell.

Chapter 52

Everything from supplies to uniforms was almost non-existence in the Sheriff's Office. When my term started January 1, all the uniforms were showing signs of wear. There were no replacements in the closet. Another of the problems I inherited was a terrible reputation for the department. It was now time to order new uniforms. After talking it over with Ron, who preferred the old style, I decided that we had just made a huge change losing almost half of the old staff so a change in staff, policy, and leader will reflect even more with a change in uniform. There were so few of us, it is important that people notice when we are around. That actually gives the appearance that there were more of us than there really was. I can testify to the fact that it worked. That is a common strategy of the Alaska State Troopers.

I did some checking and found there was no restriction on what uniform was worn by a Sheriff's Department in the State of Washington. So we placed the new uniform order, royal blue trousers with gold stripe piped in red down the outside trouser seams. The hat would be a blue Stetson, campaign style, and a lighter blue shirt. See, we were different!

Our local probation officer, Jerry Order called saying one of his clients living in Clarkston was reported to have been selling drugs. He stated he did not need a search warrant to search his apartment, but was requesting backup to go in and investigate. I took a couple of men and under his direction we entered a house a couple of blocks outside Clarkston city limits. Finding the man home, we entered and conducted the search, not finding the drugs described by the informant. The man on probation said that the drugs were in the vehicle parked out front, but it was not his vehicle. We went out and looked through the windows but could see no evidence of drugs.

The vehicle was parked in the driveway in front of his house, but the probation officer's authority did not extend to this vehicle. I called the Prosecutor's Office and requested a search warrant. After getting back with the search warrant for the vehicle, we got a locksmith to open the trunk. It only took him a few minutes and there it was, over two pounds of Marijuana, and right beside that were two boxes with hundreds of pills in each box! That was the biggest drug bust in the valley in a long time. Way to go Jerry. Any time you need help, just call.

Next up was the 1983 Asotin County Fair. Jeff Mack, a member of the rodeo committee on the fair board, was applying to the Washington Alcohol Control Board for a license to serve beer at the street dance across from the courthouse in an empty building they called the Snake Pit. He was informing me that they were also getting a license to serve beer at the rodeo grounds. I sat right down and answered back by mail that three out of the last four years the street dance at the Snake Pit had erupted into full-blown riots.

The riots resulted in damage to several patrol vehicles and fights all over town. It was just one big drunken brawl. The Clarkston Police Department was called in, 10 extra state patrol officers were sent down for the fair, and the previous year they even had to request help from the Lewiston Police Department.

That letter got the board to pull the permit, so we thought we had won the battle. The Lewiston Tribune again sent another reporter by to ask how I was going to keep things under control. I said, "No problem, we will just enforce the law. It is against the law to drink in public, and the Asotin County fairgrounds, streets, and sidewalks are all public places."

The Lewiston Tribune reporter referred to the high school dance that February, giving critical reference to how we had shut it down. One of the editorial page writers stated that Sheriff Gunkel had a .50 caliber machine mounted on top of the courthouse in Asotin. I was amazed at how many people had read the paper and asked me about the machine gun. After the second person asked about it I had to go and buy a paper to see what they were talking about.

There was a meeting called mid-morning in the county commissioners chambers. I thought the commissioners had called the meeting, but when I arrived none of the commissioners were up front where they sat while presiding over meetings, though a couple of commissioners were present. There were also three different people who had done a lot of work on my campaign for sheriff, and the rest were men and women that were very prominent people in the county, most whom I knew and respected. When I sat down, they all turned their chairs and sat down facing me, in a half circle. One of the commissioners, Erne Mason started in, "With the fair coming, we need to plan on how we are going to take care of the people during the fair. It is like a big holiday, so we would appreciate it if you would back off on the drinkers."

"Are you telling me that I am not to enforce the law?"

Everyone there made a statement of some sort that they wanted me to back off and let things be like it had been in past years. I got up to speak and everything got very quiet.

"It was just three months ago that I was in this room and I took an oath. I, Gary Gunkel, do solemnly swear that I will support the Constitution and laws of the United States and the organic act and laws of the State of Washington, and perform and discharge the duties of the office of Asotin County Sheriff according to law to the best of my ability. Do not ask me to violate my oath."

I waited a short time and when there was no response, I left the room. That was not a good political move, but it made me feel good.

Chapter 53

The County fair was to open on Wednesday. On Tuesday morning of fair week I got a call from Lewiston, Idaho PD about a homicide in North Lewiston. The suspect had just shot a man in the head with a small caliber handgun. We received information that he was going to the 1900 block on 13th street, just south of Clarkston in Asotin County.

I was in the office and the duty deputy was John Broughman. John and I got in different patrol vehicles and headed for the address. John was right behind me as we approached the property. The suspect's white pickup was in the large circle driveway that comes off 13th Street. As I pulled into the driveway blocking one entrance, I radioed John to cover the second entrance to the driveway. We got out of our cars and waited a few minutes, then I motioned to John and we started towards the residence from the two positions. Between both of us we could see the entire front and both sides of the house. There was an open hill behind the house so we would be able to see if someone tried to escape from the rear of the building. John had his riot gun with a round in the chamber and I had my service revolver, a .357 magnum Smith & Wesson. I went up to the door and John stayed back far enough to see if someone went out the back. I knocked and an older woman came to the door. I asked if Tom Johnson was there and she said yes and invited us in. I could see Johnson seated in the living room. I waved for John to come on up to the entrance of the house and I went through the door. I moved to my left, leaving room for John to enter to Johnson's right. I stepped forward and asked Johnson to stand up and upon searching him I found he was not in possession of a weapon. I asked the woman if Johnson had been out of this room since he arrived and she said he had gone to the restroom. I directed John to go to the bathroom and search for a handgun. John came back in a few minutes later holding a wet pistol with his pen through the trigger guard. He said he found it in the tank of the toilet. I placed Tom Johnson under arrest for murder. We loaded the prisoner in John's patrol vehicle and took him to the Clarkston city jail. Johnson said he would waive extradition, so I contacted our prosecutor to set up the extradition of the prisoner to be transferred from Washington State across the river to Lewiston, Idaho while in custody.

On the way to the jail I radioed our dispatcher to notify the Lewiston PD that we had captured their suspect and had found a hidden handgun. Then after depositing the prisoner in jail we returned to the office and to the county fair.

Word had come to the office from an informant through the Clarkston police department that a hit man may be going after Sheriff Gunkel during the Asotin County fair. With no interest in becoming a martyr, we finally located a bulletproof vest at the Whitman County Sheriff's office to borrow. They brought it down for our fair. I put it on the first evening and wore it for a half hour. That thing was hot, heavy and uncomfortable. I did not need something like that to keep me safe.

The Washington State Patrol assigned 10 patrolmen to Asotin County for the weekend of the county fair, because of the high volume of drinking drivers on the roads during past fairs. In addition, we had 12 men in the Sheriff Posse that were about one fourth through their certification training program for state certification. We used them as night watchmen, under the supervision of our deputies.

Jeff Mack, working with the Asotin County fair board putting on the rodeo and the street dance went back to the Alcohol Beverage Control Board again trying to get a permit to serve beer. He told them he had hired a newly formed security company from Lewiston, Idaho. There was not time to communicate and receive an answer by mail, so I called the Beverage Control office and asked what they knew about the security company that the fair board had hired. They said not much, only that the security company consisted of six people, which should ensure keeping things under control.

I told them I had done a background check on this company. All of the security guards would be armed while working. Two of them had been convicted of felonies with several misdemeanor crimes. Because I knew that they are convicted felons, I would have to arrest those two, and put them in jail if they showed up with firearms. None of them had any professional training to perform duties as security officers.

I had also researched and found that there was a good security outfit in the valley, but I guess they were busy. The supervisor from the Washington State Beverage Control Board responded, "OK, we will reject their application to serve alcohol at the fair this year."

Finally some good news, our new uniforms had arrived about a week before the fair. Our officers were in the new uniforms and the humorous reports were that the sheriff's deputies were reported to be everywhere. We were also getting lots of free advertising from the Lewiston Tribune, letting the people in the valley know that it is against the law to consume alcoholic beverages on public property, which included the fairgrounds and the streets and sidewalks of Asotin County.

On Friday night the fair was busy with lots of people in attendance. Thankfully, the phone was not ringing in the office. We were not getting any calls and the Washington State Patrol was not finding drunks on the highway. Neither were we.

I was walking through the rodeo crowd down near the roping arena as they were getting the next batch of calves ready to go. Jeff Mack stood up and yelled "Hey sheriff!" I stopped, and spotted Mack about 30 yards away across the seating area that was full of people. They had set up for spectators at the end of the arena. Jeff waved a large Pepsi cup he had in his hand and when he saw I had spotted him he raised the cup and took a long drink, then threw the cup on the ground. He waved to me again. This caused the people in the whole area to break out laughing. I smiled and waved back as I continued on, and this drew a larger roar of laughter. I just kept going.

This struck me as funny, these adults mostly in their 40's and early 50's out here acting like a bunch of kids caught with their hands in the cookie jar, some of them drinking beer disguised in Pepsi cups.

The next morning was the county fair parade. This event is always a headache for the sheriffs' department monitoring the parade route as it winds around with thousands of fairgoers coming into town to watch. That year, four young guys had used a pickup for a float, which was decorated with signs designating it as the "Open Container Patrol." The young men were the hit of the parade as they were busy running through the crowds along the parade route confiscating open containers of beer, and then depositing them into their pickup.

The numbers were unbelievable for Friday. There were no fights anywhere in Asotin, or around the fairgrounds. The 10 state patrol officers down for the weekend could find no drunk drivers. The area down where the carnival was set up was directly behind the courthouse, along the highway next to Asotin Creek. The area in front of the courthouse where the Snake Pit had operated furnishing booze for the street dance in past years was devoid of drunks! This was the area where so many fights had erupted into full-blown riots three out of four of the previous county fairs. It was a pleasure to be able walk through this area seeing young boys and girls walking with their parents, grandparents, high school kids in small groups and young families all safely enjoying themselves. There was no indication of alcohol consumption in or around the carnival concessions and county courthouse.

Saturday had its usual Pepsi cup disguise with beer during the auction, but again, there were no fights in or around the auction barns. The rodeo was outstanding and trouble-free. One of those 10 state patrolmen finally made one drunk driver arrest in Anatone, an unincorporated area with 30-some people 25 miles out of Asotin.

The people responsible for the change of direction of the Asotin County Fair were the citizens in the community. They just needed someone to take a stand. There are only seven officers in the Sheriff's

Department and no one did anything intentionally in front of us. We depended on the community to keep us informed so we could ensure their safety. This was the result of community involvement. Unless the community wants change there is none.

Chapter 54

One of the problems for law enforcement was the county had no jail for prisoners. Past attempts at passing a bond to build new sheriff offices and a jail had failed. The county commissioners were starting another attempt to pass a bond for a jail without new offices for the sheriff. The proposal called for the new jail to be built in Clarkston, where the dispatch would be in the same building as the jail on city property. The past sheriff had fought the idea of building the jail in a different location, preferring it be located near the courthouse and sheriff's office, not six miles down the road. The county commissioners drafted me to help pass the bond by attending public hearings at different locations and talking in support of the bond. We desperately needed jail space so I agreed to support the jailhouse initiative as it moved ahead.

Before the Asotin County fair, we had received approval for another deputy position that was mostly paid for by the Army Corps of Engineers, to help with the alcohol problems in the park that had developed during the prior few years. This position also enabled me to bring more pressure to the DWI driving problems the community had encountered over that time. We were making a huge impact as evidenced when the 10 extra highway patrol officers came to town over the fair weekend and were not able to find any drunk drivers. Where did they go? We had been putting them in jail!

But now this had brought other problems to light in Asotin County. My new deputy, Mike Carpenter was working the night shift and getting most of the arrests when the bars closed. In the State of Washington, any arrest that results in a conviction or guilty plea, automatically causes the driver to lose their drivers license for 90 days. Deputy Carpenter came into my office complaining that these drivers still had their licenses, and as far as he could determine they never had lost them. I gave Mike permission to investigate and determine just where the system was breaking down.

Mike began his investigation at the District Court office. The public disclosure law allowed Mike, as it also allows any citizen, to go into the court files where he found the copy of the arrests and all information including the breathalyzer test administered and the status of the arrested person. Further investigation revealed that every file in the two large drawers of the cabinet still had the yellow copy of the disposition page on the carbon copy of every person that had been arrested. Deputy Carpenter next contacted the Department of Operators Licenses in Olympia. First he gave several names and operator license numbers to see their status. None of the people had any record of arrest on their record. None of their licenses had been revoked or even suspended. This was the second and third drunk driving arrest for some of those people. The yellow carbon copy was supposed to be sent to the Department of Licensing every time they were arrested so they could enforce revoking and suspending operator licenses.

I went straight to Prosecuting Attorney, John Lyden and told him what was going on. He listened with no expression on his face, and I got the feeling he knew exactly what was going on. John answered, "What do you want me to do about it?"

I responded, "You are an officer of the court! Why are you letting this continue?"

John's response, was, "The judge does not agree with the law. He says we have no public mass transit system here, and it is not fair to our local drunks as they cannot get on a bus and get to work."

I reminded him, "We arrest people all the time that do not believe in the law they violated. So what gives the judge and prosecuting attorneys in this community the right to disobey the law?"

I pressed him to speak to the judge. John hesitated and answered, "I will talk with him." The next day he came by and told me he had spoken to the judge and that things were not going to change.

I again asked, "Are you going to do anything about it?"

"There is nothing I can do about it."

I felt like I had just been kicked in the stomach. The criminal justice system in this area was corrupted to the point that they felt they could do anything they wished, despite what the law of the state required. The prosecutor refused to be true to the oath he took when sworn into office. They were setting themselves above the law.

That left me only one way to go and that was to make a rock solid case against District Court Judge, Donald E. Moore. I would start with a group of citizens that I had organized as the Sherriff's Advisory Committee. We asked the judge to come to our meeting. I thought if this group could change his point of view and learn directly from him that they could hold him accountable and encourage him to abide by the law. I informed the committee what had happened when I had spoken with the prosecuting attorney, so they agreed to keep him answering questions.

The questions were about over and this judge was very good with words. So if I wanted to bring out the truth I had to step in. "Judge, may I ask you a few questions?"

"Yes sheriff, what can I help you with?"

"Why did none of our local drunk driving cases make it to the driver's license headquarters in Olympia?"

His answer, "I do my part on the bench, and the office staff does the rest."

"That is not what your staff says, Judge."

The Judge lost it. He spun around as he had started to leave, and looked right at me and said, "The Sheriff better stop rocking the boat, or someone is going to get wet!" Then he left.

There were 22 people at that meeting, and they all heard the judge threaten me. This is exactly what I did not want. There is only one District Court Judge, and one Superior Court Judge in Asotin County. And now I was forced to go after the District Court Judge.

We just lost the first drug case we had made a month before. I had not looked closely at the search warrant or the affidavit until after it was thrown out for insufficient probable cause. Prosecuting Attorney Lyden had not entered more than half the probable cause information that I had provided him in my report. He had left out the probable cause of a witness being able to smell the marijuana being smoked by the defendant, who was selling it. What is going on here? This was my attorney. We were supposed to be working together. I had just learned how important it was to participate more directly.

I received criticism for two reasons: one for going into the city of Clarkston and making a drug case when the Clarkston Police Department had not contacted the complainant. The Public Defender winning the case for his client also said in a statement to the Lewiston Morning Tribune that he liked me and had backed me in the election, and would be glad to loan me a book on search warrants.

We are all a team, I told myself, so I thought, Gunkel keep your mouth shut and keep smiling. Then along came John Mason, the Fish and Game Warden for the State of Washington. He told me he had a search warrant for Jason Anderson house along Asotin Creek to look for marijuana. I asked him where he got his information and he said he'd seen it himself. Then he went on to explain what he really wanted was to get into Anderson's house because he believed that Jason Anderson had stolen a .22 caliber rifle from him and he was hoping to find it there during the search. He wanted me to come along; I believe to protect, him from Jason Anderson, but also to add substance to the search. I told him to get his search warrant and then come back and see me.

At 3:00 p.m. Mason came in with the search warrant. I assigned a couple of deputies to accompany us and we drove the three blocks to the suspect's house. Warden Mason knocked on Anderson's door and served the search warrant. We went through his house in about 45 minutes finding a small amount of marijuana, several rifles, a .22 caliber pistol, but not the game warden's rifle.

I was in my office two days later. a little after 10:00 a.m. when, a reporter from the Lewiston Morning Tribune came to see me. I had seen her around a few times, but she was new. She introduced herself as Joan Abrams. a reporter with the Lewiston Morning Tribune. She said there had been a meeting about one of our drug cases upstairs that morning."

"Yes, I heard there was going to be one. What happened?"

She said, "The Prosecuting Attorney, John Lyden said you had served the original search warrant instead of the copy, so now he had to dismiss all charges."

I said, "What!" coming to my feet. "Are you sure he said I served the warrant?"

Joan seemed taken aback by my question. Checking her notes, she said, "Yes, that is how he phrased it."

"You know that is the 5th straight drug arrest that we have lost?" She nodded. I said, "This is a real surprise, because I never had anything to do with this case. John Mason, the Fish and Game guy was with the suspect a few days ago and witnessed the marijuana in his house. What he really wanted was a rifle that had been stolen from him, and he thought it might be in this guy's house.

"Joan how would you like to do some investigative reporting?"

"I would like that," she said.

"I am having some problems with Prosecutor Lyden and District Court Judge Moore. I am getting some evidence together that the judge does not agree with the law, so he is withholding evidence. I want them to be conducting their duties as the law requires. In a few minutes, we are going up to the county legal library and I will show you how to look up the administrative code the judge is violating. I will be having a press conference releasing my information."

Joan Abrams was well informed and on her way to getting this case together when she came out of the legal library. She could see our case clearly.

I called the District Court office and got Mary Gene Seay, the District Court Clerk. I told her that I was coming to get copies of the eight cases I had looked up a few days before. She told me she could not give them to me, and I responded that the public disclosure statute says anyone has access to those papers. "You are not allowed to keep them from the public." I grabbed the book with the public disclosure law and started up to the District Court Office.

As I came up the last step out of the stairwell I looked down the hall. Mary Gene Seay saw me and hurried out of her office and ran into the Prosecuting Attorney's Office. As I started that direction, she went to the far end of the office and turned right into the Deputy Prosecutor's office. As I went through the door the clerk pointed to Deputy Prosecutor, Bill Acey's office. I walked to the door and stopped just inside. Mary Gene Seay had gone around Acey's desk getting as far as possible from me. I looked at Bill and said, "I came up to look at the DWI arrest files. Mary indicated I could not see the files. I brought the public disclosure statutes," with my finger holding the document open to the page. I looked at her and asked if she wanted to read it. She stated she did not know how to read that stuff. I looked at Bill and asked if he would explain it to her.

Bill looked at me and answered in a raised, belligerent voice, I will not explain anything to her. I looked at Mary, then back to Bill still sitting behind his desk.

"OK, I try not to do anything when I am mad! You get word to Judge Moore that if he does not get those driving records to me before noon tomorrow, I will go to the Courthouse in Whitman County and get a search warrant for the District Court Office in Asotin

County. All I am doing now is putting together the eight cases I started this investigation on to accompany my letter to the Judicial Qualifications Commission. If I have to go to the next county to get access to these records, I will do an investigation on each record the judge has in those two file drawers." I looked at Mary, "You are more familiar with those files than I am. There are probably 150 to 200 cases upon which I could bring charges."

Bill Acey leaped to his feet and in a loud voice yelled, "FLY AT IT!" With that I turned around and left the office.

My day at the office started at 7:00 a.m. It was 7:06 a.m. when my phone rang the next morning. I answered, and Judge Donald E. Moore came on the phone. "Sheriff Gunkel, this is Don Moore. I am calling to let you know those papers will be available for you as soon as my clerk opens the office at 8 a.m."

I responded, "Thank you, Judge Moore."

The following excerpts from the Lewiston Morning Tribune Friday April 20, 1984

Article by Joan Abrams:

STATE LACKS DWI RECORDS OF EIGHT IN ASOTIN COUNTY

Asotin County Sheriff, Gary Gunkel, Thursday produced driving records of eight people convicted of DWI. None of these certified driving records; received by Sheriff's Office on April 4 from the state Department of Licensing, indicate any conviction for drunken driving. All eight convictions were made between January 1 and March 14 of this year. David Kirk, administrator of the DOL at Olympia, said convictions should appear on driver's records within a week to 10 days from sentencing. A check by the Lewiston

Morning Tribune of the court records of all eight DWI offenders Thursday show they had pleaded guilty and were given deferred sentences of one year. All records of those convictions, including the yellow copy of the disposition intended to go to the DOL, were still contained in the case file.

Court Clerk Mary Gene Sea stated the cases were still pending, and until the judge had fully disposed of them (after the year's deferment) they would stay there. If an offender successfully completes the deferment period, the record of conviction is never sent to the licensing office, she said.

Seay said that the DOL doesn't want anything until you have your final disposition that is until the judge has finished with the case. Seay also commented on the Sheriff's investigation by saying, "Any man who would try to boost his own reputation by destroying another man's is no man. The judge will be able to answer the allegations satisfactorily."

When asked Thursday if it was his intent to not enter the conviction on offenders record, Moore answered "that he understood, from the clerk that that's the way the DOL wanted it handled."

But that is not the way the DOL says it should be done: A conviction of DWI carries a mandatory 90-day license suspension under Washington State law. The DOL is in charge of imposing those suspensions.

A deferred sentence does not mean an offender will be excused from the license suspension, according to James Silva, an Assistant Attorney

General assigned to the DOL. Silva stated, "It appears to me that the tickets should have been sent in if there's been a guilty plea."

"If there has been a guilty plea, which under State law is the same as conviction," Silva said, "then the judge must send the disposition to the DOL. And even if the deferred sentence period is completed successfully, the record of the conviction must remain on the driver's record for five years,"

Moore admitted Thursday, he never researched the rules and now his procedure has changed.

Joan Abrams is now a real investigative reporter. On receiving the hard copies on my end, I finished my reports and sent my reports along to Esther Garner, Executive Director of the Judicial Qualifications Commission in Olympia, WA.

The Judicial Qualifications Commission does not notify anyone of their meetings or the decisions they make. When Judge Moore came back from his meeting with the Qualifications Commission he stated he could not comment on the meeting, but wished he could. Judge Moore finished his term in office as District Court Judge, then retired.

And then in our Superior Court, a 22 year old man that was arrested for taking indecent liberties with a with a minor girl and pled guilty in 1983, had been sent to Eastern State Hospital in Medical Lake for treatment as a sexual psychopath. The hospital staff had informed the court earlier that an evaluation had determined that it would not be safe for him to be at large.

In the hearing it came out that the 22 year old said he did not think he could gain any more benefit from the hospital, and the hospital agreed by granting him a four-day release, so the process had started to see what the court system was going to do with him.

My question to the judicial system is why should he come back to jail? I thank God that the state of Washington still gives the people the right to elect the people in the judicial system. It is just hard for me to believe that after our judicial system was told by the doctors at Medical Lake that in their judgment this person was a sexual psychopath, that they would even consider giving him leave was amazing.

A reporter from the Tribune came to me and wanted my response to the judge rescinding the granting of a four-day release. My answer was no comment. I had highest respect for Superior Court Judge, Jones. He was a true gentleman, and had retired for health reasons. But it seemed unfair to me in that when one of my deputies needed time off to attend his father's funeral, and the county only allowed him three days.

I had been looking at an old case, and this reminded me of the "Boston case" at Clarkston in which a man had ordered his mother's murder, was freed on his own recognizance, and they never saw him again.

Further information from the Tribune regarding the "Boston case" the Prosecutor was Jones and Patrick McCabe of Pomeroy was the judge when the Boston case was in court. According to court records, Jeffrey Boston, then 33 years old put out a $5,000 contract on his mother in the mistaken belief that her early death would increase his inheritance. She was shot to death at her Clarkston home in 1977, the two gunshots blending in with July 4 fireworks.

Chapter 55

Chief Deputy Ron Laverne and I were working with the Drug Task Force in Lewiston. Two State of Idaho detectives had started the drug task force working only drug cases. This cooperative relationship magnified our efforts, as the sister cities of Lewiston, Idaho and Clarkston, Washington share so many issues. Chief Anderson from Clarkston also joined the cooperative, melding the bond between city police department, county law enforcement and state agencies. The first drug bust with the task force was on Thirteenth Street just south of Clarkston. We had set up a buy, and sent an undercover agent in with a wire on, to make a buy . . . But they were out of drugs. It was very frustrating trying to work with these bad guys; they were terrible businessmen.

Meanwhile, another drug case came along that just seemed to fall into our laps at the sheriff's office. There was plenty of probable cause, so I personally had decided to write the affidavit for search warrant and the search warrant. The last five drug cases were lost because of problems with the affidavit for search warrant or the search warrant. With first-hand knowledge of the problems with Asotin County Prosecutor John Lyden's warrants, I bypassed what had developed into a weak link. Little did I know that those long hours I had spent getting the affidavits, search warrants and criminal complaints correct, would pay off for Asotin County.

When I had finished putting the reports together, I took them in with the affidavit for search warrant, and the search warrant that I had prepared, I delivered them to Prosecutor Lyden and he grunted, cleared his throat a couple of times then was quiet. I asked, "Is there anything that needs changing?"

Prosecutor Lyden once again cleared his throat and said, "If that is all you have, it might work." The only thing that was different was that I had included ALL the probable cause in the case report instead of leaving half of it out as he had done in previous cases. Finally, we won our first drug case, after losing five in a row.

The search warrant produced a bust that included lots of drugs, and it had no problems withstanding the legal challenge in court. One difference was that we were able to move on this case because we did not have to buy drugs to make the case. The county commissioners provided us with $300 in the first sheriff's budget I inherited to buy drugs with. I believe that such lack of support probably had something to do with the fact that there were no drug arrests in Asotin County. The only drug cases in Asotin County were a few that had something to do with alcohol, such as DWI, or minor consuming.

It was for that reason we had made the decision to accept the invitation to join forces with the Idaho Drug Task Force. Transactions would cross the state line and we needed their additional cash to make a large enough drug buy to get the big dealers who were bringing drugs here from out of the area. It was our belief that the dealers could not get their money at the bank, so when they have to get more drugs to fill such a large order, they would go directly to their supplier and that is when we could nail them. The last buy the task force made with this dealer was considerable. We let them walk with our money. This provided us with the probable cause to nail this one down. We had ordered up thousands of dollars worth of drugs. Our contact met the bad guys in North Lewiston and there was a partial exchange. Then the bad guy took off in a light green sedan for Spokane, a hundred miles north.

Our team had set up four vehicles and drivers to follow at a safe distance so as not to be made by the suspects. The primary tail at the start was myself using my personal airplane, the Piper PA-12, specially equipped to fly at slow speeds. Ron Laverne served as my spotter. We circled slowly at 3,500 feet. We were in radio contact talking to the head coordinator in vehicle #1 who was now just starting up Highway 95. He was staying behind the suspect a quarter to a half mile back, just catching sight of the suspect occasionally. The other three vehicles were another half mile back, staying out of sight. Every five miles or so, the coordinator would have the current vehicle that was directly behind the suspect vehicle drop back to the last position, trading the lead observer position.

With the airplane and light traffic, the coordinator could keep all but one of the other vehicles out of sight, greatly reducing the chance of getting made by the suspect. After getting to the top of Lewiston Hill, I held my elevation at around 2,500 feet above the suspect and slightly to the right. I was able to keep visual contact with the suspect until he pulled off the freeway using the Division Street off ramp. As we approached Spokane, the four vehicles took over the surveillance. I then withdrew from the surveillance team. This had put me very close to Felts Field in Spokane, so I contacted the tower, landed, and taxied to a parking area near the tower. We waited for our ride.

So far we had been successful keeping the vehicle under surveillance all the way to what appeared to be the drug house in North Spokane Valley. Then our suspects drove back to a large restaurant near the IMAX movie theater to meet our contact. In the restaurant our undercover guy exchanged money for drugs, and then our multi-agency team moved in on the bad guys and arrested them. Our coordinator had set this up earlier with the Spokane Sheriff's Department, who awaited our arrival into Spokane County. As soon as they got together, our coordinator and a Spokane county investigator sat down with a prosecutor and went to a waiting Judge. We received the necessary warrants to conduct the search. With combined manpower of our five officers and the four deputies from Spokane County, we went back and did a search of the drug house. We arrested the three people found in the house, a large amount of marijuana, cocaine, and some hashish. The total street value of the drugs was well over $4,000. We recovered $6,000 in cash, much of which was our buy money. Also seized was one vehicle and we arrested five bad guys. Since the bust took place in Spokane we did not get the credit, but this arrest really dried up the drugs in our valley. It turned out that this group was keeping several small drug pushers in the Lewiston-Clarkston Valley supplied with anything they wanted.

Ron and I caught a ride back to Felts Field and our airplane. Our ride home was much shorter, less than an hour, where it took just over two hours tracking the car to Spokane.

The time spent with the drug task force was well worth it. We learned a great deal about interagency collaboration, with each department contributing and sharing resources. The Idaho State officers also contributed greatly. We knew what to do, but the polish and training along the way created a team that made this large project much easier. We really appreciated the time spent training and bringing us up to speed. Because of the makeup of our team, there were no jurisdictional problems. We were able to take what we learned back to our departments and apply the new experience to each of our respective departments.

Jean Holman, our Civil Service Deputy took a call from the Bureau of Alcohol Tobacco & Firearms out of Missouri, leaving me the following message.

> "There was a Truck and Trailer load of very high grade marijuana which had come out of Asotin County early last fall, to our area in Missouri. The buyers on this end were so impressed with the quality that they had put in an order for two truck and trailer loads of marijuana for the coming growing season. I can't tell you more. That is all I know. Good luck."

"Jean, would you mind calling the county commissioners office and get me on their agenda for tomorrow. The subject will be getting an aircraft line in my budget. I do not need more money, I just need to transfer some funds to that line from one of our other items."

Jean asked "Do you want it in closed Executive Session?"

"No, we want the whole world to know we are flying to find growing operations. It pays to advertise. Anyway we can shut it down will work."

We were a small department with very little manpower and no money. But soon, our office received complaints from a couple of local pilots saying they were scared to fly in certain parts of the county. They were concerned that marijuana growers would start shooting at their airplanes. Then a local news reporter came to me wanting a response. I told them, just let me know where those areas are and I will eliminate the problem.

Chapter 56

The City of Clarkston and the Asotin County Commissioners went together with the project to get a jail built. The bond issue passed and it was decided that the jail would be built in Clarkston on city property, and be operated by the county sheriff. The sheriff's office is located in Asotin near the county courthouse. A new 16 bed jail was now under construction.

The Clarkston City Police Department had been operating with a six bed holding cell, and the next closest jail facilities were in Colfax, which was in Whitman county 45 miles away, or in Pomeroy in Garfield county 45 miles away. We would occasionally have to use Spokane county jail, 100 miles away for long-term prisoners. We had been spending lots of time transporting prisoners, so we were really looking forward to the new jail facilities.

The opening of the jail ended a 10 year drive for a new county jail. Sheriff Herb Reeves began the drive for a new jail, but the two men that should have received most of the credit for getting the jail built was Clarkston Chief of Police Robert K. Anderson and County Commissioner Bernie McCabe. The county could not fund the jail even with the large grant they had to build it. It took the cooperation of the city and county working together, sharing some of the expenses, and agreeing to move the jail to Clarkston instead of near the courthouse in Asotin.

When the jail was nearly finished the local judges started postponing the jail time they were awarding to the newly convicted persons until the new jail was finished. When the jail was finally finished, it took months to address the backlog of prison time to serve.

Celebrating the Opening of the Hoosegow Hotel

(Named and described by Johny Johnson, Lewiston Morning Tribune writer)

Paying guests test new Asotin jail and jailers.

We still have a few rooms available for anyone wanting to see our jail from the inside out. For only $20 we will put you up for the night, feed you supper, breakfast, and give you a T-shirt that reads, "I spent the night in Asotin County Jail."

For reservations call the Asotin County Sheriff. You will have your fingerprints taken and a mug shot to take as a souvenir.

I was locked in twice, once with two women, then another time within a hallway that did have a phone in it. When I picked up the phone I had to make a long distance call to the dispatcher in the control room. She was just on the other side of the door. The only way I could talk to her was to make a collect phone call. Dispatcher Bonnie Albertson answered the phone, and when she was asked if she would take a collect phone call from Gary Gunkel, there was a long hesitation . . . "Oh no!" I was thinking, "It could be a long night in this hallway," but then I was able to let my breath out as Bonnie finally accepted my call, and let me out. Phew!

Clarkston, Chief of Police Bob Anderson, showed up with his security blanket and a great big teddy bear. The prisoners all ate together in a large day room. They were allowed to watch the black and white TV and then everyone went into the largest day room for the evening program.

One of the things the prisoners did not expect was to become a captive audience (pun intended). I had promised Guy Trotter, who always wanted to be an evangelist, an audience for his message. He was the only conservative in that den of liberals at the Lewiston Morning Tribune. The Tribune only let him write one article a week.

I went into the room leaving the door open. Chief Anderson, started to edge towards the open door and then made his rush yelling, "Let's get him!" trying to capture me before I escaped out the open door. With the crowd right on my heels I raced through the door and was able to swing the door closed just in front of Chief Anderson. As it locked, I was able to make my escape. Wow that was a close one!

A short time later, a stolen dogwood tree showed up in the jail that was supposed to have been planted across the bridge, as you would enter Lewiston. According to the jailhouse rumor, it had been left unplanted when they had struck rock and went after a backhoe. When they returned the tree was gone. Clee Manchester, the Jail Commander took Clarkston city council members, Delbert Ells and Ronda Clovis to the telephone where they called Lewiston Mayor Mueller. The mayor soon showed up with his young son Jason and a Lewiston policeman. After identifying the tree that stood about 10' tall, they found they could not get it into the car. Ells promised to haul it back in his pickup when "released from jail the next morning."

Next, a coconut frosted cake arrived for Clovis. There was a file in the cake. But the new jail had no bars. So the prisoners ate the evidence. About this time, jailers Bruce Peters and Don Schmidt who were taking dinner orders entered a corridor and left the door open. Chief Anderson closed the door and locked them in.

The cake with the file was traced to Bette Lynch of Clarkston. She was contacted by phone but refused to go to jail. She must have had a guilty conscience as she showed up later and joined Clovis and McDonald housed in the three cell work release block.

Several prisoners woke up in the middle of the night by a huge black dog with large white spots dancing and playing thc star spangled banner on a squeezebox. Wake up time came at 5:00 a.m. Outside the city was mostly asleep. The sun was rising and another night in Jail was over

Chapter 57

Back to work on another beautiful, August morning with an early morning temperature of 75 degrees, promising a hot afternoon of 100 degrees or more.

I liked flying early in the day in the Snake River canyon and the other canyons, along the borders between Idaho, Washington and Oregon. In the afternoons there were usually thermal winds in these canyons making marijuana patrolling difficult. I would take off from Lewiston, Idaho and fly over to the Asotin County border on the Washington side of the river heading south.

By getting an altitude of 1,500' to 2,000' I could work the Asotin County side of the river from the river's edge well up into the breaks along the river. I would survey the main canyon and any side canyons that came into it, especially those that had water in them. Any green growth received a closer look.

Where the mouth of the Grande Ronde River enters the Snake River, I crossed keeping to the west side of the Snake River going to the Oregon border, and checked those canyons along with the others in the area. So far I have been seeing lots of deer, a few bighorn sheep and some elk, with an occasional small herd of cows. Most of the cattle were in the higher and cooler, Blue Mountains until fall.

This area is very rough country with steep canyons that are hard to penetrate on the ground. I could find no growing operations in this area using the airplane. Several miles up the Grande Ronde River were a few ranches that were accessible by road coming down to the river, from a small town called Anatone. The road is a public road maintained by the county. On reaching the river the public road turned right and went upstream a few miles. There were a few public access areas to the river. The road also went left down river, but most of this road was private. I had permission from Phil and Betty Johnson to go to the end of this road where they owned 100 acres. I paid several visits to this area with a fishing rod, doing a little fishing and a lot of hiking checking green patches I had spotted from the air.

The ranch, located where the road reached the river, was raising a large field of corn, approximately 15 to 20 acres. There was very little tillable ground in this area of the Grande Ronde. This required a lot of time to check out, as the corn could be a cover for Marijuana. As I flew over the corn patch I was looking closely at the interior part of it, but saw nothing that peeked my interest. It would be investigated more closely when I was on the ground.

This area was traveled very little. I always used my personal rig, or borrowed a friend's vehicle. On this kind of investigating I did not know anyone down there, but everyone knew I was the sheriff, and they stayed clear of me.

As I flew over the road coming down from the high country to cross the Grande Ronde River I could see why they called it Rattlesnake Grade. That road zigzagged back and forth around the mountainside then back for several miles. There was a road going up the side of the river that got into an area called Grouse Flats, as you climbed the ridge. There were several ranches scattered across the mountainside that leveled off into several different benches with some grain fields. The largest ranch in this area was the Four O Cattle Company. It spread out for miles in timber, grain fields and lots of grass mixed in with timber. A lot of their property sits in some of the finest clk country in Washington and Oregon.

I had a good look from the air at most of those properties located in Asotin County. I heard they thought I was trying to catch them growing marijuana, as there was lots of airplanes flying over their property especially in the late summer. Most of that air traffic which they thought was my plane was actually other airplanes searching for elk. The newspaper was responsible for giving them the idea

311

that I was after them, as they wrote several articles about me flying searching for marijuana plantations.

I did spot a remote garden near one of the properties. I made the long drive back into the mountains and looked a long time before locating one of the prettiest vegetable gardens I have ever seen.

I learned that most of the marijuana hauled by truck and trailer was grown in an area called Big Springs, not too far from the Grouse Flats area. That was the year before I was sheriff.

Each air search for marijuana took four to five hours of flying time. If I observed any suspicious growth it would also require at least one more trip back on the ground to double check my observations in the air. That would add at least three more hours. The time factor really limited the amount of flying and searching I could accomplish.

That fall we received another call from the Bureau of Alcohol and Firearms in the Missouri office. "We have just received word from our informant that the people in Asotin County were not able to deliver those two truck and trailer loads of marijuana. They said that the new sheriff had taken over and he was all over them. Good Job!"

Chapter 58

Lorie McCroskey, a local businessman that was heading up our block watch program, was going full speed. I went with Lorie to the first couple of meetings, introducing him and the block watch material to the community. Lorie was in the landscape business specializing in waterfalls and small ponds, with bio-systems that would support fish. He would get the block watch set up and install a block watch sign at his own expense. Then as the material instructed, he would get together with those in each home showing them how to make their home safer from burglaries and damage. Often it might just be a light or two, or if there was a window that might be inviting to a thief there are different plants that have stickers or thorns to keep the thief away. Another tool is a light that comes on when censing movement. If they asked for help then he could let them know about his business.

We were getting lots of new block watches established because other people wanted in. They liked the joining together with others in the neighborhood so they could all help each other watch for intruders. This helped promote a cooperative relationship between the public and the sheriff's office, while bringing results. We are catching burglars and that was making the neighborhoods safer. Others in the community seeing our success wanted the same benefits in their neighborhoods. The way we made a difference in our county was by working with the people. They were ready to help, and law enforcement can always use help. Asotin County was poor, so the extra help came in the way of volunteers. The neighborhood block watch program started with seven, but grew to over eighty with more forming every week. These people would meet at least once a month for a potluck dinner, and exchange notes as to who might be leaving town that month. This way everyone could help watch over their neighbor's property. As you can see there are literally hundreds of hours spent working with others in our communities.

The block watch was the cornerstone for what I called my kitchen cabinet members. In the county I had several of these locations. I felt comfortable stopping by to find out what might be going on in their corner of the world. One of these was near Clarkston High School. I thought of Marie as one of my generals. She and I had many visits that lasted an hour or more and she turned into a very good friend. She reminded me of my mom.

Marie and I met again, several years later when I was doing a survey and knocked on her door, in a different area of town. An older lady answered the door and appeared she was hard of hearing. I introduced myself, and she responded, "Oh, I know Gary Gunkel, he is a good friend of mine. Then I knew it was Marie! Not only was her hearing bad, but she could not see very well. I tried to tell Marie that it was indeed me, but she thought my hesitation was because I did not believe her. She grabbed my arm to lead me into her home saying no, Gary Gunkel is really my good friend. Come on in I will show you he is my good friend as she lead me into her kitchen. Right above her table was a framed paper hanging on her wall. I looked at it and the tears started to form in my eyes as I looked at a certificate from the Asotin County Sheriff's Office that Marie was certified as a Block Watch Captain in 1983, signed by me. Marie said proudly, "See! I told you Gary Gunkel was my friend."

Now, I was glad that Marie could not see very well as the tears were running down my face. I responded that yes Marie I am Gary Gunkel and I really am your good friend. I remember all the times I used to come into your kitchen and we would talk. We used to have lots of these conversations, didn't we?

I was supposed to be somewhere else, but right then I realized I was actually right where I was supposed to be. Thank you, Lord for giving me another chance to visit with my good friend Marie. I really saw the devotion and strength that our volunteers gave to the sheriff's department.

That first dance I shut down because the kids were drinking really demonstrated the big problem of alcohol in Asotin County; that and the 23 alcohol-related fatalities in our county the four years before I became sheriff. Another lady volunteer, Jo Jackson stepped forward to help. We had found packed away in storage an old McGruff, The Crime Fighting Dog, costume.

Deputy John Broughman our crime prevention officer joined forces with Jo and together they put together a program addressing theft, with the emphases on booze and drugs. Jo, said, "Take a bite out of crime." During the course of a year the McGruff team, including Super Pup, was in every school in the county, first grade through the elementary grades. The hours donated by just that one volunteer amounted to hundreds of hours, and Jo refused to take money. That was her donation to our community.

In 1986, deputy John Broughman won statewide recognition as the top crime prevention officer in the State of Washington. His partner, Jo Jackson, volunteer and our friend, contributed enormously as the team won the hearts of the students and community. They also put on the bicycle safety program.

Another new program we started in our county was the Chaplain's Program. Several of the pastors in local churches had come forward to assist in delivering emergency messages, or to help a victim or deputy when needed. We encouraged our chaplains to ride along with a deputy once a week, or when they had time. The chaplains worked out a schedule covering each month, so there was always someone on call for an emergency. Working with these guys was a joy.

Volunteers are the key to bringing crime under control, and getting citizens involved in their own community. For the victims of crime, enter the Victims Advocate program. The way the criminal justice system works the criminal gets all the attention and the victim often is left frustrated and emotionally abused. Using a real case, but changing the name, the Smith family's house was burglarized. Later, Smith reported to a deputy sheriff that he will never report another burglary to the sheriff's office again. Not realizing how the system works, Smith said, "The Sheriff turned the burglar loose within two hours, and now my kids are having nightmares thinking the burglars are back. And we still do not have our stolen property back, so that is the last time I will do that again."

To rectify that problem I decided to launch a new program I'd heard about in the Southwest United States. It was called the Victim's Advocate Program. I received the program all laid out on paper. I could find no one else in the State of, Idaho, Washington or the whole Pacific Northwest that was using this program. As far as I was concerned it was the pilot program in our area.

After advertising, 20 volunteers showed up and we started weekly classes. For instructors we used the prosecuting attorney, the district court judge and superior court judge to teach the processing of criminals through the court system. We also used the parole officer, a deputy sheriff and the juvenile court system to learn their roles in the criminal process.

Then we brought in people that work with abused people and furnish housing and protection for those people. In their classes they learned the many different programs and other resources available in our community. Lots of the problems can be taken care of by just knowing the resources available. We also brought together the other social services operating in our community. In general, we learned about the different programs in our community and how they might help our victims.

The once a week classes took almost four months to get through. Twelve of our advocates were ready to go. Nine of the advocate's were senior citizens, who, at that time, had a program that provided free gas for those in the community that were using their personal vehicle in social services as volunteers. This was very important for us as we had problems getting gas enough the first couple of years just for patrol vehicles.

Every month we had volunteers working hundreds of hours, donating to the sheriff's department by the various programs we were sponsoring. Some of the training was done from within, but mostly by other experts working in different areas around our county.

Chapter 59

The Asotin County Civil Service Board, which is appointed by the County Commissioners, is responsible for maintaining a list of qualified applicants for the Sheriff to select from when filling a civil service position. Upon request, they immediately began advertising and testing applicants.

With their permission, I used an emergency hiring clause and interviewed Mike Carpenter, one of their new applicants. I had met Mike about a year earlier and was impressed with him and his ambition. I told Mike that he would have to go through the civil service testing and end up in the top three positions so that I could legally keep him on the job. Mike made it easy for us and ended up in the number one position after all the physical and mental testing.

We hired two more deputies as soon as the civil service board was able to complete the testing and establish a list for me. After the list was finally established, I also hired deputy Derck Laws, and deputy Dean Grover. Then deputy John Broughman was hired.

Deputy Michael Carpenter, our first new hire was one of the automatic non-civil service appointments allowed the Sheriff. The agreement between Mike and I was that Mike would go through all the civil service testing, and we would change his status to civil service when the list was established.

That allowed us to get Mike down to Swallows Nest Park, and the green belt along the highway as warm weather began. Our plan for solving the drinking problems was to greet the first of those bringing beverages containing alcohol, and have them dispose of the booze or get a ticket. That was all we had to do to get everything under control, in the parks, and green belt. Ticket or Dump it! We also used the same procedure on first time keggers we came across. Ticket or Dump it, unless they were already under the influence, then we arrested and transported. We appealed to everyone for help to get first hand invitations out to all keggers. We were serious about stopping teenage fatalities, which had become the norm the prior few years.

It was a busy time getting new deputies trained and through their probationary period. It did, not always go as planned. We had a drug case underway and had just received a search warrant. I was bringing in a couple of off-duty deputies to execute the search warrant, when new deputy, Dean Grover came up and asked to be included on the search team. I responded that we already had a team together, when Deputy Grover interrupted, saying that he was the only officer in the sheriff's office that was qualified to go on the search warrant. Surprised, I turned around asked, "Just what qualifies you above all the rest?"

His reply was, "I am the only guy here that has ever killed anyone."

"And who did you kill?"

"I was a sniper in Viet Nam, and I killed a lot of people."

"Why does killing someone qualify you to go on a search warrant?" I could not believe I was having this conversation! I thanked Deputy Grover for his input and got on with the business at hand.

I had been out of town attending a Sheriff's—Chief's of Police Association meeting, just prior to that incident and a couple of the larger departments had just started using psychological examinations as a tool in all new hires.

I called the Spokane sheriff's department and got hold of the people administrating examinations on entry level personal. They had added psychological testing to take care of potential problems like I was experiencing with Dean Grover. They pointed out after discussing my problem with Deputy Grover, once you are aware of a possible problem in your department you could be liable if you do nothing and Grover should use poor judgment.

The only way you can start administering psychological testing is to establish testing on all deputies that have not completed their probation period. I called the psychologist that Spokane was using. I explained my problem to the psychologist without giving him the deputy's name. I told him that I had no problems with Viet Nam veterans, but I wanted to learn if this man was a danger to our department or the community. I sent the first two deputies up to Spokane for their psychological evaluations, Mike Carpenter and Derck Laws.

Following their testing, I received a call from the psychologist about the Viet Nam sniper, saying there was no problem with him. "He is solid, and I have no problems with him." Confused, I asked for the candidates name and learned it was Mike Carpenter. "OK, I will get our other two guys up there tomorrow. Thank you."

This was going to be interesting as Grover was the sniper I was concerned about and he had not been in for his testing yet. Turning to Chief Deputy Ron Laverne, I said, "Now what is going to happen? I had no idea that Mike Carpenter was also a sniper in Viet Nam."

Ron responded, "Are you kidding? Mike has never mentioned anything to me about it either."

When the psychologist called the next day, he asked why I had not told him that we had two Viet Nam snipers. I told him I did not know there were two. The psychologist went on to tell me that Dean Grover was a ticking time bomb, and could go off at any time. "At this point in his life I would not recommend law enforcement for him as a career. It could be tough for him and his personal life, as well as detrimental to the community."

As soon as I received a written report from the psychologist I wrote a letter to Deputy Grover that he had not successfully completed his probation period, so I had to terminate him immediately. He went straight to the Union who told him they could not do anything unless I gave a reason why I terminated him. Grover came back to me demanding that I tell him why he was terminated. I would only state that he had failed to successfully complete his probation period, as required in our operations manual. If I were to say anything more, then we would be involved in a long complicated court battle.

Dean Grover went to the Clarkston Police department and applied for a job. They hired him and he went to work right away.

Another change took place in the political community going into 1986. It was an election year. Just before the end of 1985, Prosecuting Attorney, Bill Acey requested a special investigation from the State Attorney General's Office to investigate the possible misconduct against deputy Mike Carpenter for mishandling a breathalyzer test. The same allegations that brought in the Attorney General's investigation also brought District Court Judge, Don Moore into action by coming forward and ordering a retrial of the case involving deputy Carpenter. That case had taken place a full year before, and had been cleared. Now before any investigation into possible wrongdoing, Judge Moore had ordered a retrial. There was no wrongdoing. That was the finding of the Attorney General. Are we not innocent until proven guilty? District Judge Moore; are you not the same judge that was withholding records on DWI convictions?

When Bill Acey came to me that he was going to bring in the Attorney General's Office, I was not happy. We had already done an internal investigation and had hard evidence that what Clarkston police officers had alleged had happened was not true. New cameras had been installed and proved that memory was not quite as accurate as the camera.

We had videotaped several of Carpenter's breathalyzer tests and arrests without his knowledge. The policy was we taped every DWI breathalyzer, regardless of who it was. We found no indication of untruths on Mike Carpenter's part. In fact, one of his arrests tested .09 on the breathalyzer, not quite reaching the level required by law of intoxication considered under the influence. Mike Carpenter entered the correct reading. We not only videotaped Carpenters tests and DWI arrests, but we had been videotaping everyone's arrests and breathalyzer tests, even before the jail was finished. And again this arrest had taken place the year prior. Why did they wait until an election year to file the complaint? Oh right . . . Politics!

As a result of the reports, the Attorney General's office was coming to town to see if Sheriff Gunkel or his deputies had been doing anything wrong! These complaints had all happened months before, and were investigated at that time and found groundless. One of these complaints was against one deputy who completed an arrest of three very loud high school boys in Clarkston, who were arrested in a scuffle that took place in a quiet neighborhood late at night. That investigation uncovered 11 different witnesses scattered over two blocks that said to the last person, Deputy Derck Laws did a very good job. He did not use excessive force. He did not hit one of the drunken boys over the head with his gun. He was able to make the arrests, and finally restored peace to the neighborhood. The complaints came only from the drunken teenagers.

Gregory P. Canova, the Assistant Attorney General leading the investigation came to the Sheriff's office and there were two polygraph tests applied, one to deputy Carpenter and one to deputy Laws. The examiner kept complaining about the noise level from outside the testing room, and disrupted the examination by stopping the test. He then moved the equipment to another room, which also had noise issues similar as the original testing room. Both deputies failed one question each.

Deputy Carpenter was cleared of all criminal misconduct in his case! Asotin County Prosecutor, William D. Acey reported he was troubled that disciplinary action was not recommended by the Attorney General's office, despite the fact their investigation uncovered no evidence of wrongdoing. I was curious why Bill Acey had actually asked for the investigation the first place.

I contacted Spokane to make appointments for two polygraph examinations and sent Deputies Carpenter and Laws to Spokane.

Included in the examination were the same set of polygraph questions they had flunked in the Asotin County test. This time we used the same examiner that Spokane County used for the new examinations. I had them re-examined because of previous complaints from the State Patrol examiner that our facilities were not suitable for a polygraph examination, as there was too much outside noise. In Spokane, both deputies passed the polygraph test by the most highly rated examiner in Eastern Washington.

We had used the same evidence at the time the charges had been made a year ago on our internal investigation, and amazing as it may sound we arrived at the same results. Our deputies did nothing wrong! When I first decided to run for sheriff, I met Chuck Cassell and his wife Laura. Chuck owned and operated Valley Real Estate that we bought our ranch through, and he helped in plotting strategy, securing money donations, and doing everything they could think of to help me to win the election. After winning both the primary and general elections, Chuck tried to make my entry into local politics as smooth as possible by introducing me to the Prosecuting Attorney, John Lyden. John was very polite, but very cool towards me.

After that meeting, Chuck got very sober and serious. "Listen Gary, you are the first Republican Sheriff since 1917. You have just beaten Democrat, Chief Deputy Stanley Booster the person the Democrats had decided to make sheriff after Herb Reeves retired. They feel like they have been humiliated. Mark my words, when your re-election comes around they will throw everything including the kitchen sink at you. Be very careful."

I had forgotten that conversation, but now it jumped right to the front and center. John Lyden had become the Superior Court judge and Bill Acey was now the Prosecuting Attorney. Donald Moore, the District Court Judge, an apparent casualty to our battle over DWI cases had chosen to not run again.

In the Lewiston Morning Tribune, on July 15, 1986 under the title:

COMPLAINT: Lewiston Man wants Gunkel investigated.

Prosecutor William D. Acey requests that the Special Prosecutor place Sheriff Gunkel under investigation, to see if he has done anything wrong.

I was concerned for the approximately four-year-old Roberts boy who seemed slow or shy. I had stayed out of the investigation, not even looking over the shoulders of the two deputies I had working full time on the case. I had not made any contact with the Roberts' or anyone working on the case until I heard that a special DSHS investigator was going to the Roberts residence to question their son using anatomically correct dolls to see if there were grounds for molestation.

A year or so before I became sheriff, our son Mark was 11-years-old and in the rabbit business. The Roberts, living in Clarkston, had the best price on rabbit food in the valley, so that is where I bought food for Mark's rabbits. Every time we went there the Roberts' young son was out in the rabbit area. Apparently I was one of the few that always had taken time to talk to him. He always seemed delighted to see me, and I counted that boy as a friend. It appeared that the young boy might be mentally challenged. I called Jerry Evans the DSHS investigator asking the reason DSHS requested a deputy sheriff to accompany their investigator to question the young boy. Jerry explained that he needed complete control of the interview with no interruptions from the parents. The deputy was strictly a peacekeeper, not an investigator. He was there to stop any interruptions from the parents, but at the same time to not upset the young boy. I explained the past relations we had with the Roberts. I asked, "If he would like me there as the boy knew me and trusted me, or if he thought I might be a distraction to his investigation."

"Having you there, and being trusted by the boy, would be appreciated by me during the investigation." I agreed to be there. "Oh, and sheriff, would you call and set the time for 10:30 a.m. at their home as that would make the boy feel more relaxed. Thank you."

Clark's complaint stated, "I was told that Gunkel had alerted the Roberts by phone to the rape complaint and advised them to destroy evidence, and then pulled investigating deputies off the case before it was fully investigated."

In the sheriff's office I saw the two deputies who were working the case, so I stopped to tell them the change in plans for the interview by DSHS. I explained that it was DSHS decision that I accompany him instead of a detective, as this was a peacekeeping mission for us with DSHS doing this stage of the investigation with their anatomically correct dolls.

Later, both deputies were upset, saying that I had alerted the Roberts by phone (I did contact them at DSHS's request to set the time we would arrive for the DSHS meeting). I never pulled the deputies off the case, and I was at the interview conducted by DSHS only as a peacekeeper. If the boy's mother or father had molested him we needed to get them, and get the boy out of there. If they did not molest him we needed to be in a position to protect him. Either way, it was my purpose to serve as an advocate for the boy.

After Jerry Evans completed his investigative session, it was apparent that he was able to answer the molesting question beyond a doubt. Jerry was very good at what he did. And I felt good to be a part of that team. Upon completion, he thanked me for the help and said having me there helped to get the boy to communicate with him.

Chapter 60

John Mason, the Fish and Game Warden was the Democrat Sheriff candidate, and we were scheduled to speak at a Sheriff's forum for the upcoming election. I was not looking forward to the event. This one was set for early afternoon at Tri-State Hospital, in a large room that was open for community use. When I first went in about 20 minutes early, the place was already jam packed with no empty chairs. They were bringing in more chairs and setting them up. This would have been one of those times I would have been delighted to offer my chair to a woman, and get out of there. The hospital administrator had spotted me and had started towards me. Oops, it is too late, they caught up with me.

Looking back out into the full parking lot, I understand why there are no parking places there or for several blocks up or down Highland Ave. They had placed all the chairs there was room for, and it was standing room only. They closed the doors. I had discovered a game and was getting a kick out of the results. I would smile at a person, and would know instantly how that person was going to vote. Either their eyes would dart right and left or just towards the floor and they would look very uneasy. Or there would be an instant smile, with maybe a little wave. Body language was easy to read. I am glad it was not a jury, because the results looked about three to one against me.

John spoke first, stating how he would restore dignity to the Sheriff's Office by doing this and that. I had decided that I would not play cat and mouse with him. I would use a different approach rather than you pick at me and I will pick at you.

I had selected 24 chairs that were up front, and in the center, so when I was introduced as the sheriff and republican candidate up for reelection, I was ready. Smiling I asked for cooperation so I could illustrate better to the audience what the numbers actually said. I pointed out 24 seats and was finally able to get those people on their feet . . . oh no, I said to myself, but some of those around me caught it also. One man, Duke, from the City Clerks office, was in a wheelchair. He could not get to his feet.

First I apologized to Duke. Then I said, "This actually is working out better than I expected, as you will see. The four years before I was elected sheriff there were 24 people right here in our county that were killed in automobile accidents.

"I wanted to illustrate to you what 24 live men and women actually looked like as we come together this afternoon. Thank you Duke, now you can join the rest of the room.

"For everyone else still standing, please remain standing for just a couple of more minutes. Did you know that the other 23 were all killed in accidents involving drugs, mostly alcohol? Look again at 23 people killed the last four years that will never be seen again in our small community. There are only 16,000 people to start with, and we had lost 23 killed by drugs in only four years! Please sit down. Thank you for the help.

"Now I want to read to you a letter that I got just last week."

Dear Sheriff Gunkel,

I am writing you this letter to thank you for saving my life. I have done many dumb things during my life and now it is clear to me how close I have come to being killed.

Because you took a stand and would not back down you got my attention and have saved my life.

Please do not release my name because I am
an inmate at Walla Walla State Prison in Walla
Walla, Washington.

Thank you,
(John Doe)

Being Asotin County Sheriff that election year was like going
through a minefield. Every step, every turn there was someone
after you. Several attorneys were attempting to bring criminal
charges against me, and a lawsuit was filed against Ann and myself,
going after our personal property. The State Attorney General's
office completed an investigation on two different deputies on two
different cases attempting to implicate me, at the request of the
County Prosecuting Attorney. In still another case, the father of a
rape victim filed charges against me for protecting the accused, after
the accused received two years in jail on a felony rape charge. This
occurred when someone leaked out untrue information that resulted
in another special prosecutor investigating Sheriff Gunkel.

When I take time to look for direction, Christ guides every step I make.
The problem is, I do not always look for direction. I claim no credit
for getting through all these stumbling blocks with no violations, no
guilty pleas, and no lawsuits lost, and no plea bargains made. But in
the end, I was cleared of all accusations the day before the election.
All that garbage does not win elections, as the competition knows,
but we "won" the primary election, and again, what is the meaning
of winning? The general election was upon us.

After the primary election one of the members of our Sheriff
Chaplains, Frank Needles, the minister of First Christian church of
Clarkston said he had decided to leave our community and wrote me
a letter starting off by saying it would do no good to attempt to come
over to his house as he would no longer be in this community by the
time I received his letter. He went on to say, the differences in our
ideology became obvious at a meeting a little over three years ago
making it impossible for him to work with me, so he was resigning
his position with the Sheriff Chaplains. Three years ago?

This man was a pastor in his church and I felt bad that he was afraid to talk with me. Frank was going to great ends to let the world know that he did not believe along the same lines that I believed. He also met with a reporter of the Lewiston Morning Tribune, his last days in our community setting this up. I felt I had a special relationship with our Sheriff Chaplains Association. I felt that Christ was the center of our organization, so his letter was a real shock to me. I felt the need to talk with my own pastor, Paul Barber, of the First Church of the Nazarene in Lewiston. All this negative campaigning was getting to me. I was getting the feeling that I could trust no one. I was a member of the church board and had worked close with our pastor on several church projects. He knew how I was put together.

The following Sunday I had the honor of being directly encouraged by pastor Paul during his sermon. There were always hundreds of people that attend the Sunday morning services at the First Church of the Nazarene, and this day was no exception. For most of the service pastor Paul was looking directly at me.

Reverend Paul Barber started by laying the foundation for his subject. England's "Sir Winston Churchill was one of the strongest Christian leaders of the modern world. On October 19th, 1941 he was in Harrow School in England where he had attended and graduated from the military school and academy. He was there to deliver an inspirational message. England was locked in a war with Germany, and France was the last large nation of the mainland in Europe which had just fallen, even with England's army helping France. England's Navy was barely able to evacuate the English army that was in France and also able to evacuate what was left of the French army. Although the French and the English were fighting the Germans together, there was no way they could slow down Germany's war machine.

"Germany had rolled across France, defeating France's army even though reinforced by some of England's Army, in a matter of days.

"England was now the only country left in Europe and they were under constant bombardment from the German Air Force around the clock.

"England was feeling very lonely. The United States of America had their problems with Japan, and had not yet entered the war against Germany. There appeared to be no way out. It was a very dark time for England, and a solemn auditorium at Harrow Academy."

Pastor Paul continued. "After being introduced, Sir Winston Churchill went to the speakers table and remained quiet. He just stood there and looked at the packed auditorium." Pastor Paul was looking straight at me. You could have heard a pin drop. "Then the Prime Minister said, '**NEVER, NEVER, NEVER GIVE UP!**' Then without another word he went over to his seat and sat down. The place erupted with cheers that went on, and on!"

Pastor Paul concluded, "When you are doing God's work, never, never, never give up!"

I felt a rush of emotion thinking to myself, *I have not ever had that problem before, and now I know that I will continue on, allowing Christ to lead my way.*

Chapter 61

A couple of years earlier, on a late afternoon in summer I received a call from Joe Wilson of Sillcott, saying that a man approached his 13-year-old daughter who was swimming at the beach in Chief Timothy Park, six miles west of Clarkston, and offered her a white substance he said was cocaine. The duty deputy was on another call so I rolled on this one.

I drove out to Chief Timothy Park on Highway 12, and contacted the witnesses and took statements from them making contact with the suspect. I found he had been offering his white substance to several people, claiming it was cocaine. After advising the suspect of his rights he told me the substance was white aspirins that he had smashed up, producing a small clear plastic bag with a white substance in it and tried to sell it as cocaine. I asked him if he knew that it was also against the law to sell an imitation drug, and he said yes he did, that he had just got out of jail a few weeks ago. I took the bag of white substance as evidence and arrested the suspect for attempting to sell a counterfeit drug. I transported him to the Asotin County jail where Terrence M. Hanson was booked in on a felony charge. While in jail the suspect apparently got the name of the main witness, Joe Wilson's daughter and placed a phone call making threats. This all took time developing and now about election time here comes the Hanson show.

Hanson was always trying to get out of jail. He was trying to get out on bail, then on his own reconnaissance. Now there was another problem and that was the Washington Parole Board was involved. Hanson was controlled by the parole board which would not release him, When that did not work he was able to get on the phone and was trying to hire a hit man to get the witness. We accommodated him by setting up a contact with our undercover "hit man" and Hanson hired him and set things up to kill the young girl.

This took time, and that prolonged the case. Then we were able to file additional charges of intimidating a witness. Hanson's attorney in the meantime was still trying to get him out, so when the case was brought before Judge Moore, his argument was he must be safe for the state parole board to release their hold on Hanson. Asotin County Prosecuting Attorney, Bill Acey attempted to keep Hanson in jail until after his trial, but Judge Moore said Hanson could be released on a $10,000 public recognizance bond because he had been in jail so long. The conditions of parole were that Hansen would not leave the company of his sister or brother in law. In early November, Hansen was released at 4:45p.m. then less than nine hours later, because of an Asotin County Sheriff Department stake out, a deputy arrested Hanson near his sisters residence on Poplar Street. Hanson waited until 2:00 a.m. when the others went to bed, before leaving. Hanson told the deputy he was just going after a pack of cigarettes.

Hanson had been turned loose two months before his trial. He had been tried earlier, but that trial had been called a mistrial as one of the jurors told the judge she thought Hanson had offered her drugs under the same circumstances similar to those in the current trial.

Among previous convictions was one for first degree burglary. Hanson entered his parole officer's residence armed with a sawed off shotgun. Off to jail again. He was released from prison just two weeks before I arrested him at the park in Asotin County. This was a very dangerous man.

Election Day arrived! I got up early and checked with Ann to get any last minute changes in time, scheduling or surprises. Everything seems to be going smoothly, so off to the office, to return phone calls, then out for a campaign meeting, then home for an early lunch.

Election afternoon I took my pickup, with side boards and a mobile radio and started working in residential neighborhoods collecting yard campaign signs. I kept working steadily, but would take time to say hello, and thank you.

By working hard it made the afternoon pass quickly, and at the same time run down all my campaign signs in the county, or most of them. I finished just before dark, took the load of signs home, grabbed a quick shower, change of clothes, and we were off to Chuck and Lora Cassells with some friends to listen to the election results coming in.

The first returns were from the smaller precincts, and showed I was trailing. As the larger precincts started filing their results, I would gain a little, but then continue to fall even farther behind. Our friends there with Ann and I tried to encourage us but I said there is no sense denying the truth, we are not going to win this election. That relieved those in the room as the results were pointing to a loss. I was disappointed not to have won, but I was really glad that it was over.

It felt like a huge weight had been lifted off my shoulders. All the negative garbage had been tough on our family, but I felt as though I had let down those people that had worked hard for me and who wanted me re-elected sheriff.

I congratulated Don Steal on keeping my chief deputy Ron Laverne as his Jail Commander, and for keeping Clee Manchester, my Jail Commander and making him his Chief Deputy. We must have been doing something right in the newly elected Sheriff's estimation.

I want you all to know that we thank you from the bottom of our hearts for the hours we worked together, and for all the things we accomplished.

Chapter 62

The election was over and now we had to decide what we were going to do. I had been thinking of Pastor Paul and his sermon. I have almost two months left in my term as county sheriff. Lots of elected office holders just quit when they become a lame duck office holder, and concentrate on other things. I know there are three more suspects we have reports of selling drugs in our county, But I also know that these reports run about two to one of being not true. Christ put me in the sheriff's office to clean up these problems in our county. So we will continue on with our work until December 31st. Never, never, never quit!

The very next morning I called a meeting with Ron Laverne and Clee Manchester in the sheriff's office. I knew that everyone was wondering what I was going to do. That was easy . . . I was just going to keep doing what I've always done while being Sheriff. We are going after the bad guys.

First of all, I wanted them both to know that I was glad they had stayed in positions of authority at the Sheriff's Office. Then I told them I planned on keeping busy the next two months. I knew of at least three more suspects selling drugs in the area. Ron said yes, he was aware of the three suspects still remaining and one looked like he may be a mid-sized grower.

The first drug suspect that had been reported selling drugs was located in an above average neighborhood in the Clarkston Heights. Driving by, the location appeared well kept. The back yard was fenced and completely private, the people living there did not have any reports of police calls. We went to the person making the report, and found that there may have been some misunderstanding, so Ron and I had nothing. We had spent several days doing research on the residence, with negative results. So to lay this question to rest, we went to the residence in full uniform. I knocked on the front door and when a young woman answered the door I introduced myself and Ron to the young lady. She was surprised when a smiling sheriff, and undersheriff, came to her front door and requested her to submit her home to a voluntary search for illegal drugs. She said ok, which blew us both away. So I advised her of her rights, and when I asked if she would like to talk to us, she responded, sure. Wow the direct approach again!

First we walked around her backyard and found a well kept yard with a freshly mowed lawn, and no sign of growing marijuana. Then through her house, opening a drawer or two, there was a place for everything, and everything was in its place. We thanked her for her co-operation and left. There were no illegal drugs in that residence. Now we have two drug reports left.

There was a small house on Sillcott road about six miles east of Clarkston. It was 5:35, just a little after dark on that December evening. Ron and I were both in uniform as we went to the front door. When a young man opened the front door I introduced Ron and myself from the Sheriff's Office and told him we had a report that drugs were being sold from the residence. He looked a little startled, but was quick to say there were no drugs there and that no one was selling drugs there. I thanked him for his time, and we left.

We drove the patrol vehicle back to the road and stopped out of sight, and turned the lights off. A few minutes later someone came out and got into an older pickup. The vehicle lights came on, started out the driveway and turned towards where we had stopped along the side of the road. As he drove by, Ron said, "can you believe it? His left tail light is out." I turned on the overhead lights and pulled out behind the pickup as he pulled over to the side and stopped.

I walked up to the driver's window as Ron went to the passenger side of the vehicle. He rolled down his window and before I could say anything he reached over and picked up a small four inch seedling that had just enough growth to tell it was marijuana. He said that was all he had, and I could look in his place if I wanted. We ended up issuing him a citation for possession of a controlled substance, and operating a motor vehicle with a tail light out.

Those of us in the criminal justice system in the valley were aware of Terrence M. Hanson as he had established a record of disturbances in his different court hearings. Hanson's first hearing was his arraignment on October 7th, 1986 on drug charges. He had to be removed from the room at the judge's order after he became profane and verbally abused court officials. Hanson created another disturbance at the conclusion of his jury trial on November 25th when he was convicted of attempting to sell counterfeit drugs. He was also scheduled to be tried in Asotin County Superior Court on related charges of intimidation of a witness and first degree solicitation to commit kidnapping of a material witness in the drug case.

These last cases had been transferred to Walla Walla County, to get a fair trial. Hanson's attorney requested one last hearing trying to get Judge Jones to make the Sheriff let him use a phone at the jail so he could contact his mother, who Hanson reported was dying. During the conversation back and forth his voice was getting louder and louder. Now there were also a lot of obscene words coming from Hanson's mouth and his voice volume level had reached a shout. As Hanson pushed back the table in front of him and his attorney, Hanson was on his feet heading around the table and at the Judge. I had been in the courtroom at the Judges request seated off to the side, and Deputy Tom White was standing by the main exit from the courtroom. Both Tom and I started moving about the same time, but I was closer so was able to get there just ahead of Tom. Hanson was wearing handcuffs, but they were cuffed in front of him, so he was able to fend us off. I think that I was just ahead of Judge Jones asking me to remove Hanson from the courtroom. We quickly got Hanson to the doors going out of the courtroom and he slowed us down by grabbing one of the doors and getting it partly closed. We cleared that door and had two flights of stairs to get down to the first floor. Now that I think about it, the judge did not give me a court order to let Hanson use the phone. Hmmm, I wonder if it just slipped his mind?

There was a microphone on in the courtroom to let the Sheriff's Office in the basement know if there was trouble there. Deputy Mike Carpenter and Reserve Deputy Bill Jollymore arrived from the basement at about the same time we arrived at the glass door to the parking lot.

We were walking at a rapid pace when Hanson attempted to push me into the glass portion of the door. I did not give way and he could not alter my direction so he attempted to pivot off me and knock Deputy Carpenter into the glass. That did not work as I altered my speed so that Mike missed the door completely, but our prisoner could not change his direction in time to miss. His left shoulder struck the door splintering the glass giving him several cuts on his upper arm and the side of his face. On the way to the hospital, Mike Carpenter and I were the latest additions to his list of persons to kill when he got out of prison. One was the judge, the prosecutor, and last the sheriff.

I could not believe how fast things were coming at us. It was December 23rd, 1986 and we were wrapping up all kinds of things I had started and wanted to finish before my term was up a week later.

I came out of the back of the courthouse heading for my patrol car and ran into County Prosecutor, Bill Acey as he was heading into the courthouse. He put out his hand saying "Gary, I have been wanting to talk to you since the election. You have really done a great job while being sheriff, with all the programs you have started. By starting a State certified reserve officer training program meeting all the requirements of state certification was amazing for only having seven commissioned officers to work with. Then getting help from the private sector with your block watch, which grew all over the county, generating eyes and ears watching and listening, giving you an inside view of what was going on that no one else has been able to develop.

"Then this last year you came out with the Victims Advocate Program that has been needed for a long time, but no one had recognized the need but you. So many times when you get a call the good guys out there need help, but no one gets around to help them."

"Bill you are the prime reason that I was able to get the reserve officer training program going by helping in the different classes, never turning me or Ron down when we needed an instructor. That did encourage others to join in teaching the different classes, involved. The Victims Advocate took lots of recruitment, and organization."

"Gary as far as I see you are the first law enforcement agency in the State Of Washington or the whole northwest corner of the US that is doing it. You are the first, while being one of the smallest departments."

"Well, it did not originate with me, I sent off to a sheriff in Arizona and received the complete program broken down with the entire training program."

"But one of the amazing things is, you put it together with 100 percent volunteers. Then training, learning all the different assets already in place, just working with the victim, and assisting persons in need. When there was an arrest your Advocates were able to work with the legal system doing a good job in keeping the victim educated and informed as to what was going on. You did an incredible job with very little. If only you could have . . . you know, just . . . I am sorry."

Bill continued on into the courthouse. "Thanks for the compliment Bill," as I thought, that is the question I have asked myself time after time. What would I have changed if I could have?

But there is one to go! We have been working these drug cases all along, and this is the last of the three that were called to our attention by the citizens and other informant networks in our county. Of the last three, this is the one that we have spent the most time trying to develop. We have been working on gathering information to get probable cause for a search warrant. Our information indicated a growing operation, big enough to more than fill a pickup canopy with large plants nearing harvest time.

For the last couple of weeks we have been operating an observation post next door to the suspect, watching for anything that might help us. The suspect lives in a home with a daylight basement, the windows in the daylight basement seem to have a covering on them. That is where we believe the growing operation is set up. Our contact actually shares a driveway with the suspect to get to the rear of their homes. The side where the suspect lives goes to a parking area behind his house, and the area where our contact lives has a garage behind his house. Our contact has a window at the rear of his house that is right across from the parking area of the suspect's residence. This is where our observation post operated.

We are running out of time, with Christmas Eve and Christmas Day taking us up to the weekend. So I set another meeting with chief deputy Laverne for Monday morning the 29th of December. "It is now or never, Ron, we are out of time. Do you have any ideas?" Ron smiled and said, "Fresh out."

"The way I see it we need to get it done today if at all possible. We do not have probable cause to get a search warrant, so we have to think outside the box and get him to bring the marijuana to us."

After four years I had the reputation of being a tough sheriff, but especially tough on drugs. Everyone knew that I was aggressive in going after those that were outside the law, and backed down from no one. We used search warrants frequently. I am a firm believer of "it pays to advertise".

I made sure that those in the press had every opportunity to know that we get the bad guys, with a high frequency of convictions, and they did appreciate all that I gave them to write about. They could have been a little nicer on how they wrote about me, but either way, this case demonstrates how that strategy helped us.

My idea was to use a mystery caller that would call the suspect, saying, "I was in the courthouse this afternoon and saw Gunkel in there getting a search warrant for your house here in Clarkston. I just thought you would like to know, and then hang up.

"You know Sheriff, I think that might just work." We went ahead and worked out the details, figuring that the best time to set it up would be about 3:30 pm. We wanted the daylight to be able to see and recognize the marijuana with normal light, not artificial light. We also wanted the driver to turn his lights on when he left his driveway, so we could tell if he had a light out, or did not signal for a turn. We needed probable cause for a traffic stop, so if it was time for lights that would up the odds to get probable cause for the stop. On the 29th of December, it started getting dark a little after 4:00 p.m.

Ron went a block north of the suspect's residence, and I went a block south to wait for the call. We were using a tactical radio frequency and the call came out to Ron and I that the phone call had just been made and the caller had responded, "Oh man, thanks for the call, I got to go!" Then shortly afterwards the suspect came running out the back door carrying a large potted plant and put it in the back of his pickup. He then hurried back to the house again. It took a short time and he had rearranged his load to get all his plants in his truck.

He pulled out and headed south, towards me. It was dusk and I could see his lights coming. As his pickup went by my position I saw that the right rear taillight was out. I pulled out behind him, amazed as everything was falling into place perfectly. I called in his license number and then turned on the overhead lights, and the pickup pulled over to the right side of the road. After approaching carefully, I looked through the side canopy window and there was nothing but marijuana plants about three feet tall crowded inside. As his hands came into view, I asked too see his driver's license. As he was removing it from his wallet I invited him to step out of his vehicle to see why I had stopped him. He started to the rear of the vehicle and as we arrived I pointed out his right taillight that was not working. The driver sounded relieved. Then I pointed to the glass window of the canopy on his pickup. "That certainly appears to be marijuana plants in your vehicle." Aahh, "You will receive a citation for operating a vehicle without a taillight, and I am impounding your vehicle as it is being used to transport illegal drugs, and I am arresting you for possession of an illegal controlled substance. Marijuana."

The arrested man wanted to talk to his attorney, so I transported him a couple of blocks, to Highland Market and asked who his attorney was. He responded, Bill Acey, requesting me to dial for him. By using the phone book at his request I dialed Bill Acey, the recently elected Prosecuting Attorney. Then it was off to book the prisoner. And that was the last drug dealer that we knew of working in our county.

Just in time, the next day was New Years Eve, 1986, the last day of my term. We processed the evidence, and put the reports together. The next afternoon, I moved out of the office. Just like that, I finished an incredible four years, not giving up and working right through the last day.

The Final Chapter

As I look back I'm quite proud of what we did. What could I have done differently? A few things perhaps, but I don't know that I'd change anything. In fact, I find that I seldom had much of a choice. I had taken an oath to enforce the law, fairly and impartially, regardless of who has done what, removing any obstructions we find along the way.

Occasionally the system seems to break down, and then we need to slow down and figure what, or who, caused the problem. I have found that prayer is an incredible tool in solving why it is not working. For me I need to pray for direction then check all possible remedies and move forward slowly and impartially enforcing the Law. This sometimes requires bringing charges against people in high places who have lots of power and influence. There is little room for mistakes at times like that. You get all the direction that is available. I find no times would I have changed what I did, but a few times I wish I had used the prayer option earlier. With us keeping the heat on, we can get things under control. Using this approach will for the most part cause all things to go away, by keeping on enforcing the law fairly and impartially.

The last morning, Johnny Johnson, reporter for our local Lewiston Morning Tribune came by and asked if I'd had time to clean everything up and was ready to leave office?

"You know, Johnny I have been thinking about that, and the promises I made. First of all I promised to clean up the teenage drinking at dances and the keggers. In Asotin County there has been only one fatality accident involving alcohol in the last four years, and that was a drunk that came out of a bar in Lewiston and going up river was in a one car roll over, killing himself. The four years prior to my term there were 23 deaths involving alcohol.

"We cleaned up the Asotin County Fair, removing the Snake Pit, the fights and rioting. The fairs are now family safe.

"We removed the alcohol in the green belts and parks along the river, removing the female topless and nude bathing.

"We installed 24-hour patrol with only seven officers including the sheriff. We kept the coverage all four years. As we got contracts adding people it became easier to maintain the coverage.

"Deputy Michael Carpenter arrested 69 DWI's from January 1, 1985 through mid-December. That was more DWI's than the whole nine man Clarkston Police department made. They had only 64 DWI arrests during the same period. Another deputy, Derck Laws had 52 DWI arrests with another 12 DWI's arrested by the other officers in the sheriff's office. That alone is an impressive record, but when you look further into what was going on by the team of officers, reserve officers, Sheriff's Posse and office staff, it is incredible when you consider the total number of arrests of burglars and different individuals arrested for larceny and drug cases in 1982. The year before I became sheriff, there were a total of 80 arrests department-wide. Once our team was established and went to work, arrests rose from 80 the year before I was sheriff to a high of 340 arrests in 1986. And our convictions averaged 95% to 98%.

"Now that it's over, Ann and I are looking forward to getting out of town, without feeling guilty. My work day averaged 11 hours a day, with most of my days off only six to eight hours, of work."

Ann sat down and wrote the following final tribute herself to the Editor of the Lewiston Morning Tribune. That was very unusual for her.

L. GARY GUNKEL

Dear Editor,

In answer to all the articles and letters in this paper against Sheriff Gary Gunkel, as his wife, I want to set a few things straight, as I don't even recognize the man your paper was writing about.

1. Illegal search warrants and harassment of teen-agers: First, he just does not go out looking for teen parties to raid, he answers calls, complaints, and tips. He has been the leader of youth groups and activities and actively supports youth sports in the valley. The Prosecuting Attorney has the final say on all search warrants. The Sheriff's Office gives him all the information and he does the rest. Why don't we hear about the high percentage of convictions achieved?
2. Unfeeling and out to get everyone: There is the Christmas he bought a tree for a young mother caught trying to steal one for her five-year-old son. Many trips up the river during flood time to check on people. Employees feel free to come to him with their personal problems because they know he will listen, cry with them or laugh with them, and help in any way possible.
3. Dishonest: If he was dishonest he would have been sued and lost many times. It appears he only gets sued and charges brought against him during election years.
4. Integrity: If he did not have high standards or was a lesser person, he would have succumbed long ago to the level of his opponents. Only his disclosures would be proven facts, not political rhetoric.
5. Low esteem and lost confidence in the Sheriff's Office: I answer the phone many times a day, and hear someone say how happy they are with the sheriff and what he is doing. I open many letters with words of thanks. There are lots of good solid citizens out there who want the

law enforced fairly and impartially, and that's exactly what Sheriff Gary Gunkel did.

Ann Gunkel

Romans 11:36

For from Him and through Him and to Him are all things. To Him be the glory forever!

Amen.